THE ART OF PHOTOSHOP®
FOR DIGITAL PHOTOGRAPHERS

FROM IMAGE CAPTURE TO ART

DANIEL GIORDAN

SAMS

800 East 96th Street, Indianapolis, Indiana 46240 USA

THE ART OF PHOTOSHOP®
FOR DIGITAL PHOTOGRAPHERS:
FROM IMAGE CAPTURE TO ART

Copyright © 2006 by Sams Publishing

International Standard Book Number: 0-672-32713-9

Library of Congress Catalog Card Number: 2004094242

Printed in the United States of America

First Printing: September 2005

08   07   06   05   4   3   2   1

Trademarks

Warning and Disclaimer

Bulk Sales

Sams Publishing offers excellent discounts on this book when ordered in quantity for bulk purchases or special sales. For more information, please contact

U.S. Corporate and Government Sales
1-800-382-3419
corpsales@pearsontechgroup.com

For sales outside of the U.S., please contact

International Sales
international@pearsoned.com

Acquisitions Editor
Linda Bump Harrison

Development Editor
Alice Martina Smith

Managing Editor
Charlotte Clapp

Project Editor
Dan Knott

Production Editor
Heather Wilkins

Indexer
Ken Johnson

Technical Editors
Matt Detrich
Doug Nelson

Publishing Coordinator
Vanessa Evans

Multimedia Developer
Dan Scherf

Interior Designers
David Giordan
Cindy Lounsbery

Cover Designer
Daniel Giordan

Page Layout
Eric S. Miller
Stacey Richwine-DeRome

Graphics
Tammy Graham

CONTENTS AT A GLANCE

TABLE OF CONTENTS

ABOUT THE AUTHOR

Daniel Giordan is an artist, author, and designer who currently resides in Columbus, Ohio. As a fine artist, Dan's work has been shown throughout the United States, including the Museum of Fine Arts in Boston and several New York and Boston galleries.

Dan is also the Director of Design at AOL Web Properties where he oversees the Web design and brand development for online brands such as Netscape, Compuserve, AOL Instant Messenger, and other AOL properties.

This is Dan's 13th book on Photoshop and digital design. Recently published titles include *The Art of Photoshop* and *How to Use Photoshop CS2*. He has also written for numerous magazines, including *Photoshop User*, *Dynamic Graphics*, *Photoshop Fix*, *Digital Camera*, and *Adobe Magazine*.

DEDICATION

For Barbara, my indulgent muse.

ACKNOWLEDGEMENTS

This was a big project…probably the most complex and involved computer book ever written. It involved traveling to Tuscany in Italy to capture and organize a vast array of images, cataloging these images into a cohesive group, and weaving them into a narrative that taught photography, Photoshop, and design. I wanted the layout of the pages to be impactful, and I wanted the book to have the feel of a first-person travel diary. That's juggling a lot of different variables in a single volume.

As a result, kudos must be distributed far and wide to the team of people who helped pull this together.

First, I want to thank Sams Publishing as an organization and Associate Publisher, Mark Taber, in particular for supporting this project. This book broke the mold even more than did the original *Art of Photoshop*, and Mark saw the potential and helped shape the final result. In addition, Linda Harrison was a fantastic help as Acquisitions Editor. This was our first time working together and her first project after moving to Sams from a different imprint. I can't think of a more challenging project, especially since she was new to the organization. This project would not have happened without her focus and dedication. In addition, the Sams team did their usual bang-up job, including Alice Martina Smith, my long-time colleague and Development Editor extraordinaire.

On the technical side, Matt Detrich did a great job double-checking my photo technology facts and figures. Doug Nelson was also a help on the computer technology side. Thanks also go to Richard LoPinto, Steve Heiner, and the guys at Nikon for serving as a resource for technical information and general equipment support. You guys are a big reason why Nikon is a leader and innovator in the digital imaging arena.

As I look back over the course of this book, I'm amazed at the sacrifices my wife made in helping me complete this project. Barb allowed me to burn our vacation time to spend two solo weeks in Tuscany, gathering the images for this book. She then had to endure the months of writing and development that inevitably pulled me away and forced more work on her. Thanks Barb, I love you lots and appreciate all that you do for me.

Finally, I can't write an acknowledgement without thanking God. He's the absolute facilitator and the source of all my strength. I can't wait to see what He's going to do next.

WE WANT TO HEAR FROM YOU!

As the reader of this book, *you* are our most important critic and commentator. We value your opinion and want to know what we're doing right, what we could do better, what areas you'd like to see us publish in, and any other words of wisdom you're willing to pass our way.

You can email or write me directly to let me know what you did or didn't like about this book—as well as what we can do to make our books stronger.

Please note that I cannot help you with technical problems related to the topic of this book, and that due to the high volume of mail I receive, I might not be able to reply to every message.

When you write, please be sure to include this book's title and author as well as your name and phone or email address. I will carefully review your comments and share them with the author and editors who worked on the book.

Email: graphics@samspublishing.com

Mail: Mark Taber
             Associate Publisher
             Sams Publishing
             800 East 96th Street
             Indianapolis, IN 46240 USA

FOR MORE INFORMATION

Visit the Sams Publishing website at www.samspublishing.com and type in the ISBN of this book (excluding hyphens—0672327139) or the title *Art of Photoshop for Digital Photographers* to access more information about this book and the downloadable images.

INTRODUCTION

There's an old saying that "Sometimes the worst thing in the world is to get what you want." This just might be the case with the *Art of Photoshop* books as they continue to grow in complexity, detail, and nuance with each new volume. And yet, I guess I wouldn't have it any other way. I consider dynamic imagery and compelling source material to be requisites for any design book.

When I started writing, my books were straightforward text-based volumes with the occasional screen shot. The layouts were done by someone else and the images were scavenged from whatever royalty-free stock photo house we could find. As I continued writing, things slowly began to change. I started taking my own photos for the *How to Use Photoshop* books, and took control of the layout with *Art of Photoshop*. With this book, I've added a new thematic variable that I hope results in a cohesive volume that is even more instructive and informative—Tuscany.

Initially, this book presents itself as a digital photography travel book, drawing its inspiration and photo resources from the Tuscan region of Italy. In addition to featuring the images I shot during a photo trek through the area, the book also includes stories and commentary about how the images were captured, technical challenges, and overall aesthetic impressions. Thus, the book you're holding is an instruction guide for how to capture digital images, an inspiration for what to shoot, and a behind-the-scenes commentary on how the general impressions of a region translated into tangible digital images.

All the images in this book were captured with a Nikon D2H digital SLR camera and a wide range of exter-

nal lenses. I used a Manfrotto Carbon Fiber tripod, an electronic cable release, and a host of various filters and attachments.

I mention this so that readers will have a point of reference regarding the equipment used to create the images in this book. Users who don't have an SLR camera, tripod, or other accessories mentioned here will experience different results, although the basic photographic principles are the same regardless of what equipment is used. As mentioned elsewhere in the book, my suggestion is that you use a digital SLR as a bare minimum, along with a stable camera support and cable release. This combination will allow you to follow most of the procedures outlined in the upcoming chapters.

Each image that appears in the book is accompanied by a profile of how it was created. Specifically, it lists the camera used, f-stop, shutter speed, and focal length. Occasionally, I used exposure compensation on an image, and this data is listed as well, using an "EV" designation followed by a positive or negative compensation value. In addition, all images were captured at ISO 200 to ensure optimum resolution detail, except as otherwise noted.

This book is also about Photoshop. Although the first part of the book looks at how to take a good picture, the second part features explorations that show you how to bring those images into Photoshop and push things further. Some of the explorations teach alternative photo techniques such as cyanotypes and hand coloring, while others are more artistic and painterly. Part 2, "Photoshop Explorations," is not exhaustive by any means, but it does provide a solid base for how you can transform a photograph into a digital design.

The final part, "Gallery," presents my own vision for exploring and interpreting the Tuscan region. It presents a suite of eight finished works, along with step-by-step details for how they were created, following the familiar format of the original *Art of Photoshop* book.

If you want to follow along with the steps in the presentations, you can download low-resolution copies of all the source images used in the projects (low-resolution versions of the finished art are also available) from www.artofphotoshop.com.

The result is a book that provides a glimpse into my impressions of the Tuscan region and how those impressions were channeled and molded into finished works of art. It should serve as an example and inspiration for how you approach your own work and the external world as you experience it through your camera's viewfinder.

WELCOME
TO TUSCANY

On the surface, I was touring
Tuscany to capture images for a
digital photography book.
In the process I discovered a
personal perspective and an
intimate connection with this
timeless region.

ENUTO

WELCOME TO TUSCANY

Thinking Outside the Guidebook

I was on my own for three weeks; just me, a cheap convertible rental car, and about 60 pounds of camera gear. It was the first time I had traveled alone to a foreign country, and I was expecting a very different sort of trip. My past travels to European and tropical destinations have been group experiences, either with family, friends, or as part of a tour. Barb and Josh agreed to stay home and let Dad go off to do his photography thing (at the cost of a family Disney cruise, I might add), allowing me to plan my expedition to Tuscany on my own terms.

The fact that I was alone made this a very different trip. Although traveling companions can be good from a coping and security standpoint, they inevitably color how a new region is perceived. If your traveling partner dislikes the French, is paranoid of pickpockets, or keeps their nose forever embedded in a guidebook, these perspectives indirectly become *your* perspectives.

In addition, everyone always has a personal quest that requires extra research and inquiry, if not an absolute change in plans. For me, it was finding a really good *Bisteca Fiorentina* while I was in Florence (translation: I wanted a good steak). This goal ultimately resulted in my seeking out the people who might possess this insider knowledge, consulting a few maps, and making an evening cab excursion. My wife's personal quest might be finding the perfect doll to give her niece for her birthday, or doing an extensive review of all the gelato shops in Siena. Now don't get me wrong, I'm not saying that it's bad to have personal quests or wanting to experience specific things when you go to a new place. In fact, it's probably a requisite for making a personal connection between you and your new surroundings. I'm only saying that when you travel with other people, a group experience tempers your own personal response to the region. And my goal for this trip was to connect on a personal level, documenting my own unique perspective.

8

Planning Ahead

As my wife will attest, when I'm on a photo shoot, I'm oblivious to time and schedules. I stop even more frequently and resist anything but the most loosely formed itinerary. On several occasions in Tuscany, I would literally drive a hundred yards, stop, set up, and shoot. After breaking down all my equipment, I would drive another hundred yards and stop again. My peripheral vision was always glimpsing something that I had to investigate or explore further. Dragging anyone else along, even another artist or photographer, would have driven us both crazy.

As a result, with my Disney extortion paid and my family safe and secure with a *sans-Dad*, Ohio-based itinerary of their own, I set out in late August to experience and document the region around Florence and Siena.

The planning for the trip actually began in the spring. After researching points of interest as well as areas to avoid, I settled on an itinerary with an initial focus on the region of Siena and its northern hill towns. From there, I would travel south towards Pienza, Montepulciano, and the Orcia Valley.

I could have stayed in one place and taken day trips to all these sites pretty easily. Siena is no more than an hour's drive from Florence, and my southern destinations were less than an hour from Siena. Thus, staying in Siena could have given me access to all these areas. On the other hand, as I studied my hotel options, it seemed like there was a stark delineation between authentic city-based hotels that gave immediate access to an entire town, and resorts in the country that provided panoramic views of rolling Tuscan landscapes. Because much of my photographic work centers around landscapes and urban textures, it seemed natural for me to spend part of my time in the city and part in the country. In retrospect, it was a good decision and it worked out well.

Going Home

If you've ever been to a place that was truly different or that touched you deeply, you'll understand when I say that it was really hard to tell people about what Tuscany was like for me. Oh sure, I could show them the pictures and tell them about tiled roofs and rolling hills, but the reality is that people could glean all that from a travel brochure. But when a place resonates on a deeper level, it's a bit harder to articulate what you experienced without getting really personal and introspective.

At least I could use my cameras to frame and capture the world. Handing my pictures around or pointing to the PowerBook screen, it was implicit that for me Tuscany looked like *this*. *This* is what impacted me. *This* is what I saw and felt. But this visual residue still falls a bit short of the whole perspective, especially when it comes to emotional responses.

My immediate family strongly identifiies with the Italian culture. My dad came to the United States from Italy when he was three years old. On arrival in the States, my grandfather changed his name from Giordano to Giordan, in a feeble attempt to Americanize what was once a classic Italian surname. The bastardized result of "Giordan" remains as a confusing souvenir of the occasion and is equally difficult to pronounce for people of both languages.

Italian was never really spoken among my relatives. Those who knew it quickly forgot it through lack of use, and others like my dad quickly adopted English as their primary language.

When my grandfather died in 1956, most of the ties to our Italian way of life died with him. Relatives knew little about where we actually came from, or the whereabouts of any remaining relatives. "We lived in Florence and Naples," my dad would say, parroting back the line that must have been told him by his mom or dad. Ask for more info, and he would shrug his shoulders and say he didn't really know.

Even so, and in spite of all this veiled information, I felt like I was going back to my homeland; that I was going to reconnect with my people and my heritage.

Finally, as an artist trained in the traditional skills of drawing and painting, it's hard for me to maintain a neutral stance regarding Tuscany and its role in the Renaissance. This was the birthplace of western art; the iconic images left behind by Mike, Leo, and Raphael are powerful examples that can't be ignored. At the same time, as we push the artistic boundaries of the 21st century, experiencing these masters begs the question of how Renaissance art is relative for today and how we should relate to it within the context of a digital world.

I was going back home, and I was taking a pilgrimage to one of the true holy places of western art. It was unavoidable that I would come face to face with myself in the process.

A Tentative Start

When my plane finally arrived in Florence, after transfers in New York and Paris, I should have known that my bags would not arrive with me. Looking back on my itinerary, I had scheduled too many transfers too close together. In addition, I had missed my connecting flight from Paris to Florence; arriving three hours later than scheduled ensured that my bags would be listed among the missing.

Of course, I say all this in hindsight. At the time, I was happy to have finally arrived and was looking forward to getting my bags and my car and driving the 45-minute route to Siena. As the last of the bags were retrieved by their owners, and those of us orphaned by our bags were left to console each other, I was forced to accept that my journey was not yet complete. The woman at the counter told me that my bag would arrive in five hours. Did I want to wait or would I like them to drive it to my hotel? I was told that it would arrive at my hotel by courier by 9:00 AM the next morning. I could call that evening at 8:00 PM to ensure that it arrived, and it would all be taken care of. I was tired, and they made it sound so simple, so I agreed and started for Siena to get some rest and wait for my bag.

When I called at 8:00 p.m. to check on my bag, I was told that it had arrived and that it would arrive at my hotel by noon the next day. "Noon?" I asked. "I was told it would be here by 9:00 a.m." The guy on the phone told me that the courier didn't open before 9:00, but that it would go out as soon as possible, definitely by noon. Thus, at noon I was holding a lost-bag vigil in the small, dark lobby of my hotel, waiting for the courier who opened at 9:00.

When I mentioned the delivery delays to the woman who ran the hotel, she took a moment to give me a quick lesson on Italian culture. She had a heavy accent, and a perpetual cigarette dangled from the corner of her mouth. The glowing tip bobbed and danced as she rambled on in her broken English. As she spoke, I couldn't help thinking about how much this small, thin, energetic woman reminded me of my aunt Minnie.

The cigarette was bobbing away, and a coarse, animated voice was telling me how Italians were well-intentioned procrastinators who eventually got the job done. "Oh sure, they tell you 9:00 a.m., 12 noon, 3:00 p.m. They say lotsa things. But everyone here moves at much slower speed. More relaxed, you know? But it's okay, your bag will come eventually. Today's only Sunday. Maybe Wednesday, maybe Thursday, but they will bring it."

Now I was really getting scared. My desire to get my bag involved more than just a simple desire for a clean change of clothes. To save space, I had packed my tripod and a few crucial pieces of gear in my suitcase, and the Palio was going to be run at 6:00 p.m. the following day.

14

The Palio and the
Gangs of Siena

First run in 1656, the Palio is a medieval horse race run by representatives from the various neighborhoods of Siena, known as the contrada. Consider this excerpt which explains their social and political position, as written by Kristin Jarratt in the "In Italy Online" website:

> "The backbone of Il Palio are Siena's 17 contrade, which we would liken to city wards or administrative districts. These well-defined neighborhoods were designated in the Middle Ages, basically to aid the many military companies hired to defend Siena's fiercely earned independence from Florence and other nearby city states. Over the centuries, the contrada has lost its administrative function and become an area held together by its residents' common emotions and devotions. Its role has broadened, so that every important event—baptisms, deaths, marriages, church holidays, victories, even wine or food festivals—was celebrated by, and only by, the contrada. Even today, it is not considered a good idea to marry out of the contrada, and if you do, it's probably wise to sleep at your parents' house the night before the race."

The Palio was serious business in 1656 and it's serious business now. You could get beat up or seriously hurt if you wore the wrong colors in the wrong neighborhood during Palio time. The whole atmosphere is kind of like the street gangs of Los Angeles taking a sudden interest in the Preakness.

The main square in Siena is the Campo, and it's the site of this ritualistic spectacle. The cobblestones are covered with a deep layer of dirt, and railings are erected that turn the square into an approximation of a racing oval (despite the squared corners and blind spots that make the race more of a suicide run than a sporting event).

The people were in a fanatical frenzy as the start of the race grew closer. The costumes, flags, and pageantry are faithfully preserved from Siena's past, and it feels like more of a ritualistic reenactment than a casual summer festival.

Watching the jockeys ride bareback around the hairpin turns inspired vivid flashbacks of the opening scene on ABC's *Wide World of Sports*, when the skier wipes out on the ski jump as the announcer talks about the agony of defeat. I was struck by how raw and ferocious the atmosphere was. The horses ripped around the corner, riders and horses flipped and tumbled to the ground, and the densely packed crowd erupted and screamed. Il Palio exudes a palpable undercurrent of violence that makes it feel more like a bullfight than a horserace.

Anyway, it's now 3:30 and my bag still hasn't shown up. Aunt Minnie has stepped out for the afternoon, and a girl named Danielle has replaced her at the front desk. Danielle is a student at the University of Siena, having come to Italy last year from South America. She tells me that the people of Siena are very closed and insular. Even though she speaks

perfect Italian and blends in visually, she is not accepted here. "The people who were born here, whose families have lived here a long time, they do not accept outsiders like me and my friends," she tells me. "They will tolerate tourists because you spend money, but they are closed and exclude the outsiders who live here."

Siena was originally an Etruscan settlement that later became the Roman city of Sena Julia. Throughout the Middle Ages, the city came under the control of the Lombard kings, and they were constantly fighting with neighboring towns—including Florence, which was their biggest rival. The city set up numerous alliances to resist aggression from its enemies. The Spanish, the Florentines, and even the French have tried to overrun this tiny hill town, which resulted in a legacy of heroic struggles. Throughout history, the Sienese have stood together to preserve their identity, which was closely tied to their security. Apparently they are still closing ranks against outsiders, even today.

The pieces were all starting to fit together. The contrada were neighborhood groups that had a direct military function for keeping the city safe and ensuring the survival of Siena. It's somewhat ironic that they split into such tightly knit factions while ensuring the town's survival and identity.

My bag showed up around 4:15 or so, and I breathed a huge sigh of relief as I unpacked my gear and got cleaned up. During the course of my stay, I found

that everything I'd been told about Siena was indeed true. The Sienese were a proud and passionate people who followed their own schedules and timelines. With a few exceptions, I found the people to be distant or aloof, fiercely proud of their heritage, and closed to outsiders. Their whole identity was wrapped up in the fact that they live in Siena and were somehow linked to the city's historic legacy. The Palio gave them a chance to connect with that legacy in a direct and personal way. It's a one-of-a-kind experience.

Obligatory Pilgrimages

The art in Tuscany is unique and spectacular. As an artist visiting the region, there are certain things you just have to do. The list of requirements includes traveling to towns that would be unknown if not for their one masterpiece, visiting countless works of art and architecture, and standing in admission lines for hours to pay homage to the contents of the Ufizzi gallery. You don't have much choice in the matter; if you're one who appreciates art, you simply must do your aesthetic duty.

And I certainly did mine. I dutifully read all the guidebooks, which set the Renaissance masters on their well-deserved pedestals. I plotted where the masterpieces were, which ones I could see in a given day, and ranked the works as well as the artists themselves in proper hierarchical order. I reacquainted

myself with the Sienese School of painting (which I had barely studied in art school), and checked off favorite sites and excursions remembered from a previous visit. In the course of the three months that I prepared for this trip, I must have accumulated a collection of 8 or 10 guidebooks on the region, and amassed a list of dozens of Internet bookmarks. They all contained 80% of the same material but each one had a slightly different perspective, or included a few different listings that were worth adding to my list.

All this notoriety, combined with the general guidebook consensus of what was worth seeing, set my expectations pretty high. I think that anyone who travels to Tuscany and has even casually thumbed through a single guidebook would have elevated expectations. This really *was* the Art Mecca. You can imagine tourists disembarking from plane after plane, clutching their guidebooks and looking around expectantly: "We're in Florence now, and we're going to see the greatest art in the world."

And so they stand like cattle in all the admission lines, and they shuffle past the art, taking it in as best they can. I'm sure some are disappointed by the inevitable letdown that can only follow such aesthetic anticipation. I mean, after all, it's just a piece of marble, or a bunch of colors on a panel. Others may react effusively, as though they had just met a movie star or some other famous celebrity. "Oh my, doesn't *David* look thinner in person? Well, they say the guidebook does add 10 pounds...."

A small minority is reported to have physical symptoms in response to these sublime works of art, feeling dizziness or nausea as a result of their confrontation with such beauty. The supposed malady is known as the Stendhal Syndrome, named for the famous novelist who reported nervous exhaustion, agitation, and heart palpitations in response to Florence's church of Santa Croce in January 1817. Others have reported hallucinations, fevers, tears, and convulsions (although some suspect this was in response to the high prices at the museum restaurants).

Although most of these symptoms can be chalked up to traveling stress and anxiety, the fact that these symptoms are ascribed to works of art in the first place indicates that we are bestowing great power on these objects. Our high expectations are either affirmed or refuted, and some people are sure to react strongly in either case.

As I walked into Santa Croce, which was on my "favorites from my last visit" list, I was happy to see that my admiration was not just a distorted memory blown out of proportion by the guidebooks. The cathedral was filled with amazing examples of art and history, and as I took it all in, I confess that I was beginning to feel a little Stendhal-ish myself. The frescoes and sculptures were amazing, and the list of historic figures entombed there is awe inspiring. Dante and Michelangelo's tombs are right next to each other, making you wonder if they bought the

20

adjoining plots early in life to ensure that they got the best spots.

And then there's the architecture itself, which is so high and perfectly proportioned. Inspiration is everywhere, and the place has the buzz of significance. As I sat in a pew and took in the vast interior, I couldn't help but think about the artists and dignitaries represented here, and how they must have been revered in their own time, even as they are now. I asked myself the typical questions: How did they build the ceiling so high? How long did it take to build? And who decided on the final aesthetic look and feel?

At that point, I stopped in mid-thought and reminded myself that I was in a house of worship. This place was supposed to point me and all the other visitors towards God, and instead I was sitting there thinking about all the guys who built it, decorated it, or were buried in it. It felt wrong, as though in my zealousness I had overshot the mark and missed the entire point.

Now I'm sure that some would argue that the art, architecture, and this place as a whole, was transcendent (or perhaps even "transplendent" as Woody's date from *Annie Hall* would say). They would probably assert that the absolute genius represented here gave a glimpse of God's divine nature, and perhaps even of God's general grace towards mankind. And I might consider that to be a valid justification— if it weren't for those pesky guidebooks.

Today's guidebooks mythologize the artists, shifting the focus in many cases from the significance of the work to the celebrity of its creator. In their time, these artists were pretty famous as well; if not like rock stars, then at least like the designers from *Trading Spaces*. Everyone knew who they were, and they were probably the headline attractions at all the Home Improvement conventions around Tuscany, Umbria, and the Veneto.

As I thought about it, I realized that there were similarities between the Renaissance artists and the digital photographers and artists of today. Both seem to work magic and do the impossible; one with pixels and Photoshop, the other with perspective, *camera obscura*, and a new style that seemed to replicate life itself.

The perspective and realism of the Renaissance created an art that looked "real," even as today's Photoshop artists create fabricated images that look so "real" that the very concept of photographic reality has been obliterated. Both groups of artists were on the leading edge of technology for their day. They were visionaries that threw the doors wide open and created a dazzling array of artistic opportunities for those who would come after them. It makes me curious about what today's Raphael might look like, and leaves me wondering where I put my guidebook to the digital landscape.

Prologue

The trip is now a distant memory. Ten months have passed, and I've moved from Tuscan exploration to the dogged discipline of writing the book you're now holding. The images have all been captured, the book is almost finished, and I'm just now starting to piece together what this entire experience has meant to me.

I loved spending time with the Italians. I saw reminders of my family everywhere I went, whether it was Aunt Minnie, Uncle Frank, or even my dad. When you're a kid, you wonder about where your family comes from; it was always frustrating that none of my relatives seemed to know. Grandpa came over in 1933, and I've always wondered if he left because of the political unrest and fascist climate during that time. I'll probably never understand the specific motivations that caused a man to move his family halfway around the world. Perhaps it was a dramatic situation, perhaps not. Although I can't say I've gotten any specific answers, I at least have a sense for the country from which they came.

The people of Siena clung to their identity fiercely and passionately. I used to feel the same way in clinging to my identity as an artist. When I was younger, being an artist was the most important thing in my life, perhaps the only thing. But now I think I'm more concerned with my identity as a person, being true to my beliefs and my family. Don't get me wrong—the art is still important, and it's an undeniable part of me. It's just not anything I feel that I have to prove anymore. It's as if I've made the transition from aspiration to inspiration. I'm curious, and exploring, but I'm also content where I am.

As I sat there in Santa Croce, thinking about how the aspirations of men had shifted the focus away from God, I noticed a shaft of bright sunlight streaming through a rose window, high on the wall of the right nave. It cast a rainbow-colored highlight that stretched across the stonework, spontaneously illuminating the interior. As I took it in, I never once asked myself how long it took to create it, how it ranked with similar sunbeams, and what page it was on in the guidebook. I just sat there on that tiny wooden bench, taking it in. And it was perfect.

TECNICHE

Part 1

DIGITAL PHOTOGRAPHY TECHNIQUES

When the original *Art of Photoshop* book was published a few years ago, some of the most frequent comments were from readers asking me where I sourced my images. They would say that it was fine to teach them curves or filters, but they recognized that if the source image wasn't of decent quality, artists were severely limited in what they could achieve.

The chapters in this part are dedicated to basic photographic principles, as well as the specific, actionable techniques for taking better digital photos. The chapters cover the basics of exposure, composition, depth of field, and general technical skills that will enhance the quality of your images.

Chapter 1

DIGITAL CAMERA BASICS

If you're like me, you tend to pick up books like this and skim over the first few chapters; especially if the word "basic" is attached to the chapter title. You assume that you have the basic stuff down already and that nothing important could possibly start before page 79. Well, before you start flipping ahead, consider the possibility that there's valuable information right here. This chapter provides a baseline for the entire digital photography audience, filling in the knowledge gaps for creative, photographic, and technical applications.

The reason for the knowledge gaps is that people are flocking to digital photography from all directions. There's the film-based photographer who's looking to go digital and understand Photoshop; there's the Photoshop guru who can finally afford a decent digital camera, and there's also the flat-out newbie who doesn't know photography or Photoshop. As a result, lots of people know some of this stuff, but it's a much smaller percentage of people who have it all down. (If you happen to be one of those people who are well versed in f-stops and preferences files, skip ahead at your own peril...I'll catch up with you later.)

① **Bronze Patina**
Nikon D2H
1/250 sec, f/8
Focal length 400mm

② **Yellow House**
Nikon D2H,
1/100 sec, f/16
ISO- 640
Focal length 135mm

A Simple Message

Most people are familiar with the phrase "garbage-in, garbage-out" as a way of saying that if you start with poor-quality source material, you're likely to end up with a poor-quality end result. This emphasis has always been important for film-based photography; slides and film negatives are far less forgiving of exposure mistakes than their digital file counterparts. With film, the image is set in stone, and the quality and craft suffers if the exposure and focus aren't exact.

In contrast, digital photography offers some pretty solid advantages. You can adjust the exposure of some digital files as much as two or three f-stops and still get a decent print, and Photoshop does amazing tricks you could never accomplish in a dark-room. You would expect that these advantages would be propelling photography to new heights of quality and innovation, but instead all people seem to talk about is whether digital photography is as good as film. As good? As good?! Digital photography should make everyone better than they were with film...the technology has caught up, the advantages are huge; we just need to wait for our expectations to follow.

Digital Photography Pros and Cons

Along with advantages come potential pitfalls because the immediacy of digital photography threatens to make us sloppy. We see the image instantly, we can reshoot at will, and the individual shot is almost trivialized. Why take your time to compose and shoot properly when you can just do it over if you don't see what you're after? People are cutting corners, not cleaning their equipment, shooting casually, almost glibly, with the assumption that they can make up for their mistakes in the computer. And although the computer does improve the raw image file, it often creates parity with film rather than creating

improvements because of the sub-par raw images created by this casual approach.

It's very difficult to create meaningful images with poorly captured images, no matter how fast your computer is or how well you know Photoshop. Start with a solid image that is thoughtfully composed and exposed. Afterwards, open the image and process it skillfully in Photoshop. Embrace both aspects of the process and you will find the medium to be an articulate and expressive tool that's poised to surpass the current limitations of film. To address the first part of this equation, this chapter and the three that follow it focus on helping you capture the best images possible.

Five Habits to Optimize Image Quality

The first step in consistently capturing good images is to develop sound habits that you apply instinctively, each time you take pictures. We're not talking about understanding exposure, composition, or any other specific techniques just yet; the list that follows is more fundamental than that. Follow these suggestions and internalize them as habits. They can make the difference between a good shot and a great one.

Clean Equipment

Make sure that your lenses, filters, and eyepieces are clean and free from dust, smudges, or fingerprints.

It sounds obvious, but because many digital cameras are smaller and easier to carry, they also become easier to smudge, scuff, and knock around. Keeping equipment clean is less of an issue with large and medium format cameras, in that their size (and cost) makes us approach them more methodically. Reach into your camera bag (or your pocket) to grab your camera, and you can easily fingerprint your lens or accidentally change the settings.

The casual, portable nature of digital cameras turns their lenses into dust magnets. Dust on a lens translates into dust on the digital image, and cleaning up your dust spots in Photoshop is tedious and time consuming. Because of the immediate nature of digital technology, you're going to shoot a lot of images; retouching all those images is time consuming. In the long run, a dirty lens eats into your productivity.

Be especially careful with your lens because dust and fingerprints on the glass translate into soft spots and blurred image areas. Always carry a small bellows or lens tissue to keep the lens free of dust. In addition, make sure that you keep the eyepiece and LCD image display area clean. Many manufacturers seem intent on placing the image display area so that your finger or your nose leaves a smudge every time you have the slightest interaction with the camera. This obviously makes it harder to view the image you've just captured, and puts the onus on you to clean it more often. If you don't clean your camera regularly, all this dust and oil accumulates over time, making it even harder to clean, while impacting performance and reliability.

Tripod and Cable Release

Camera shake is perhaps the number one enemy of sharp pictures. You can have the highest quality lens and the perfect lighting conditions, but if your camera is moving as you take the shot, your images will be disappointing. Camera shake happens for two reasons: The most obvious is when you're shooting at a

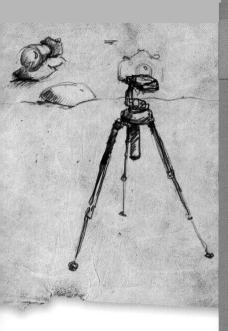

slow shutter speed and you move the camera slightly while the shutter is open. The second instance is movement created as you trigger the shutter. This can happen at much faster shutter speeds and tends to be slightly less noticeable, although it still impacts overall quality.

The solution is to use a tripod whenever possible; if your camera accepts a cable release, you should buy one and use it to trigger the shutter. I know it sounds like a pain to carry a tripod around, but there are ways of coping with it (see the PhotoTip on tripod options on the previous page). The cable release is easier than the tripod to carry and works wonders when combined

So you want sharper images, but think tripods are too bulky and heavy to lug around on a regular basis. I thought about this a lot as I traveled through Tuscany shooting the images for this book. Although many *tripods* have attained "boat anchor" status, other alternatives can help stabilize the shot while being easier on your back.

If your budget allows, buy a tripod that's made from lightweight materials that still deliver strong, rigid support. I travel with a Manfrotto Carbon One tripod, which is made from braided carbon fibers and features a lightweight magnesium head. The result is a fully functional professional tripod that's super light, while still supporting bulky dSLRs and medium format cameras.

If your camera is lighter, consider a *video tripod*. These units are usually smaller, thinner, and much lighter than their traditional counterparts, and they work just as well as long as you don't try to support anything too heavy. You might opt for a tabletop tripod that is just a few inches tall, or a modified tripod that clamps to your car window (if you need to shoot as you drive). Finally, if you want stability and mobility, think about using a *monopod*. All these tools provide increased support and stability while allowing you to maneuver around your subject or recompose the shot with ease.

Many professionals also like using sandbags or beanbags to stabilize the shot, placing them on a stable surface and nestling the camera or lens into the bag. The bag conforms to the lens, minimizes any vibrations, is easy to carry, and features minimal set up or tear-down.

I have accumulated all these options over the years and find that the biggest challenge is anticipating which piece of equipment I should take into the field or location shoot. To be honest, I haven't figured that one out yet. I'm a bit obsessive and end up taking too much gear just to be on the safe side and to make sure that I get the shot. Sadly, it appears I've come full circle, lugging around lots of lighter stuff to ensure that the elusive shot doesn't get away.

with the tripod. An added benefit of using a tripod and cable release is that it slows you down and makes the process of capturing the image more methodical. As a result, you will find that you're a bit more thoughtful regarding composition and framing, and just a bit more discerning in general when you approach a potential image ("...is this shot *really* worth setting up my tripod for?").

Focus Control

Although autofocus capabilities have matured in recent years, the systems can still lock in on the wrong area or be fooled by an absence of sharp edges. If your cam-era allows it, consider changing to Manual Focus mode and focusing by hand. This is sometimes the most direct way to ensure a clean, sharp image, especially if you're shooting close-up images or are using a nar-row *depth of field* (see Chapter 3, "Focus and Depth of Field," for more on depth of field).

Exposure Options

Develop an understanding of how your light meter works and plan your shot accordingly. Consider shifting to *spot* or *center-weighted metering* to optimize exposure or explore exposure alternatives. Also consider exploring various f-stop and shutter speed combinations to optimize sharpness and depth of field. For more on exposure, see Chapter 2, "Digital Exposure."

On the other hand, if you have only one shot at the image; *bracket*, bracket, bracket. Manual focus, cable releases, and tripods are great when the subject isn't going any-where. When you have to react fast, set the camera to bracket all expo-sures. Remember that you can also go into the digital camera's setup menu and specify the degree of exposure variation from shot to shot, allowing you to fine-tune the process to the lighting conditions. See the section, "Bracket in Uncertain Light," later in this chapter, for details on brack-eting.

Tourists at the Duomo

Tourists at the Piazza del Duomo

The Piazza del Duomo is one of my favorite places in Florence. It's a bustling square that features some of the most stunning architecture and monuments the city has to offer. There's the Duomo itself, also known as the Church of Santa Maria del Fiore, her majestic dome and carved façade holding court as the center of attention. Opposite the cathedral stands the octagonal baptistery, with the magnificent bronze doors by Lorenzo Ghiberti and sculptures depicting John the Baptist. Flanking the cathedral is the magnificent bell tower (campanile), which rises majestically above the Piazza.

Add to this a healthy dose of gift shops, cafes, and street vendors and you have a tourist magnet of the highest order. The broad steps of the cathedral invite people to come and sit, rest their feet, and nurse their gelato. So they sit for a minute and then pull out their cameras—some trying to capture the aesthetic beauty, others just looking to record the fact that they were there. Most would swoop in, looking at maps or clutching guide books, look up, and impulsively snap a picture. Many who had a digital camera would shoot and move on without even looking at the preview screen, as blind to their results as their film-based compatriots. In the 30 minutes I sat watching, I didn't see a single person study the scene, consider the lighting conditions, or use a tripod or any other camera support. I know a half hour isn't that long, but I still was able to watch hundreds of people pass by during that time.

The fact is that I wasn't there to do a behavioral study, I was evaluating the scene to determine what lent itself to a good photograph. I was looking for shooting angles, patterns in how the light cast shadows, close-up and panoramic compositions, and details that might reveal themselves with just a little more looking. I have to force myself to do this sometimes because there's a part of me that's just like the other tourists—wanting to impulsively react to capture the object, recording the moment as a souvenir. When I go to a new place, I have to consciously slow myself down and get past the tendency to record objects and places.

In the end, I decided that the square was currently too crowded for wide shots and complete buildings (I'd have to come back early in the morning for that). Instead I looked up and shot the sculpted façade of the Duomo, and close-ups of Ghiberti's Gates of Paradise portal. I chose a spot in the shadow of the baptistery, set up my tripod and 600mm lens, and pointed the camera skyward. The shots were tack sharp thanks to my cable release, and more compelling thanks to patient and thoughtful framing.

Sculptures gracing the façade of the church of Santa Maria del Fiore and the adjoining baptistery.

⑧ **Pienza Chapel**
Nikon D2H,
1/60 sec, f/4.5
Focal length 75mm

Use a Laptop

If you're doing an important shoot that will be very hard to replicate, hook the camera up to a laptop and review your images on a big screen in real time. I carried my PowerBook with me on several shoots in Italy and was thankful that I could zoom in to check exposure and image sharpness in real time. This allowed me to see the full image and fine-tune the results as I was shooting. The result: no surprises. I knew what I was getting while the camera was still set up. If an image wasn't right, I recomposed, waited for the wind to die down, or made some other revision in order to get it right.

Previewing Tips: Critical Evaluation

Artist and author Jack Davis likes to call the digital preview process "chimpin'" because you always see digital photographers gathered around their cameras, pointing at the preview screen and going "Ooooh! Ooooh!" (like a bunch of monkeys). Although we like to share the digital preview screen with those around us, it's even more important that we've checked it with our own discerning eye and are satisfied with the results. As you look at the image in the preview, ask yourself the following questions.

Is the Image Framed Properly?

How's the composition? Did you fit everything in the frame or did you cut off someone's head or feet? If you didn't frame the shot properly, erase the image and shoot it again. Even if you did get everything in the shot, ask yourself the tougher question of whether you created an interesting composition. What about a lower or higher angle of view? Could you use more space around the subject, or could it be cropped tighter? Challenge yourself in this area; you'll be surprised at what a little critical thinking can do. (For more on image composition, see Chapter 4, "Composition.")

Monochrome Stairway

Siena is a classic Tuscan hill town, with winding streets that twist, turn, and defy any semblance of a grid or logical organization. The streets are made of tiled stone, which runs right up to the edge of the stone buildings, which are topped with tiled (stone) rooftops. There are no patches of grass here, no breaks or interludes to this monochrome, petrified uniformity. It's as if the city planners took all the green grass and vegetation and shipped it outside the cities to create the glorious countryside. The palpable light, fresh air, and panoramic vistas that surround the cities present a dramatic counterpoint to the gritty stonework and historic nuance of the hill towns themselves.

The buildings and walls all look alike, and the doors and windows blur into an endless, nondescript parade of rectangles and squares, set into the corridor-like streets. The doors are generic portals that give little away as to what is behind them—open a door, and you might find a workshop, health club, hotel, or apartment. The streets are broken up every few blocks by city squares that feature fountains, churches, or other communal items (all made of stone, of course). After spending time in Siena, I was left with two prevailing thoughts: I was dying to see anything that was not made of stone, and I was curious to see what was behind a few of these mysterious doorways.

On my second day, as I was lugging my gear down to the main square (Il Campo) to shoot the practice runs for the Palio horse race, I pulled up short and backtracked a few steps to one of those innocuous doors that had been left slightly ajar. Slipping inside, I was presented with a fairly simple lobby with two archways providing access to stairs and a closet of some kind, lit by a stark, bare light bulb. I loved the symmetry of the two arches, as well as the textured walls and red and white tiled floor. I quickly set up my tripod and Nikon D2H and composed the shot.

Upon review, I decided that the image worked better as black and white because the monochrome aesthetic emphasized the texture and high-contrast lighting. Chapter 5, "Tone and Color," features details on how to convert color images to black and white. This image is a good example of when and why you should use it.

Siena Lobby in Color

Siena Lobby in Monochrome

Is It Sharp?

Sharpness is the hardest aspect to evaluate, especially on that little LCD screen. An image can look just fine on the back of the camera, but might reveal soft, blurred edges when you open it on the computer. It helps a little if your camera allows you to zoom on the image preview, but it's still hard to see exactly what you have because you never see the image at a true 1:1 pixel ratio. This is a great reason to tether your camera to a laptop while you're shooting because sharpness is the hardest thing to evaluate in an on-camera preview.

Preview Exposure with Histograms and Clipping

Don't trust your eyes to look at the LCD screen when determining whether you have the proper exposure. The LCD preview almost always looks good, even when the tonal range is deficient in the shadows or the highlights. The best way to evaluate exposure is to check the image *histogram*.

Although it might seem a bit confusing, it's crucial for all digital photographers to become familiar with how the histogram works. The histogram is the most reliable reflection of the information that resides in your image. It's more reliable than your monitor, a digital proof, or even the prepress guru at the service bureau. All those other options are subjective, but in the digital realm, the numbers don't lie.

A histogram will tell you if you have image data in the highlights, shadows, and everywhere in between. It even tells you how the pixels are dispersed throughout your image. Histograms are covered in depth in Chapter 2, but I mention them here so that you understand their role as a key factor in the image preview process. When evaluating exposure, use the histogram, not your eyes.

Some cameras also allow you to preview the highlight areas in the image that register as pure white

(255). If you take advantage of this camera feature, you can catch over-exposed images where you might have blown out the highlights in pursuit of shadow detail. The "clipping area" is usually shown in the preview window as a flashing area of flat color. Histograms and clipping can be shown in the preview window of most cameras, and can be controlled and modified by the camera's preferences menu.

Are There Any Color Casts?

If an image shows a *color cast*, it probably indicates that the camera's white balance is not set correctly. Most digital cameras come with an auto white balance feature that cali-brates the chip to the current lighting conditions, color correcting the image for you on-the-fly. If your camera lets you set the white balance manually, you should check the settings. Color casts can also occur if the image is severely underexposed. If necessary, check to see that the proper exposure is set, and modify the exposure settings as needed.

In a similar vein, ask yourself if an image might look better in black and white. If an image has high contrast, has a lot of texture, or has subject matter that lends itself to a *monochrome* look, consider desaturating the image (in either the camera or later in Photoshop) to a black-and-white shot. The trade off is that shooting black and white in some cameras lets you capture a wider tonal range; desaturating in Photoshop gives you additional control over emphasizing specific areas with the tonal range.

Capturing the Elusive Shot

It's one thing to be able to check the preview and discern whether you've got the shot, but it's quite another to have time left to do something about it. Many shots present themselves for just a brief moment before they disappear forever. As a result, anticipating when a shot will appear and being ready for it is a very important skill to cultivate.

10 Siena Flags (detail)
Nikon D2H,
1/40 sec, f/4.2
Focal length 48mm

11 Siena Flags
Nikon D2H,
1/40 sec, f/4.2
Focal length 48mm

Bracket in Uncertain Light

Bracketing is a great safety net you can use to make sure that you've exposed the image properly. It's a process where the camera captures the primary exposure along with an image that's slightly lighter and one that's slightly darker, with intervals that are determined in your camera's setup menu. You can createthe variation in exposure by adjusting f-stops or shutter speeds, although f-stop variation is the most common approach to bracketing. If you're shooting candid, dynamic subject matter in uncertain lighting conditions, bracketing your exposures casts a wide net to give you the best chance of success.

Burst Exposure for Fast Action

If you're shooting a moving subject such as a sporting event or stock car race, *burst exposures* dramatically increase your chances of getting the right shot. The process involves shooting a series of images in rapid succession, freezing the action several times in the course of a single motion. Want to catch the baseball pitcher's arm at the apex as he's throwing his fastball? Set the camera to burst and time his motion, pressing the shutter at the appropriate time. When you review your results, choose the one image from the burst sequence that is closest to what you were after.

Figures ⑫ and ⑬, showing the pigeon and cat sculpture, bear this

out. I had noticed that the birds liked to fly up to the fountain and hover a bit before landing and taking a drink. I set up my tripod and framed the shot, waiting for the birds to come in. The frame rate was set to 8 frames per second, and I was able to fire off three shots with a quick press of the shutter. Although Figure ⑫ captures the bird in profile and higher contrast, Figure ⑬ perfectly frames the bird in the doorway (which is shaped like an old fashioned birdcage). I go back and forth and still can't decide which image I like better.

Burst capabilities vary from camera to camera. As I write this, I'm using a Nikon D2H, which has a burst

rate of 8 frames per second, with an image *buffer* of up to 40 frames (the buffer determines how many shots you can shoot in succession before the camera has to write the images to the card). As of this writing, the D2H is at the high end of the digital camera spectrum, but many other dSLRs sport decent burst rates that can help you pin down that elusive moment.

Plan Ahead

One of the simplest things you can do to capture fast action or fleeting images is to do the Boy Scout thing and be prepared. This means giving yourself time to set up and shoot a few test images, being well versed in all aspects of the equipment, and learning to anticipate exposure for different lighting conditions. It sounds like a simple or obvious suggestion, but I've seen too many people show up late for an event or fumble with settings when they should have been taking the shot.

Elements of Photographic Quality

What makes a good photograph? The quest for photographic quality can be elusive, in that we can identify the components that contribute to a good image, but still have the final product fall short of its potential. As is the case with all artistic mediums, there's an intangible combination of inspiration, timing, and craft that make an artistic photograph.

In fact, laying out the steps for capturing a good photograph can be almost as elusive as the photographic muse itself. This book tries to assist you in that endeavor by teaching technical knowledge and showing inspirational images. Although it might be difficult to specify the exact path to photographic excellence, it's pretty safe to say that this path passes through the technical domain defined by sharpness, exposure, and composition. It's important to understand how these three components combine to create a quality image.

14 Olivetto Wall
Nikon D2H,
1/250 sec, f/3.8
Focal length 35mm

15 Lanterns
Nikon D2H,
1/100 sec, f/5
EV +1
Focal length 75mm

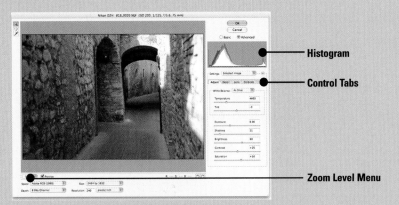

Histogram

Control Tabs

Zoom Level Menu

Using Photoshop's Camera Raw Plug-in dialog box.

at the edges of digital images. It appears as colored fringing that corresponds to either a red/cyan or blue/yellow polarity (that is, the fringe is red on one side of the image and cyan on the other). Click the Lens tab and adjust the Chromatic Aberration R/C or B/Y slider as needed. This is another adjustment that requires you to set the magnification to 100%. If the distortion is irreparable, Adobe includes Vignette sliders that allow you to create a feathered crop around the edges of the image.

The Calibrate tab allows you to tweak the hue and saturation for each RGB color channel; it also includes a separate control for the shadows. Use this tab if your camera consistently distorts a single color, such as blues and violets, which many cameras do. To tweak the global color balance of a specific image, use the White Balance, Temperature, and Tint controls in the Adjust tab.

When the preview image looks perfect, click OK to launch the image, or Option+click (Ctrl+click in Windows) OK to save the Camera Raw settings with the image file without actually opening the image.

When you open a 16-bit image in Photoshop, the Camera Raw Plug-in dialog box opens, giving you a wide range of editing options.

Beneath a composite histogram on the right of the dialog box are four control tabs that allow you to modify tone, sharpness, lens distortion, and color balance. The Adjust tab controls the tone within the image. Start by tweaking the Exposure and Shadow sliders to adjust the overall tonal range and the shadow tones. Set these variables first because they can clip the highlights or shadows, resulting in data loss. When moving these sliders, hold down the Option key (Ctrl key for Windows users) to view any clipped information being reduced to flat black or

white. With the overall range set, you can modify the Brightness, Contrast, or Saturation sliders without fear of loosing any information.

The Detail tab controls sharpness and is pretty straightforward in its application. Start by setting the Zoom Level field to 100% and then adjust the Sharpness slider to sharpen the image. If the image starts to get too crisp—which can happen along high-contrast edges—increase the Luminance Smoothing slider. If the image starts to pixelate and get chunky, increase the Color Noise Reduction slider.

The Lens tab controls a type of lens distortion known as *chromatic aberration*. Chromatic aberration is a misalignment of color channels that is sometimes visible

Sharpness and Detail

Sharpness refers to the areas of the image that are in sharp focus. When evaluating your images for sharpness, the two main questions you need to ask are whether the subject of the shot is in focus, and whether the focus area is sharp enough.

When locking on a focus point, many autofocus cameras look for parallel lines or distinct edges in specific zones of the viewfinder. As a result, the camera often misses the mark, focusing in front of or behind your subject, leaving the desired subject soft and blurry. Each time you examine a shot, you should look for the focus point that the auto-focus system decided on. Is the sharpest area of focus positioned appropriately in relation to your subject, or is it a bit soft?

Generally speaking, you want the subject as sharp as possible, so you may want to consider reshooting the image if the subject isn't as sharp as you'd like. It's easier to soften sharp objects in Photoshop, so you should always try to get the sharpest image possible. Even if you're going for a soft hazy effect, capture all the detail you can in the original shot. Post-processing in Photoshop is a great place to add back a bit of blur if that's what you're after.

Using quality lenses, putting the camera on a tripod, and using a cable release are great ways to increase the overall sharpness of your images. Don't rely on Photoshop to save the day, because even though Photoshop can do some amazing things to sharpen images, there's still no replacement for shooting a tack-sharp image through the lens.

Exposure

Good *exposure* is so important to photography that you could easily devote a couple volumes to it. In fact, I devote the entire next chapter to the art and science of proper photographic exposure and barely scratch the surface. Within the context of image quality, exposure determines whether you have enough tonal variation and information to properly describe your subject.

16 D'Orcia Hills
Nikon D2H,
1/320 sec, f/8.5
Focal length 230mm

**17 D'Orcia Hills
(detail)**

**18 D'Orcia Hills
(detail)**

The operative words here are "properly describe." It might be enough to show the subject in full silhouette, or it could be that the entire scene needs even illumination. Each subject is different, and the "proper" way to render the subject is subjective. Experiment with exposure variations and think through the best way to describe the subject. See Chapter 2 for details.

Composition and Cropping

There are two ways to approach composition and cropping, and I admit that I use both approaches as the situation dictates. One approach is to treat the viewfinder as the final image and compose accordingly. The advantage to this method is that you capture the image at the camera's maximum resolution. When you crop, you obviously reduce the overall pixel size of the image, limiting its enlargement possibilities.

The problem with composing the final image through the viewfinder is that the optimum composition isn't always evident. Perhaps the shot works better in a vertical (portrait) orientation rather than a horizontal (landscape) orientation; perhaps the object should have more space around it. In addition, there will be times when you have to react quickly and get the shot without thinking too much about composition. Take the shot and make sure that it's sharp and well exposed; cropping and composing can be addressed later in Photoshop. See Chapter 4 for details on composing and cropping images.

File Format Pros and Cons

All the technique in the world won't help you if you capture the image in the wrong file format. With a world of format options available, the challenge is to determine the proper file type and compression scheme for the type of work you're doing. This is a challenge because you hear so many differing opinions. Some people will tell you that JPEGs are fine, while others shake their heads in scorn if you capture in anything

other than uncompressed 16-bit TIFFs. Who's right, and how do you go about making a decision?

What Are My Choices?

The primary variables in this process are file format, bit depth, and compression schema. Before you decide on a strategy for format and compression, you first need to understand what these variables mean.

File Format

File format (also called *file type*) refers to the type of file generated by the camera as it saves the image. The file type determines the amount of information in the file,

how it's structured, and how it can be accessed and edited by programs such as Photoshop. For most users, the choice is between TIFF files and JPEG files.

The TIFF file is the standard format in the imaging world, making it the obvious choice for many digital photographers. The problem with TIFF files is file size; they tend to get pretty big. You can compress TIFF files using a lossless compression mode called LZW, which makes the files a bit more manageable and easier to store. Lossless compression means that the image quality is not degraded in the process of compression, and for many it's the perfect compromise between compression and optimum quality. The downside to LZW files is that they are still much larger

than their JPEG counterparts, and they take a bit more time to open and close in Photoshop because Photoshop has to run the compression and decompression algorithms in each instance.

Many digital camera users love to save files in JPEG format because the files are extremely small, and you can fit hundreds of files on a single media card. The downside of JPEG files, of course, is that you do loose a bit of detail. Is it enough for you to notice, and does it really matter? I'll explore these issues more in the next section, so stay tuned.

20 Window
Nikon D2H,
1/60 sec, f/8
EV +1
Focal length 14mm

21 Pienza Texture
Nikon D2H,
1/60 sec, f/4
Focal length 28mm

43

㉒ Palio Procession
Nikon D2H,
1/60 sec, f/5.3
EV +1
Focal length 300mm

㉓ Palio Banner
(crop1)
Nikon D2H,
1/125 sec, f/5.3
ISO 640
Focal length 78mm

8-bit Versus 16-bit

More advanced cameras allow you to capture images in 16-bit mode, as opposed to the standard 8-bit mode used by conventional digital cameras. The number of bits in an image (referred to as the *bit depth*) determines the number of gray tones it can support. 8-bit images support 256 shades of gray, as calculated by two to the eighth power. As the bit depth increases, the gray scale expands exponentially. In 12-bit images, the number increases to 4,096 shades of gray, and in 16-bit images there are 65,536 shades of gray.

But wait a minute; you might be asking what a grayscale range has to do with a color image. In an RGB image, each color channel is rendered in a grayscale model that represents the distribution of the channel color (red, green, or blue) throughout the image. In Photoshop, select Window, Channels to open the Channels palette and click the red channel; you'll see a grayscale image representing the red distribution. In an 8-bit image, that red channel is composed of 256 shades of red; in a 16-bit file, there are 65,536 shades of red. More shades mean smoother transitions and gradations, less banding, and a much smoother image.

The bit depth is critical for image editing because each time you edit in Photoshop, you erode image quality, literally throwing away pixel information. Stretch a curve or Levels slider, and you create gaps in the tonal range as the histogram expands and shifts (a phenomenon known as *combing* because of the comb shape it creates in the histogram). This process diminishes quality in both 8-bit and 16-bit images; however, the 16-bit images look much better because of the additional image data resident in the file.

If the quality loss is so significant, why don't more people notice it? One reason is that the overlap of image data across color channels tends to mask banding within each individual channel, creating a quality loss that's often felt rather than pinpointed directly. Also, the more

editing you do, the more chronic the problem becomes.

Another reason you might not notice the quality degradation is that many people using 8-bit files don't even try to do the things a 16-bit file can do. Try increasing the exposure by two or three stops on an 8-bit image, and things get ugly in a hurry. The image can pixelate in the shadows, take on color cast, or create flat, solarized areas that are void of information. People train themselves not to try these kind of corrections, even with 16-bit images. I find the extra latitude provided by 16-bit files to be indispensable when I work in Photoshop, especially when I'm exploring expressive exposure options within an image.

The downside is that 16-bit files are *much* larger than their 8-bit counterparts. For example, a 16-bit file that's 23MB reduces to just 11MB in 8-bit mode. Not only that, but each time you add another layer, the file size bumps up even more. That same 16-bit file with three total layers weighs in at a whopping 84MB; and that's just three layers. With 10 layers, the file balloons to 299MB. Change the file to 8-bit, and the total size drops back down to 23MB, including all 10 layers.

Thus, on the one hand, 16-bit files show better quality, especially if you're doing post editing in Photoshop. On the other hand, 16-bit files are huge. Many people choose to shoot and edit in 16-bit mode and then convert to 8-bit in Photoshop by selecting Image,

Mode, 8 Bits/Channel, to save file space. This is a viable option as long as you realize that downsizing the file results in a loss of file info that can never be regained.

Compression Options

Compression can be a good thing. It makes files small and compact, easy to store, and easy to attach to emails. Compression can also be a bad thing. It can erode image quality, making things looks fuzzy and grainy. There are several compression schemes available today, but for the digital photographer, the only real options are JPEG files and LZW compression for TIFF files.

24 Palio Banner (crop2)
Nikon D2H,
1/125 sec, f/5.3
ISO 640
Focal length 78mm

25 Siena Boy (crop)
Nikon D2H,
1/60 sec, f/6
Focal length 80mm

26 Siena Boy
Nikon D2H,
1/60 sec, f/6
Focal length 80mm

TIFF image files optionally use LZW lossless compression, meaning that there is no quality loss caused by the compression, and the file is kept in its original state.

Compression works by recognizing repeated pixel values in an image, replacing the many instances in shorthand fashion with just one instance. As a result, LZW is most effective when compressing images with large flat areas of color. Featureless areas compress better than detailed areas. In addition, LZW is more effective for grayscale images than color, and it might not be effective at all for 16-bit images.

The JPEG file is named for the Joint Photographic Expressions Group,

which documented and defined the file format. JPEG files allow for a high rate of compression, resulting in files that are much smaller than TIFF files, even if those TIFF files use LZW compression.

However, JPEG files sacrifice a small amount of quality as a result of the compression process. But this small degree of quality is not the primary drawback. The dangerous thing about JPEGs is that the degradation in quality occurs *each time an image is opened and saved*. Open and close a file once, and you don't see much impact on overall quality. Open and save it 10 times, and it will look exponentially worse than the first time you open it. Thus, like the proverbial frog sitting in the simmering pan of

water, the quality erodes over time in such a way that you don't even notice it—but by the time you do, it's irrevocable.

How Do I Decide?

All the file formats and compression options described thus far are good choices, depending on the circumstance in which they're being used. Obviously, you don't want to post a 16-bit TIFF file on the Internet, and you wouldn't want to repeatedly save the only copy of your wedding pictures as JPEG files. The best approach is to keep a series of files, each in a different format, for the various stages of work you're doing.

Master Files

The first step is to create and maintain pristine copies of all the images that are important to you. Think of them as master files you can copy and manipulate as needed. These mint-condition originals should be captured and maintained using the highest quality resolution and the broadest exposure range, being careful not to clip the highlights or flatten the shadow areas. Because I use Nikon equipment, I save all my files as .nef files, which are pretty small while still maintaining the 16-bit depth and all the original file data. The important thing is to save your files in the 16-bit RAW format supported by your system.

Edit Files

Whenever you want to modify an image, duplicate the master file and begin editing from there. You might feel strongly that you know just what you want to do with an image and that it's safe to edit the master file, but I advise against it. I've made the same mistake many times; I edit the original and end up wishing I could go back and crop a different way, or set a different exposure emphasis. These digital files are going to be around a long, long time, and hard drive storage is cheap. Duplicate the file and save the original master; doing so keeps your options wide open and is always the safest way to go.

Special-Purpose Files

After you've edited the file the way you want it, you might find yourself saving multiple copies of the same image for special purposes. Perhaps it's to post on the web, attach to an email, or reduce to a smaller size. This is the time to turn to lossless compression such as JPEG. You already have the original master as well as an edited copy, so it's less critical if you over-compress these iterations. In Photoshop, select File, Save As or File, Save For Web to open the appropriate dialog boxes.

27 **Galgano Window**
Nikon D2H,
1/160 sec, f/9.5
Focal length 24mm

Using a Flash Effectively

A flash is one of those features that is either indispensable or infuriating, depending on your experience level and the quality of your equipment. Whatever your current disposition, it's important to know how to use your flash effectively across the entire spectrum of shooting scenarios.

Most consumer cameras come with a built-in flash, which places a restriction on how it can be used to illuminate an image. Higher-end prosumer and professional cameras offer the option of using an off-camera flash to boost the illumina-

tion power and angle of the light, along with a list of other features that increase the creative options even more. This section looks at the pros and cons of the various flash options along with how to get the most out of each of them.

Making the Most of Your Camera's Built-in Flash

Most built-in flash units are marginally functional and difficult to control, with the primary drawbacks being flash coverage and the placement and direction of the light.

The flash coverage determines how far the light goes and how well it illuminates the subject. Most built-in flash units can light a scene with-

in a range of 10 to 15 feet, but light coverage begins to fall off quickly after that, making it difficult to properly expose subjects that are further away. In addition, because the flash is built in and pointed directly at the subject, the light is often harsh and directional. Shoot a subject in front of a wall, and the hard shadow outline will be cast on the wall, as well as strong shadows cast by features on the subject.

When shooting portraits and candid images with people, built-in flashes tend to create red-eye in subjects because of the close proximity of the light source to the lens. Although you can correct red-eye in Photoshop, doing so is an annoying

additional step that emphasizes how little control you have over lighting when you use a built-in flash.

To address the harshness of the illumination and to combat red-eye, you can try to create a makeshift flash diffuser to spread the light more evenly in the scene and make it less directional. To do this, use a white, semi-translucent material, such as a loosely crumpled piece of lens cleaning tissue or even a thin piece of tissue paper. Ball up the material and place it over the flash, being careful not to cover any part of the lens. Secure it with tape if you want, or just hold it. Although the material will scatter and diffuse the light, it will also block some of it, resulting in a

darker-than-expected exposure. If your camera has exposure compensation, increase the setting an f-stop or two, experimenting to get the proper light balance. In the end, this process is a poor substitute for a more advanced flash system, but I wanted to hold out some sort of option for those who might be struggling with existing equipment restrictions.

Options and Settings for On-camera Strobes

Moving to an external off-camera flash immediately addresses the red-eye problem while providing additional power and extended flash coverage. Off-camera flash units also

30 Santa Anna Fresco
Nikon D2H,
1/60 sec, f/4.5
Focal length 78mm

31 Galgano Chapel
Nikon D2H,
2/3 sec, f/11
EV -0.67
Focal length 14mm

feature the ability to aim the flash output vertically or horizontally to control how light is cast into the scene.

The Nikon SB800 strobe I used in Tuscany has a coverage reach of 186 feet at ISO 100 and is intelligent enough to provide a wide range of lighting enhancements, from fill flash in bright light to wide angle coverage; it also can increase or decrease flash output in various increments. Similar features are common in other external flashes, although you should check the

manufacturer's specifications to see exactly how the unit will perform.

The SB800 flash unit also features a wireless mode that allows multiple SB800 flash units to communicate with each other without wires or cables, has flexible output and exposure locking, and allows you to modify flash output with an easy-to-understand +1/-1 feature similar to the exposure compensation feature found in most digital cameras (for more on exposure compensation, see Chapter 2). Expect many of these features to become commonplace as the digital photo market continues to mature.

Special Flash Features

If you're using a digital SLR, you might find that an external flash offers a host of creative options to broaden your photographic range even further. Today's cameras support flash features for red-eye reduction using a preflash, flash exposure bracketing, and rear-curtain sync controls.

Rear-curtain sync exposes the image under natural light and fires the flash at the very end of the exposure, creating an expressive result that combines a dynamic blurred image with a crisp flash image in a single frame.

Rear-Curtain Effect
Nikon D2H,
4 sec, f/13
Focal length 80mm
Nikon SB800 flash

It's best to experiment with this feature to achieve best results because it takes some getting used to in order to anticipate how the system will record the action in the scene. In some cases, you might find that intentionally moving the camera while making the exposure creates an interesting abstract result, especially if you're shooting static subject matter. In Figure 32 I allow for a fair amount of camera shake with the shutter open, before framing the subject and firing the flash to complete the image.

Taking the Flash Off the Hot Shoe

If you have a flash extension cable for your dSLR, or if you have an all-in-one camera that supports an external flash, you can position the flash off the camera body. The primary reason you'd want to separate the flash from the camera is to control the direction of the light even more, to create more distance between the flash and the lens (to minimize red-eye).

The basic techniques for landscape photography are to watch the light, use a tripod, and be prepared for any situation that might arise. The fact that you're traveling outdoors, often in unfamiliar territory, makes things less than predictable. Follow the tips in the beginning of this chapter along with those listed here to create a solid foundation for landscape photography:

33 Cuna Skyline
Nikon D2H
1/320 sec, f/9
Focal length 75mm

34 San Gimignano
Nikon D2H
1/80 sec, f/21
Focal length 98mm

35 Lone Tree
Nikon D2H
1/320 sec, f/8
Focal length 105mm

- Use a tripod and cable release. I've said it several times in this chapter, but it bears repeating—it really is that important.

- Watch the light and plan when and where you're going to shoot. Light is best in the morning and evening in terms of color and direction.

- Ask yourself what direction the shadows will be pointing in the morning as opposed to the evening. What time of day does your subject get direct light?

- When shooting a sunset, don't stop with just one or two images. The light is changing constantly, as is the composition. Keep shooting!

Photographing objects and portraits requires you to control the light in terms of direction and intensity. It's important to bring out the details and create an atmosphere that enhances the subject. This is true whether you're shooting a portrait or a static object. Follow these steps for best results:

36 Lantern
Nikon D2H
1/250 sec, f/9
Focal length 105mm

- Control the light with a flash; use a fill flash setting to brighten the shadows.

37 Duomo Façade I
Nikon D2H
1/750 sec, f/5.3
Focal length 75mm

- Take the flash off the camera using an extension cord to control the direction of the light.

- Frame the object against a high-contrast background that's free of clutter or distraction.

38 Stirrup
Nikon D2H
1/250 sec, f/8
Focal length 75mm

Close-up work is tricky because of the narrow focus range and the necessity for sharp detail. It can be hard to get the right areas in focus while still setting up an interesting composition. The following tips can help your efforts:

Swirl III
Nikon D2H
1/80 sec, f/4.5
Focal length 85mm

Red Handle
Nikon D2H
1/60 sec, f/4.2
Focal length 50mm

Teal Doors
Nikon D2H
1/30 sec, f/4.5
Focal length 75mm

- Use a tripod and cable release. (Yeah, I know I'm a dog with a bone on this one, but it's really important for close-up work. Don't even try it without these two pieces of equipment.)

- When shooting a flat surface, make a decision to shoot square to the surface plane or select an angle that really emphasizes the perspective. Make sure that your choice is specific, not accidental.

- Always bracket because exposure variation creates different results in texture and lighting composition.

Chapter 2

DIGITAL EXPOSURE

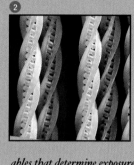

Exposure is one of those things that can be deceptively simple or complex depending on your experience level, quality requirements, and overall expectations.

This chapter starts by looking at what exposure is, including the variables that determine exposure and the range of visual effects that can be created as those variables are modified. Within this context, we'll look at how the tonal range of the visible world is compressed and abbreviated as its reflection passes through the camera lens and is printed on paper. This phenomenon establishes the primary theme for this chapter: The limited tonal range of the photographic process forces us to make decisions about which tonal areas of the image should be emphasized. Exposure directly influences this emphasis and must be controlled in order to make good choices.

From there, we'll look at the differences between optical and digital exposure compensation and help you choose the best way to make corrections, based on your equipment restrictions and the scene itself. This discussion is followed by a list of exposure correction options.

*Having established that determining the proper optical exposure is the best approach, significant emphasis is placed on exactly **how** to determine proper optical exposure, along with how to use a light meter and how to apply optical corrections to the digital workflow.*

The final pages of this chapter present tips for exposing specific types of scenes, including landscapes, objects, and close-up photography.

❶ Tuscan Woods
Nikon D2H
1/100 sec, f/5
Focal length 75mm

❷ Braided Curtain
Nikon D2H,
1/400 sec, f/5
EV +0.33
ISO 640
Focal length 75mm

Is There Such a Thing as "Perfect Exposure"?

Even if they don't know exactly how it works, most people would agree that good photography and good exposure go hand in hand. In most cases, people look at an image and, if the light balance looks okay, they nod their heads and say that the exposure looks good. In some cases, if the contrast is good and the shadows are well defined, they might even say that the exposure is perfect.

But what do they mean by that? Is there really such a thing as perfect exposure? If your objective is to capture the widest range of visible light in the image, with deep yet open shadows and well-defined highlights, then perhaps you can look at a picture and say that the exposure looks optimum, perhaps even perfect. But is this a universal assessment that can be standardized and applied to every photographic circumstance? I don't think so.

Exposure = Amount of Light and Speed of Shutter

It's important to realize that exposure determines far more than just the tonal range in the image, and that even the assessment of tonal range is subjective. In Figures ❹ and ❺, Figure ❹ features an optimum exposure, with strong tonal detail across the entire tonal range. Figure ❺ emphasizes the shadows and is more expressive. Both are acceptable, depending on your intentions.

This chapter looks at the variables that determine how an image is captured by a digital camera and how to manipulate those variables to

achieve a wide range of results. Along the way, we'll look at ways of measuring light, light meter techniques, and even apply the classic zone system to the digital process.

The concept of *exposure* can be simply expressed as light's ability to describe a scene as it falls on a piece of film or a digital chip. Variations in exposure are determined by the amount of light, how long the lens is open, and the sensitivity of the film or recording chip. The amount of light is determined by the *aperture* or lens opening, which is measured in *f-stops*. The duration for which the shutter is open is measured in fractions of seconds (or whole seconds for long exposures), and is referred to as the *shutter speed*. The

third variable in the equation is the sensitivity of the film or chip, which is sometimes referred to as the speed at which it records light. This sensitivity is described in an *ASA/ISO rating*.

The combination of these three variables determines the *tonal range* and *sharpness* for the image. If the aperture is too small, not enough light passes through the lens to capture the scene, and the image is dark and underexposed. If the opening is too large, the film receives too much light and the image appears too bright, with washed-out highlights and no shadow detail. Shutter speed plays an equally important role. If the shutter is too slow (open too long), you can let in more light, but the scene is blurry and soft. Fast shutter speeds freeze the action in

❸ **Pano Hills**
Nikon D2H
1/250 sec, f/7.6
EV -1.33
Focal length 78mm

❹ **Bench I**
Nikon D2H
1/30 sec, f/6.7
Focal length 24mm

❺ **Bench II**
Nikon D2H
1/80 sec, f/11
Focal length 24mm

The easiest way to understand the relationship between the three primary exposure components is to think in terms of halves or doubling. As settings increase in any area, the amount of exposed light doubles or halves. This approach forms the basis of gaining reliable control over exposure.

For example, ASA/ISO ratings refer to the sensitivity of film (or the recording chip on a digital camera) and set a baseline for how fast the light in the scene is recorded. The standard ASA/ISO settings are 25, 50, 100, 200, 400, 800, 1,600, and 3,200, although many digital models don't offer any settings lower than 200. Each setting is twice as fast as its predecessor, as is reflected by the numbers themselves. (Some cameras include intermediate numbers between these settings, which do not reflect the doubling/halved equation described here.) The good news is that higher settings let you shoot in lower light conditions. The bad news is that as the settings increase, the image sharpness declines (gets more coarse and grainy).

Shutter speed ratings also follow the doubling/halved equation as they move up and down the dial. The good news is that lower settings (longer exposure times) allow you to shoot in lower light. The bad news is that at lower speeds, moving objects blur and overall image sharpness is subject to camera shake if you're handholding the camera.

F-stops are the most cryptic settings of the group, and although the settings seem arbitrary, they still follow the doubling/ halved equation. The bad news is that as shutter speeds drop lower, so does the depth of field, which defines the range of focus within the image.

Because all these options follow the doubling/halved equation, they are somewhat interchangeable in how they impact the amount of light in the exposure. Increase the shutter speed by one setting or increase the f-stop, and the amount of light in the exposure is the same. Of course, you have to manage the side effects of each setting, taking the grainy resolution, blurred movement, or short depth of field into account for how it impacts the final result.

Each of these images was shot at f/4, but the shutter speed was set at 2,500, 1,250, and 640 from left to right, creating a one-stop difference between each image.

crisp focus, but require a lot more light in order to render an image that's tonally balanced. And of course, the ASA/ISO setting for the film or digital chip is the baseline that determines the overall speed of the exposure.

Another characteristic controlled by exposure is depth of field. *Depth of field* refers to the areas that remain in focus in front of and behind the primary focus point. Depth of field is covered in greater detail in Chapter 3, "Focus and Depth of Field."

In summary, exposure controls three primary variables: sharpness, tonal range, and depth of field. The "perfect" exposure is the one that manipulates these variables to serve your intentions for a given shot. Blurred subjects are dynamic and convey motion, sharp subjects convey depth of detail and information. Controlling the background and overall focus point plays a key role in overall composition and expressive narrative in the image. The perfect exposure is determined by the scene in front of the lens in combination with your artistic intentions.

The Tones and the Zones

Photographers break the tonal spectrum into *zones* that are classified and targeted in the exposure process. Ansel Adams' zone system is based on this philosophy, breaking the light spectrum into nine *grayscale* zones, with solid black at zone I, middle gray at the center as zone V, and solid white at zone IX.

These zones are distributed equally so that increasing an exposure variable (ISO, f-stop, or shutter speed) by one setting brightens the exposure, making each tonal area one zone brighter. When tones fall into the first or last zone, they flatten into flat black or flat white, loosing their ability to describe form or modulated tones. Tonal areas falling into these zones are described as being "clipped." I'll explain the process for assessing and revising tonal values later in this chapter, but for now it's important to understand that the tonal range of an image can be described in specific zones that correspond to the camera's exposure controls.

⑥ Pienza Guy
Nikon D2H
1/100 sec, f/5
EV +1
Focal length 75mm

⑦ Ghiberti Doors III
Nikon D2H
1/500 sec, f4.5
EV -.33
Focal length 78mm

Figure ⑧ shows how the zone system breaks the tonal range into nine zones, from flat black (zone I) to flat white (zone IX), with neutral gray in the middle (zone V).

Looking at Tones

As a photographer, it's critical that you play an active role in the images you capture. It's one thing to look at a grayscale zone chart and understand that a neutral gray is zone V, but it's another to look at a red sunset or green meadow and understand how that scene relates to the zone system. The easiest thing in the world is to press the button and hope for the best, but in many ways you're leaving the process to chance and will undoubtedly miss (or mess up) some great shots.

The easiest way to approach the process is not to impose a set of rules or zone-based constructs onto the scene, but rather to identify the areas of the scene that are important to you and then study the exposure to make sure that those areas are visible and detailed in the final image.

On the other hand, playing an active role does not mean you should over-analyze every shot, metering every corner of the scene and bracketing like crazy. For one thing, your camera's internal meter is set up to handle many scenes flawlessly—perhaps as many as 70%–80% of your shots will look just fine without any special work on your part. For another thing,

⑧ **The zone system breaks the tonal range into nine zones, as shown in this grayscale image.**

you could spend so much time measuring and analyzing every area in a composition that the world passes you by and you miss the shot you wanted to capture. The key is to analyze each scene, looking for exceptions to your meter's capabilities. Before you shoot, remember a few basic rules and check a few things as explained in the next sections. Your results will be more consistent and satisfying.

Make a Decision, Form a Vision

In each image, you should compose and expose based on your reaction to the scene. What's the most important area? Where is the emotion or drama? What is it about this scene that made you stop and decide to shoot it?

When you have a sense of what's important, make a decision about what you're going to do with it. We'll process this comment more in Chapter 4, "Composition," but composing your shot is also relevant to exposure in that you must make sure that the exposure enhances and communicates the important areas in the image.

For example, in Figure ⑨, I was especially interested in the texture and tonality of the column. It was located under a portico in pretty heavy shade, making the subject look dark. The first thing I had to do was look at the coloration of the column and mentally convert it to grayscale to get a sense of how the meter would see it. In this case, the darkly shaded column fell into

zone III. To lighten the subject, I opened the lens up two stops, shifting the column to a lighter shade that brought out the texture and detail.

While assessing the tones in the image, I took a mental note of the background, trying to assess what would happen to it as I made the two-stop shift (the background would also lighten by two stops, along with the column and everything else in the image). Because I knew the main area of interest was the column, I determined that the image would still look good if the background was brighter. In the context of the zone system technique, the two-stop shift moved the background from zone V to zone VII. In the process of lighten-

ing the main areas of the column, I sacrificed some of the highlight detail because the zone VII image detail at the bottom of the background was clipped to the flat white of zone IX.

Watch the Contrast

As you assess the scene in front of you, be on the lookout for high-contrast regions where bright areas and deep shadows are dominant. In scenes such as these, you might have some difficult choices to make. If the shadow detail is most important, you might want to brighten the image to catch the shadow detail. Be aware, however, that you risk clipping some of the details in the highlights, reducing them to flat white. The inverse is also true: Darkening the image to bring out

detail in the highlights can flatten the shadows. In Figure **10**, a statue in Marconi Square in Siena offers the choice of a richly detailed green patina, if only I'm willing to sacrifice the shadow detail beneath the shield and under the wing. I thought of adjusting the exposure to lighten the shadows, but that would have definitely washed out the detail in the rest of the statue. Opting for saturated color and detail, I took a hand-held spot meter reading off the bright spot on the right forearm. This rendered that tonal area as a neutral gray, capturing a full range of detail across most of the statue.

If these trade-offs are acceptable, go ahead and take the shot. If you want to have your cake and eat it too, there are a few tricks you can try to hold the detail in both the shadow

and highlight areas. See the discussion on multiple exposures in Chapter 4.

Special Lighting Situations

In certain situations, you will want to capture and emphasize the overall light in a scene. These "Kodak moments" are familiar to most photographers and might even be deemed cliché by some. If you simply rely on the overt lighting elements—such as the atmospheric quality in a sunset—your image will probably look pretty cliché. Combine this one lighting attribute with an interesting composition or a unique point of view, and you can transcend the cliché and use the special lighting situation to your advantage.

Sunrise /Sunset—A Good Color Contrast

The light at the beginning and end of the day has a warm glow that is rightly prized by photographers. As you take stock of these lighting situations, there are at least two factors to keep in mind. First, make sure that you retain the color of the light in the scene. If your camera is set to Auto White Balance, you could find that it automatically corrects for the warm yellow/orange tint to the light, making the color relationships feel like a neutral mid-day setting.

The second factor to consider is how you want to position the tonal range. The shadows will probably be dark and filled in, and you will probably have some beautiful color in the sky. The decision you need to

make is whether it's more important to emphasize the shadow detail or the saturated sky color. If you lighten the image to bring out shadow details, the color saturation in the sky goes away. Don't be passive— make a decision and go with it (or *bracket* and shoot it both ways).

For example, in Figures ⑫ and ⑬, the rich sky and extremely dark areas present a tonal range that is beyond what the camera can capture. As I observed the scene, I noted that the land was much more visible, but to capture that land, I would have to lighten the sky and reduce the saturated color. In Figure ⑫ I chose to emphasize the sky and let the land flatten to darkness. Figure ⑬ shows the same scene with an averaged reading.

Incandescent/Florescent Lighting— A Bad Color Cast

Shooting indoors usually imposes a yellow or green cast to your images, depending on whether the lighting is *incandescent* (yellow) or *florescent* (green). In most cases, these color casts are unflattering, and you'll want to remove them. There are filters that can neutralize these effects, such as a Blue 80a filter for incandescent light, and an FL-D filter for florescent light. In addition, remember that you can always rely on your camera's Auto White Balance setting to do its job and neutralize a color cast caused by artificial lighting. Also keep in mind that the flash will neutralize much of the color casts caused by indoor light sources.

⑫ **Tuscan Sunset I**
Nikon D2H
1/250 sec, f/5
Focal length 102mm

⑬ **Tuscan Sunset II**
Nikon D2H
1/60 sec, f/5
Focal length 116mm

14 **Siena Madonna**
   Nikon D2H
   1/250 sec, f/8
   Focal length 80mm

15 **Grapes III**
   Nikon D2H
   1/80 sec, f/11
   Focal length 24mm

Adjusting Exposure

It's necessary for you to override your camera's default and automatic settings if you want to make photographic choices. For example, to choose between exposure options such as shadow detail and silhouettes in a sunset shot, you must make an exposure adjustment.

There are many ways to adjust exposure. The available options depend on the type of camera you have and your desire to work with technical data. Some options require you to understand formulas and the characteristics of light, while others do most of the work for you and simply require you to press the shutter. As you consider the various exposure options, keep the following two principals in mind:

- All exposure compensation techniques do one of two things: They make the image lighter or darker.

- Exposure compensation options can be categorized as either optical or digital. Whenever possible, use the optical options first, and then move to the digital options as needed.

Optical Exposure Compensation

Optical exposure compensation refers to the physical controls that actually change the amount of light passing through the lens. The most obvious options are the f-stop and shutter speed variables discussed at the start of this chapter. Using a

flash is also an optical control. However, ISO modifications are digital compensations because they modify the sensitivity of the photo sensor rather than changing the amount of light.

It's important to start making your exposure adjustments with the optical controls first because they provide control over the relationship between the amount of light and the exposure duration. This allows you to control the depth of field, sharpness, and other image aesthetics. Optical exposure modifications also result in a cleaner image that has not been modified digitally. In many cases, this affords more flexibility in lightening or darkening the image, or making post-capture revisions in Photoshop.

Seeing the World in Grayscale

Use your camera's B&W setting to preview a scene in grayscale so that you can look at the image in the same way your light meter does—using shades of gray.

Let's say that you want to expose for the shadows in an image. If you use a digital control such as exposure compensation (as explained in the following section), the sensitivity of the photo sensor is increased to record more detail. In the process, the image becomes more grainy, making it more difficult to lighten the exposure further (in Photoshop) and also limiting your ability to make oversized prints.

You're better off exposing optically, controlling the amount and duration of light so that the chip records the target tonal area of the scene without increasing the sensor's sensitivity (which can degrade image quality). As an analogy, think of the difference between turning up the volume on your stereo to hear the

Here's a great trick about mapping the world of color to the grayscale world seen by your camera's light meter. Set your camera to Black and White or even Sepia mode and take a trial shot of the scene. Look at the result to understand how the colors translate to grayscale tones. What tone is the red fire truck that you're trying to emphasize? If it's dark, you might want to increase exposure to lighten it a bit and add some detail.

If you do that, what will happen to other colors and tones in the image? Will they fall out of range, and are they really critical to your vision for the image?

Work out your exposure strategy in black and white, then switch back to color mode and shoot the image with a better understanding of what's going to happen.

Mike's Tomb III
Nikon D2H
1/4 sec, f/4.5
EV -0.67
Focal length 78mm

Tree Vine
Nikon D2H
1/125 sec, f/5.3
ISO 640
Focal length 75mm

Mike's Tomb II
Nikon D2H
1/4 sec, f/4.5
EV -0.67
Focal length 78mm

bass line better as opposed to using an equalizer to bump up *just* the lower decibel range.

Please note that these are general statements, and that results vary between CMOS, CCD, and LBCAST sensors. Although manufacturers continue to advance these digital technologies, it's still a good idea to make exposure modifications optically, concentrating on the right amount of light for the proper duration.

Digital Exposure Compensation

Digital exposure compensation changes the overall sensitivity of the sensor, as happens when you make ISO revisions. Digital exposure

adjustments make the image globally darker or lighter. As I mentioned at the end of the last section, the best approach in modifying exposure is always to adjust exposure settings and set them in manual mode or with some form of *Exposure Lock* control.

Having said that, the digital exposure controls are there for a reason and can be used in certain situations. If I'm in a hurry, trying to catch an elusive shot, I'll use Exposure Compensation to quickly adjust the exposure. It's better than loosing the shot completely as I'm looking at the camera controls. The general rule of thumb is to make exposure changes by changing f-stop or shutter speed, or by using your camera's Exposure Lock feature. When that's

not practical, by all means use the camera's digitally based controls to get the shot.

How to Adjust Exposure

The method you use to adjust the exposure and lighten or darken the image depends on your equipment, your skill level, and your patience. The following list identifies the various methods for changing the exposure on your camera, ranging from the basic to the most complex:

• **Use the flash (optical).** All cameras have a flash, either built in or as an accessory. Using a flash will lighten the scene, but it obviously can't help if you need a darker exposure.

- **Fix it in Photoshop (digital).**
This is a viable option, especially
for corrections within one or
two f-stops of an optimal exposure. The thing to remember
here is that Photoshop cannot
correct detail that's not present
in the image file to begin with.
Beware a loss of detail in the
highlights and *quartertones*, or
shadows that are too dark. If you
ask Photoshop to lighten shadows that are too dark, you usually run into pixilated noise that
looks worse than when you
started.

- **Use camera presets (digital or
optical).** Many cameras feature
exposure presets (such as
Snow/Sand or Cloudy) that
anticipate lighting conditions for
typical scenes such as portraits
and nature settings. In the
absence of manual controls such
as f-stop and shutter speed, try
dialing these in when they're relevant to the scene.

- **Change the ISO setting (digital).** The ASA/ISO film speed
rating determines how sensitive
the film (or recording chip) is to
light. A lower setting means it is
less sensitive; higher ratings are
more sensitive. If a scene is too
dark, you can try increasing the
ISO setting. The problem with
this approach is that higher ISO
ratings in the digital world bring
increased grain, pixelization, and
overall coarseness, just as higher
film ratings create increased
grain.

- **Bracket the image (optical).**
Many cameras have a bracketing
option that automatically shoots
two other images whenever you
press the shutter. One image is
exposed a stop lighter than the
original, and one is exposed a
stop darker than the original.
You can review the three images
after the fact and choose the
exposure that's right for your
vision of the scene.

- **Use exposure compensation
(digital).** This approach uses a
basic exposure correction that
increases or decreases exposure
in 1-stop increments, based on
the internal meter's initial reading. Dial in a +1 setting to darken
the exposure by a stop; a -1 setting lightens the exposure one
stop. It's important to remember

⑲ Mikes Tomb I
Nikon D2H
3 sec, f/18
Focal length 75mm

20 Clouds III
Nikon D2H
1/30 sec, f/6.7
Focal length 200mm

21 Pienza Door I
Nikon D2H
1/90 sec, f/4.8
Focal length 78mm

that this adjustment does not impact the amount of light entering the lens; rather, it changes the sensitivity of the sensor chip. In most cameras you can go from -2 to +2. This exposure correction method is used in digital SLRs, advanced amateur (what I call *prosumer*) cameras, and even in a growing number of point-and-shoot models.

- **Adjust shutter speed (optical).** If your camera has them, you can increase or decrease the shutter speed settings to speed up or slow down the exposure duration. Decrease the shutter speed one increment (from 1/30 to 1/15, for example), to double the light

in the image, or increase one increment (from 1/30 to 1/60) to halve the amount of light. The obvious pitfall with this approach is to be careful not to use a low setting that could induce camera shake or be too slow to properly capture the motion in the scene.

- **Adjust aperture (optical).** This solution delivers the most control and is the one to consider if you're serious about gaining control over exposure and you have interchangeable lenses that provide *aperture* (f-stop) settings. Each setting on the aperture ring doubles or halves the amount of light in the exposure, just as is true with the shutter speed controls. The main difference with

aperture is that you can adjust the lens opening without impacting image sharpness as can happen when you change the shutter speed. (However, depth of field is affected when you change the aperture setting, as discussed in Chapter 3.)

- **Use flash exposure compensation (optical).** Some of the newest accessory flash units allow you to increase or decrease the flash's light intensity. Similar to the on-camera Exposure Compensation, this approach allows you to dial the intensity of the flash up or down to control the amount of additional light introduced to the scene by the flash. Nikon's SB800 flash unit, which I used

for all the flash photography in Tuscany, is an example of a powerful strobe that features this capability.

Metering Light

As we begin to consider the technical side of exposure, I should mention that many readers will be content to stop here and simply understand the various exposure options available and how they impact results. There are plenty of artists who are *not* photographers, and who are content to rely on their light meters and the basic camera controls without thinking technically about exposure. This approach to photography is valid, as long as you're content with your results.

Having said that, you know all the basics and terminology now, so I would encourage you to read on and gain a better understanding of how to take complete control over exposure.

Thus far in this chapter, we've discussed exposure in a significant level of detail. We've defined how your camera controls exposure with f-stops and shutter speeds, the kinds of exposure controls you can implement, and how shades of gray and the zone system can help you assess the tones in an image. With all this in mind, we'll discuss how to measure the light in a scene as well as how to evaluate the tonal values in the resulting digital image.

What Light Meters Do

If you're using a digital camera, it almost certainly has a built-in meter that measures the light coming through the lens and sets what it deems to be the "proper" exposure. Understanding the assumptions your meter makes is the first step in applying the appropriate level of human intervention in the exposure process.

All light meters see the world as a monochromatic jumble of gray tones. Of course, they don't really "see" at all—they simply measure the intensity of the light as it bounces off the objects in the scene, setting off an electrical charge in the meter's sensor. This method of measuring light as it bounces off the subject is called *reflected metering*.

㉒ **Sant Olivetto I**
Nikon D2H
1/80 sec, f/4.2
Focal length 14mm

23 Observer
Nikon D2H
1/60 sec, f/5.6
Focal length 400mm

24 Campo Windows
Nikon D2H
1/60 sec, f/5.6
Focal length 400mm

The meter takes the initial reflected light measurement (which is called an *EV rating*) and converts it into an exposure setting. To do this, it must know a few things about the exposure settings, and it must make one very big assumption.

First, the meter must know the ASA/ISO setting for the film or image sensor (how readily the film or sensor can read and absorb the light falling on it). When the meter knows the sensitivity of the image sensor, it makes its big assumption: The meter always assumes that the subject matter is of medium reflectance and should be rendered in neutral tones that are not considered shadows or highlights. The EV rating represents the amount of

light that will render a subject of medium reflectance.

Next, the meter suggests a range of shutter speed and f-stop combinations that will deliver the proper amount of light to render the subject as neutral, based on the ASA/ISO sensitivity. Select a desired shutter speed or f-stop, and the meter provides the other half of the equation (see the section, "Exposure=Amount of Light and Speed of Shutter," earlier in this chapter).

The Limitations of Reflectance

The first area where light meters fail us is when our subjects do not fall within the meter's assumed range of

medium reflectance. If the subject is highly reflective, such as a snow-covered landscape or a sandy beach, the meter is fooled, lets in too much light, and the scene is overexposed. Conversely, if a subject is of low reflectance, such as a black cat, the meter is fooled again and lets in too little light. The resulting underexposure renders the cat as a washed-out gray. Interestingly, the overexposure of the snow scene also results in a dull gray snow bank because the meter's erroneous assumption of a neutral gray world is brought to unacceptable fruition. Therefore, always remember to intervene and override your meter whenever your subject is overly dark or overly reflective, falling outside the middle gray reflectance zone.

The Perils of Averaging

When a meter takes a light reading, it divides the sensor or image area into a grid, takes a light reading for each section, and averages them together for a single, aggregate reading. In an effort to compensate for this, the meter sometimes tries to recognize contrast differences that would indicate a landscape, a portrait, or some other set variety of images. The problem is that these efforts are still broad approximations that can fall short of understanding the relationships between the tonal areas in the particular image you're trying to capture. The thing to look out for are areas of high contrast that would throw off the averaging. If a very bright area is

Exposure Strategy: Shoot and React

Siena Palio
Nikon D2H
ISO 1,600
1/800 sec, f/6
Focal length 75m

The "shoot and react" approach to exposure is truly unique to digital photography. When you shoot film, you usually don't have the chance to shoot, develop, print, and then decide whether you're going to reshoot. The immediate feedback you gain from checking composition in the digital camera's preview window and exposure with the histogram readout allows you to evaluate and decide whether you've got the image you're after. On the other hand, don't make the mistake in thinking that this strategy is simply about reacting to results. It also requires a certain amount of preparation and anticipation.

In Siena, I attended the Palio festival, which culminates in an amazing three-minute horse race around the historic town square. Having traveled so far just to capture this fleeting race, there was no time to shoot and react, even with the immediate advantages of digital technology. I arrived early, scouted out my place, and began shooting

test exposures to check lighting conditions. I shot the race track to test the lighting conditions, checked the histogram, and made sure that the tonal range was optimized. I then revised these exposures to find the right combination of f-stop and fast shutter speed so that I could freeze the action. After a considerable amount of testing, I was ready to shoot. I prepared as much as possible in advance, did some tests, and made some adjustments. I then reacted as best I could to capture the moment as it flew past me at 30 miles per hour.

If you're shooting fast action or candid shots of people, it's important to prepare and test so that you're ready for that once-in-a-lifetime moment. The key is not to shoot blindly; even with landscapes, still lives, or static photography, it's important to apply all your knowledge of exposure and photography.

right next to a very dark one, the meter will try to average the two, and will probably have problems describing either area accurately. The following section describes methods for overcoming averaged meter readings and other *through-the-lens (TTL) meter* limitations.

Overcoming TTL Meter Limitations

So what do you do with a high-contrast scene or with a scene outside the average reflectance range? The solution that offers the most control is to measure the scene accurately, set a strategy for which parts of the tonal range are important to you, and manually set the shutter speed, f-stop, and ISO settings to capture the desired result.

Obviously, you must have a camera that can independently control these three settings, allowing you to operate in what is called Manual mode. I'll touch on non-manual mode strategies later in this chapter, but being able to manually set f-stop, shutter speed, and ASA/ISO is a very important feature in controlling exposure. Consider upgrading your equipment if you really want to control exposure.

Take Readings for Individual Areas

To properly expose a child's face or a tree trunk in a landscape, you must isolate the meter reading to that specific area. If your camera allows you to *spot meter* specific areas, measure the face or tree and enter the exposure settings manu-

ally. Envision in your mind how the face will look at a neutral 18% gray. Is this what you want, or should it look lighter or darker? Make these decisions based on your vision for the image and set the exposure accordingly.

Use a Gray Card

One way to get an accurate exposure reading is to take a meter reading off an 18% gray card (available at most photo shops) placed in the same light as the subject. (Use the gray card to calibrate the exposure; use a white card to color balance the camera.) Set up the tripod, put the card in front of the camera, and meter the scene. Enter the meter readings as the settings in Manual mode to expose properly for the light in the scene.

Trick the TTL Meter

If you don't have a gray card and you can't spot meter, try moving close to the area to be metered, filling the entire frame with the tree trunk, snow bank, or face that is the subject of the image. Don't worry about focusing the camera, just take the light reading, being careful not to cast any shadows on the area in the viewfinder. Enter the close-up meter reading into your camera's manual settings (or adjust exposure up or down if you want to shoot the image in a different zone), recompose the scene, and shoot. As long as the light hasn't changed, the close-up area you metered will be exposed perfectly. Figure 26 shows an image created by filling the frame with the grass from the foreground, taking a manual light reading, and then recomposing the whole scene.

Use Exposure Lock

If your camera has an exposure lock feature, take advantage of it. Exposure Lock is a button that freezes the exposure settings and allows you to recompose the scene before you shoot. Thus, you can fill the frame with the desired area (or meter the gray card), press the Exposure Lock button, and shoot away with the proper exposure locked in. This feature saves you from manually setting the exposure settings for every shot, allowing you to work faster.

Non-manual Exposure Settings

Let's say that your camera doesn't have a manual mode or exposure lock setting. Although your options in exposure compensation are severely constrained, you still have ways to compensate for your meter's poor assumptions. If it's available on your camera, use the exposure compensation feature to increase or decrease the exposure settings. This feature usually allows 1/3 or 1/2 stop adjustments up or down to a maximum of +/- 2 stops. Exposure compensation is not available on many consumer camera models, but if you have it, it's the best non-manual exposure adjustment.

26 **Tree Silhouette**
Nikon D2H
1/320 sec, f/9
Focal length 85mm

You can also adjust exposure by dialing the ASA/ISO setting up or down to make the image lighter or darker. If you don't have that option, check whether your camera has exposure presets for things such as close-ups, landscapes, and portraits. These settings can anticipate and adjust the exposure for the corresponding scenarios, but these settings are something of a last resort when you want to compensate for unusual lighting conditions.

Using a Handheld Meter

If a camera with non-manual settings is at the low end of the exposure-control spectrum, then using a handheld light meter is at the high end. Handheld meters usually employ two or three metering methods that overcome many of the shortcomings of your camera's onboard meter. For starters, handheld meters allow you to take reflected light readings by pointing the meter at the subject and measuring the light as it bounces off the subject. Note that this kind of reflected metering is susceptible to false readings from objects with above and below average reflectivity, just as is true with the meter in your camera.

Remember that your objective is to record the amount of light *in the scene*; the reflection part is a necessity imposed by the meter's placement inside the lens. So how do you avoid false readings from reflected light? Avoid the reflection by turning your handheld meter around, pointing it at the camera, and record the light as it falls onto the subject, before the light is distorted by reflectance or averaged into a generic, homogenous reading. This type of measurement is called an *incident reading*, and it can produce some very accurate exposures.

Most handheld meters include some sort of dome attachment or slider used to take incident readings. The meter averages the light falling on the dome from all angles. This type of averaging is good in that you've avoided the reflectance problem, ensuring that the reading does not

A typical handheld light meter.

U sing a handheld meter takes some practice and technique to get it just right. Follow these tips when taking incident readings in both general use and specific lighting situations.

overcompensate for light or dark subjects. Just make sure that there are no shadows falling across the meter, and that the meter shares the same light as the subject.

The third type of measurement available on advanced meters is a *spot meter* option that narrows the angle of the metering cell to take readings from specific spots in a scene in as little as a 1-degree metering angle over long distances. Spot metering involves looking through the viewfinder, lining up the center spot on the subject of your image, and pushing the button to take the reading off the subject. Because spot metering is a reflective technique, it produces a reading that renders the sampled area as neutral gray. Make

Metering Angles

When taking an incident reading, make sure that you point the metering dome directly into the lens of the camera. When shooting outdoors in a landscape, you might want to tilt the meter 10–20° up towards the sky to lighten the image slightly. You might choose to slightly vary the upward or downward angle of the meter in the landscape to emphasize either the ground or the sky. Side to side angles are more critical because this lighting angle can throw off exposure considerably. Again, point the meter into the lens, not off to the side.

Strong Backlighting

Subjects standing against a bright background pose a problem in that the contrast is so great that both reflective and incident readings usually fall short of an accurate reading. One way to work around this is to take an incident reading at a right angle to the subject and light direction, so that the light and shadow fall down the middle of the dome. Another approach, called *duplex metering*, is to take a reading with the meter pointed towards the light source, take a second reading pointing away from the light source, and then average the two readings.

Shadow Information

Midtone Information

Highlight Information

sure that this is what you want, or use some form of exposure compensation to lighten or darken the area. Spot metering is also good for measuring the relative brightness between different areas of the scene.

Measuring Tonal Range with Histograms

How do you discern whether you got what you were after? Let's face it, when you shoot a digital image, you immediately check the LCD display to assess your results. Do you keep the first image, or do you need to reshoot? How do you decide, especially if you're away from your computer or out in the field as I was while shooting in Tuscany? One thing is for sure:

Don't trust the paltry little LCD screen on the back of your camera. It might show you composition and framing, but it lies and deceives when it comes to exposure—it cannot show you anywhere near the level of detail necessary for critical decisions. The solution is to use *histograms*.

A histogram is a graphic representation of how pixel information is distributed within the *tonal range* of an image. How much information is in the highlights? How about in the shadows? What's the darkest pixel? All these questions can be answered quickly using a histogram. When you're shooting in the field, you can access the histogram for the image you just shot to see whether you exposed properly for the highlights. If the highlights are clipped (too

strong) or if there is no information in the highlight range, you know that the exposure is incorrect and you should probably reshoot. The next section explains how histograms are structured and how to read them so that you can make intelligent decisions about exposure and tonal range.

Anatomy of a Histogram

The histogram is a common tool in assessing the tonal range of an image. It's in most camera preview systems, as well as in Photoshop and other image-editing software. Because the histogram is a standard measurement tool, you must know how to read a histogram correctly and understand how it relates to the image as well as your creative objectives. In a histogram, pixel values are

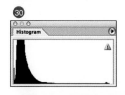

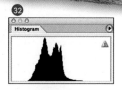

represented along the horizontal baseline, increasing from left to right. Rising up from the baseline are peaks and valleys that graph the proportionate number of image pixels corresponding to the baseline value. A quick glance tells you whether you have any peaks in the highlights or shadows, signaling that pixel data is present in that area (see Figure ㉘). Check to see whether image data is present across the full tonal spectrum, especially in the areas that interest you the most.

For a scene that's evenly lit, a good histogram shows some pixel data at both ends of the spectrum, with the highest peaks (the most pixels) in the middle. Such a graph signifies an image with moderate highlights and shadows and the majority of infor-

mation in the midrange. But what about that snow scene or that twilight image? The histograms associated with those images will look very different from the ideal ones. If there are no bright highlights in the scene, don't expect them to be in the histogram. This lecture might sound basic, if not remedial, but it reinforces the point that each histogram is unique, and there is no target histogram shape, just as there is no universal formula for perfect exposure.

Histogram Shapes

There are as many histogram shapes as there are image types. Some emphasize the shadows, others the highlights. Don't fall into the trap of making all your image

histograms look the same. What's more important is that you recognize the important areas in the image, and make sure that there is adequate pixel data in the corresponding area of the histogram. Figure ㉙ shows a standard exposure, with bell-shaped histogram. Figure ㉚ shows an image with the shadows dominant; notice that its histogram is skewed to the left. Figure ㉛ shows an image with the highlights dominant; its histogram is skewed to the right. Figure ㉜ shows an image dominated by a single flat color, with minimal highlights or shadows; its histogram is similarly flat (most of the pixels in the center of the histogram).

㉚ **Yellow Flower**
Nikon D2H
1/160 sec, f/10
ISO 640
Focal length 75mm

㉛ **Fresco Detail**
Nikon D2H
1/60 sec, f/4.5
Focal length 80mm

㉜ **Table Cloth**
Nikon D2H
1/250 sec, f/4
Focal length 20mm

In a landscape, the sky is always going to illuminate the ground below and will almost always dominate in brightness. Remember to anticipate this and compensate by making the exposure lighter or darker to emphasize the sky or ground as your vision dictates. Here are some additional exposure tips to keep in mind when exposing for a landscape:

33 San Gimignano
Nikon D2H
1/60 sec, f/19
ISO 640
Focal length 75mm

34 Monteriggioni
Nikon D2H
1/200 sec, f/22
Focal length 24mm

35 D'orcia Sunset
Nikon D2H
1/160 sec, f/4.5
Focal length 75mm

- For normal landscapes, an incident reading from a handheld meter is the best approach to getting the exposure right.

- If your camera allows (as professional cameras often do), add an extra 1/2 stop of exposure if there are large areas of dark foliage that are important to the scene.

- Reduce exposure by 1/2 stop if you want to increase the saturation of a dominant color, such as the sky.

- Take a spot meter reading in the darkest shadow areas and reduce exposure by 2–3 stops to maintain detail in the shadow areas.

- Reduce the exposure for a snowy scene by 1 stop if you're taking an incident reading or up to 3 stops if you're taking a reflected reading.

- Night shots look best when there is still some color in the sky. Reflected readings work best at night.

When you're shooting an object—whether it's a ball, a child's toy, or a portrait—you're looking for ways to articulate and describe that object, bringing out nuance or emphasizing specific features such as the texture or rich color. The biggest challenge in shooting an object or a portrait is one of lighting. Is the subject evenly lit or should you use a fill flash or a reflector to balance the light? What about the background? Does it compete or is it too distracting? Ask yourself these questions as you shoot, and consider the following tips to improve the shot:

36 Grapes
Nikon D2H
ISO 640
1/125 sec, f/11
Focal length 75mm

37 Florence Fountain
Nikon D2H
1/640 sec, f/4.5
Focal length 105mm

38 Flowers
Nikon D2H
1/30 sec, f/5.3
Focal length 180mm

39 Roses
Nikon D2H
1/60 sec, f/4.5
Focal length 60mm

- Keep the object far enough away from the background to avoid casting unwanted shadows from the light source.

- Use a reflector to cast reflected light into the shadows.

- For most portraits, position the subject against a background that's 2 stops darker than the subject's skin tone (2 zones).

- Use an incident meter if possible, pointing it directly into the camera lens.

- Dress your portrait subject in light clothes if you want dark skin tones. Conversely, dress in dark clothes to convey light skin tones.

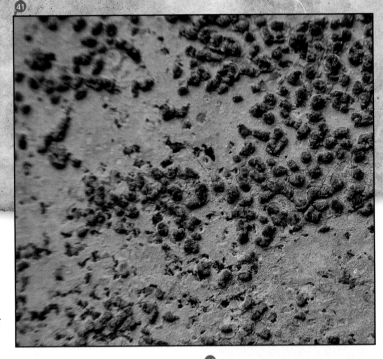

The key in emphasizing texture and detail is to reduce glare and enhance sharpness. Although exposure can't help much in the sharpness department, it can reduce glare and bring out details. Slightly underexpose images with glare for a little added saturation and detail. Your TTL meter is probably going to do well with these shots because the entire viewfinder should be filled with the detail or texture area. Consider the following tips for enhancing texture and detail exposures:

40 Cross
Nikon D2H
ISO 640
1/90 sec, f/4.8
Focal length 28mm

41 Paint
Nikon D2H
ISO 640
1/160 sec, f/6
Focal length 75mm

42 Field
Nikon D2H
1/500 sec, f/5.6
Focal length 90mm

43 Charred Door
Nikon D2H
1/30 sec, f/3.5
Focal length 28mm

- Shoot textures outside on a cloudy day, which provides even, diffused lighting.

- Position the lens at a 90-degree angle to the textured surface to maintain focus across all areas of the surface.

- Take an incident reading and underexpose by 1/2 stop to reduce glare and deepen saturation.

- If possible, set up directional side lighting to further emphasize surface texture and detail.

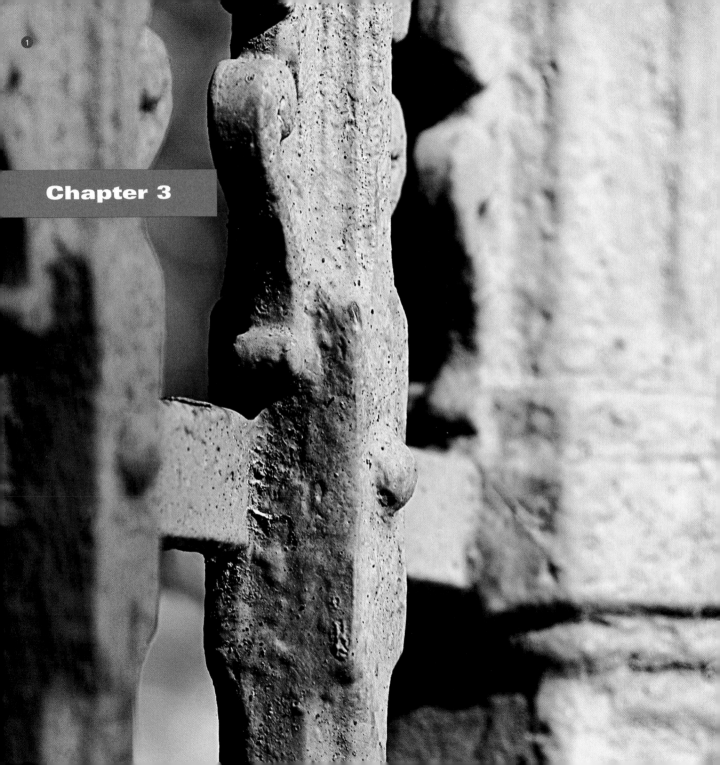

Chapter 3

FOCUS AND DEPTH OF FIELD

Focus is perhaps the most important component in the success of an image. We all focus our eyes in the natural process of seeing, although lighting conditions, attention span, and our emotional engagement with the scene impact exactly what we comprehend and react to. Thus, we use our eyes to bring the world into optical focus, but we also focus our minds to concentrate our attention on the things we're trying to understand.

This chapter looks at the act of focusing with both our eyes and our minds. Getting the camera to render the world in sharp detail is the first step, while controlling what is in or out of focus allows us to create emphasis and to control the composition of the image. This chapter starts by outlining the basics of digital focusing techniques, and moves quickly to explaining how to control depth of field effects.

The final pages of this chapter present tips for controlling focus and depth of field in specific types of scenes, including landscapes, objects, and close-up photography.

❶ Fence
Nikon D2H
1/125 sec, f/5.6
Focal length 185mm

❷ Montepulciano Altar
Nikon D2H,
1/60 sec, f/4.5
Focal length 75mm

Focus, Sharpness, and Depth of Field

Focus and sharpness may sound like the same thing, but they really are two related but separate components of good photography. Sharpness refers to the crisp clarity and detail present in a photograph, while focus refers to the controls and action required by your camera to achieve the final sharpness result.

Camera manufacturers have been on a holy quest to get us to forget about focus, assuring us that the cameras are automatic and intuitive enough to read the scene—as well as our minds. Although this is often true, there are times when the camera is less than intuitive, and we have to give it a nudge to get the focus right. To help you do that, we're going to examine the mechanics behind focusing systems, explaining how they work and when you should shift from auto to manual.

Focus is also one of the means by which you determine a photo's depth of field. Depth of field is interesting because it controls what parts of the image are in focus as well as the overall clarity of the subject. Thus depth of field plays a significant role as a compositional element, controlling where the viewer looks and the speed with which his or her eyes move through the scene. These issues are covered in greater detail in the next chapter on composition, but for now, the important thing is to understand what depth of field is and how to control it.

Types of Autofocus

All of today's cameras use some form of autofocus, where the camera automatically detects the distance from the camera to the subject and sets the focus on the fly. With each generation of new cameras, engineers continue to advance the intelligence and capability of digital autofocus, transforming it from a clumsy yet interesting concept into a functional piece of photographic technology. Having said that, although the technology has improved greatly, it is by no means automatic or foolproof. It's important to understand a bit about how the focusing system in your camera works, so

that you can get the best results and avoid focusing mistakes.

The primary types of autofocus are known as active and passive systems. *Active autofocus* sends out an infrared signal that is reflected by the subject, allowing the system to calculate the distance to the subject and set the focus. *Passive autofocus* systems determine the subject's distance from the camera based on the light and contrast in the subject matter.

Passive autofocus systems are less desirable in that they are limited by the available light; they have trouble focusing if there is little or no contrast in the subject matter or if the scene is too dark. Active autofocus works well in most instances,

although its infrared signal can prohibit you from focusing through glass windows or other transparent objects.

Autofocus cameras define active areas within the viewfinder that act as focusing zones. When one of these areas is active, it reacts to areas of contrast and edge detail, reflecting back information to both passive and active systems for the reading. The number, placement, and sophistication of these focusing zones vary based on manufacturer and price point of your camera, but it's safe to say that all autofocus implementations are a marked advancement from where we were just a few years ago.

③ Val D'Orcia
Nikon D2H
1/250 sec, f/7.6
EV -1.33
Focal length 78mm

④ Montalcino Ring
Nikon D2H
1/100 sec, f/10
EV -0.33 ISO 640
Focal length 75mm

⑤ Olivetto Trees
Nikon D2H
1/80 sec, f/4.5
Focal length 200mm

⑥ Duomo Statue
Nikon D2H
1/500 sec, f/4.5
EV -0.33
Focal length 75mm

Blurring on Purpose

Remember that it's not always necessary to keep everything tack sharp in order to create a great image. There are times when I intentionally create images that are soft, and sometimes blurred beyond recognition.

For example, many museums in Europe don't allow flash photography or tripods (even though they do allow you to use your camera on its own). I think it's their way of allowing tourists to get their snapshots without giving up anything good to the professionals. Thus, if I'm standing in front of a great sculpture and I don't have enough light to capture a sharp image, I'll introduce some intentional camera shake to make the image even more abstract. If I'm going to get camera shake, I'm at least going to get shake that's interesting. In the example shown here, I was in the museum of the church of Santa Croce in Florence, shooting sculptures from the original façade.

Intentional blur is an obvious way to imply motion within the image. A tripod-mounted camera with a slow shutter speed can keep the static portion of the scene tack-sharp, while adding blur to the moving subject. This approach allows you to blur just the subject, while avoiding the inevitable camera shake that comes from hand-holding a slow shutter setting.

In other instances, I experiment with abstraction by setting the camera to a very slow setting and shooting out the window of my car while the car is moving. Now, I don't necessarily recommend that you do this if you're the driver (I always have someone else at the wheel as I'm shooting these kinds of images). With some experimentation, you can achieve some interesting, fluid abstractions that would be very difficult to emulate, even with Photoshop's filter set. In this second example, I was shooting at 1/13 of a second at f/25, allowing for a well-exposed image with a great tonal range, in spite of the extreme abstraction.

Experiment with intentional blur in low-light conditions.

Motion-induced abstraction.

Controlling Autofocus

The skill you need with the auto-focus technique is being able to quickly identify the desired focus point in your image and select the nearest focusing zone in the viewfinder. If the subject is not aligned with the focus zone of the viewfinder, the camera will focus on the background or the foreground, and the subject will be out of focus.

If your camera is older or more of a point-and-shoot model, you might not be able to select specific focusing zones, although your owner's manual should outline where the focusing zone is and how to optimize focus. In many instances, you can place the subject in the center of your viewfinder, hold the release button halfway to focus, and then recompose your image before pressing the release button the rest of the way down to take the picture. This approach to focusing is similar to a feature called Focus Lock, which is available on many advanced cameras. Instead of pressing the shutter halfway, Focus Lock allows you to center the subject and press the Focus Lock button to set the focus, then recompose the scene as desired.

Digital SLRs and advanced all-in-one digital cameras allow you to select which focusing zone is active *as you're shooting*. Some Canon models use eye-tracking technology that allows you to simply look at a zone in the viewfinder in order to activate it (the camera tracks your eye movements to determine the focus zone you want to use). Nikon has a button that toggles through all the available zones. Most systems work well with a little practice, provided that you understand what it's doing.

When to Switch to Manual

Although autofocus can be a life-saver in certain situations when you need to react quickly to get the shot, you can also see that it has its limitations. As a result, be mindful that you can switch your SLR camera from autofocus to manual mode to set the focus exactly where you want it by adjusting the focus ring on the lens barrel. (If your camera doesn't offer a manual focus feature, it's a good reason to consider upgrading to a more advanced model.)

7 **Duomo Scaffold III (detail)**
Nikon D2H
1/250 sec, f/7.6
EV -1.33
Focal length 78mm

8 **Duomo Scaffold III**
Nikon D2H
1/250 sec, f/4.5
EV +0.33
Focal length 75mm

A Night in Siena

Porta Romana, Siena

Santo Spirito

While in Siena, I stayed in a small hotel just inside the old walls of the city, close to the massive southern gate known as the Porta Romana. I estimated its thick stone walls, rising several stories high, to be at least 15–20 feet thick. I struggled with how I was going convey this monumentality in a single shot, and didn't even point my camera at it for the first few days of my stay.

I was returning from a day's shooting in San Gimignano when I saw the edifice illuminated at night for the first time, and realized that this was the perfect way to shoot it. The darkness enveloped the surrounding distractions, and the tourists and other pedestrians were at a minimum, clearing the stage for my close-up of the Porta Romana.

I set up my tripod and cable release and began shooting test exposures. I confess that in my film days, I would have pulled out my handheld meter and taken spot readings across the scene. With the immediate feedback I get from digital, I now start with an educated guess and tweak the results as needed. This is a situation in which you have to check the histogram in the camera's LCD so that you can be sure you're getting the proper exposure.

The first exposures were shot from the side, just to get the settings right, although I knew all along that I needed to set up in the middle of the road to get the composition and symmetry right. I ended up using a wide lens set to 12mm, with an exposure of 2.2 seconds at f/4. As I set up and triggered the shutter, a single Vespa motorbike appeared and drove past me, creating the perfect light trail to punctuate the composition.

I shot several compositions that night, including the shot of the church of Santo Spirito. In this shot, I created en extreme angle of view by setting the tripod on the lower steps in front of the church, and setting an extra long exposure to exaggerate the color and to pick up detail in the sky. The image shown is straight from the camera, with no color or exposure adjustments to create the dramatic effects. Once again, I used the 12mm focal length, with a 13-second exposure at f/4.

Low Light

Low light is probably the most common reason for switching to manual focus. Passive systems require enough light to bounce off your subject and reflect back into the system, and if they don't confirm a focus point, they usually don't allow you to shoot the image. In these circumstances, the only way to shoot an image may be to switch to manual mode and do your best to focus on your own. Although active systems create their own beam of light for focusing, the beam can misfire and hit the wrong area of the image. Although the active autofocus camera will let you shoot, the results from the misfired autofocus beam

might not be visible in the dim viewfinder. Thus, with both active and passive autofocus systems, it's a good idea to take your time in low-light situations and switch to manual as necessary to get the shot right.

No Edges

Autofocus systems look for contrasting edges to determine where the subject is in relation to the camera. If you're shooting a soft or muted subject, such as a foggy meadow or diffuse sky, the camera might not be able to find enough edge contrast to set the focus. In these cases, you should switch to manual and set the focus yourself.

Some autofocus systems detect only horizontal or vertical edges and

might have a problem if the appropriate edges are not visible to the focus sensor because of a lack of contrast. Problems with edge orientation can be avoided by turning the camera on its side while focusing. In either event, you can focus on another subject at the same distance and use the Focus Lock feature or switch to manual focus.

Glass and Transparency

As mentioned previously, glass presents a problem for both passive and active focusing systems because both systems tend to get fooled by the reflections off the glass. There's not much middle ground on this one: Switch to manual whenever you're shooting through glass and set the focus as needed.

9 **Montepulciano Altar III**
Nikon D2H,
1/60 sec, f/4.5
Focal length 75mm

⑩ Shed
Nikon D2H
1/100 sec, f/9
Focal length 12mm

⑪ Shed Detail
Nikon D2H
1/125 sec, f/17
Focal length 22mm

Focus and Camera Stability

Autofocus is important for determining which part of the scene is in focus and which parts are blurry. When you have a basic understanding of how your camera's autofocus system works, you need to develop good habits for keeping the entire camera steady while shooting. Otherwise, the entire scene will be blurry and nothing will be in focus; not even the wall in the background. In short, autofocus does nothing to compensate for camera shake.

Although most of us do our best to keep things steady while shooting, there are pitfalls to be aware of. The first is when you're shooting in low light. In dimly lit situations, you must open up your camera's aperture to let in more light. You must also slow down the camera's shutter speed so that more light can pass through the lens. If you're shooting in automatic mode, the shutter speed is automatically lowered, making the long exposure far more sensitive to any movement. In addition, the slightest finger movement while pressing the shutter is more than enough to blur the image. Although some manufacturers have developed cameras and lenses that nullify a small degree of camera shake, it's still a good idea to use a tripod for any shots below 1/30 of a second (see Chapter 2, "Digital Exposure," for more on the relationship between shutter speed and f-stops).

If your subject is moving along a predictable path, you can *pan* the camera to follow the movement. Doing so blurs the background even more, while keeping the moving subject in sharper focus. For example, if you're shooting a horse race or stock car race, pan the camera to follow the subject, and the results will be sharper.

Timing

There's more to focus than simply mastering the autofocus feature and holding the camera steady. These technical skills will make certain image areas sharp, but a better question to consider is *what to shoot at*, or perhaps *when to shoot*. These

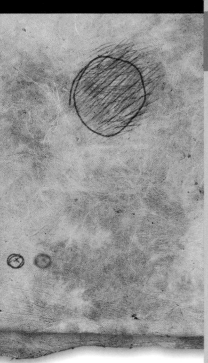

Improving Focus in Photoshop

The first thing to keep in mind is that sharpening in Photoshop is no replacement for getting the focus right in the camera. Repeat after me: *Sharpening is **not** focusing*. Your camera is capable of making judgments about the distance of the subject to the camera, and where one object ends and another begins. Because this 3D thinking isn't possible for Photoshop, the program treats the image as a flat 2D grid of pixels, unless you manually define the objects and relative distances.

On the other hand, if you're just trying to give the edges in your subject a boost, Photoshop's Unsharp Mask filter is a great tool. Follow these steps to get the best results from Photoshop's Unsharp Mask filter:

Output Resolution. Set the size of the image before you scale it up or down. Setting the sharpness and then reducing the image is likely to erase the detail you just created.

Bicubic Sharper or Smoother. When scaling the image up or down, make sure that you use the correct interpolation setting. Use Bicubic Sharper when making the image smaller to maintain image detail. Use Bicubic Smoother when making the image larger to smooth the effects of pixilation. These settings can be found in the Image Size dialog box, after enabling the Resample Image option.

The Unsharp Mask dialog box.

View Actual Pixels. When sharpening, make sure you're viewing the image at a 1:1 pixel ratio by selecting View, Actual Pixels.

Amount versus Radius. Set the ratio of the Amount and Radius sliders in the Unsharp Mask dialog box depending on the image being sharpened. For images with lots of detail, set the radius below 1 pixel and use a higher Amount setting. For softer images where you want to sharpen only major contrast areas, set the Radius higher and the Amount lower.

questions revolve around the photographer's goal of capturing the decisive moment.

The best way to capture the moment is to have an innate sense of intuition and timing. Unfortunately, these skills are largely instinctive and are developed more through experience than instruction. Having said that, using your camera's burst exposure setting is extremely helpful in capturing a number of shots in a brief time span, increasing your chances of nailing the decisive shot.

Whether you're shooting in single or burst (multi-frame) mode, it's important to get used to the shutter lag that happens between the time you push the shutter release and the moment the image is

⑫

⑫ Ufizzi Courtyard
Nikon D2H
1/90 sec, f/4.8
EV -0.33
Focal length 31mm

captured. When you press the shutter release, the camera determines exposure, sets white balance, and focuses on the subject. On some cameras, this set-up time creates a noticeable delay before the picture is taken. Sometimes you must adjust your timing to get the shot right. In certain cameras, it's possible to switch from active to passive focus mode, eliminating the pre-focusing beam that can create the shutter lag. Each camera is different though, so check your owner's manual and practice to understand the specifics of your system.

What Is Depth of Field?

When we consider the timing of a shot, we begin to move from the technical aspects of focusing to its artistic application. When you begin to explore how the focus of an image influences its artistic expression, you must consider the image's *depth of field*.

Depth of field refers to what's in sharp focus and what's blurry. The basic tenet is that all images have an area of focus, measured in distance from the camera lens. Objects in the center of the focus field are in the highest degree of focus. Objects further from the focus point are out of focus. For example, if you set

your camera to focus on a subject that's 10 feet away, that object becomes the center of the focus field. But what about the objects that are 8 feet from the camera...or 13 feet away...or 5 feet away? Are they also in focus, and does the focus effect fade gradually or stop abruptly? The answers to these questions are determined by how deep the focusing field is; that is, over what distance do things move from sharp focus to soft obscurity?

When an image has a deep depth of field, lots of things are in focus, and the transition between sharp and soft focus is a gradual one, if it happens at all. Figures ⑬ and ⑭ show the same shot of a carved pediment that stands 15 feet in front of a

stone wall. Notice that in Figure **13**, the wall and the pediment are in sharp focus, revealing a deeper depth of field. In Figure **14**, the rear stone wall is out of focus because of the image's narrow depth of field.

If the center of the focus field is 10 feet away, objects as close as 3 feet and as far as infinity might be tack sharp (in other words, *everything* in the image appears in sharp focus). Deep depth-of-field effects are often used in landscape images where you want the flowers in the foreground *and* the mountains in the distance to be as sharp as possible. A deep depth of field is also useful for still-life images, commercial photography, and other subjects for which the photographer wants to communicate all the detail present in the image.

Narrow depth of field means that the transition from the central focus point and the out-of-focus areas is quick and abrupt. If the subject is in focus at 10 feet away, the person standing next to that subject at 8 feet away might be soft and blurry. A narrow depth of field tends to isolate and emphasize the subject, rendering the subject sharply, while throwing everything else out of focus. Close-up photography is notorious for creating narrow depth-of-field images, where a macro lens can shift from sharp focus to a soft blur in just a few millimeters.

Controlling Depth of Field

When you focus your camera in a landscape, it quickly becomes

apparent that the depth of the focusing field is not equally distributed in front of and in back of the central focusing point. More sharpness is apparent behind the focus point than in front, as caused by the way the optical field is compressed as it moves away from the camera. A standard rule of thumb is that the depth of field extends 1/3 in front of the focus point and 2/3 behind.

The variable that delivers the most control over depth-of-field effects is the aperture (f-stop) of the lens. When the aperture is reduced (set to a higher number), the depth of field increases (gets deeper). Thus, an aperture of f/22 has a much deeper depth of field than an aperture of

13 **Deep Depth of Field**
Nikon D2H
1/10 sec, f/3.4
Focal length 400mm

14 **Narrow Depth of Field**
Nikon D2H
1/400 sec, f/5.6
Focal length 400mm

15 Dried Flower
Nikon D2H
1/400 sec, f/10
Focal length 75mm

16 Vines
Nikon D2H
1/80 sec, f/7.1
Focal length 75mm

f/5.6. Of course, as the aperture shrinks (the f-stop gets larger), the shutter speed slows down to let in more light. As a result, you'll find that you usually need a tripod for deep depth-of-field shots.

When you want to create an extremely narrow or deep depth of field, choose lenses with an extreme focal length. Short lenses, including wide angles and fish eyes, deliver a very deep depth of field. Long lenses such as telephotos generate a narrow depth of field. Thus, choose a 28mm lens for a deep depth of field or a 300mm lens for a narrow one.

The last thing to remember about depth of field is that the distance between the focus point and the camera determines how wide or narrow the field will be. This is why the focus markings on many camera lenses jump from a focus distance of 12 feet right to infinity while marking off much smaller increments between 3 and 6 feet. It's extremely critical to get the focus point just right when objects are closer to the camera.

Artistic Application

For many photographers, depth of field just happens, and as long as it doesn't get in the way, they tend to ignore it. This is a huge mistake in that it is one of the most powerful in-camera creative tools at your disposal. Consider the creative options described in the following sections.

Implying Distance

Depth of field is a great way to imply vast areas of space within a photograph. A background that fades to a soft blur is a basic feature of atmospheric perspective, which was a compositional tool used by Renaissance painters. The background is soft and desaturated in many old master paintings as a way of implying a distant horizon. In Figure **15**, the sunflower is in sharp focus as the background goes to a soft blur. Although this effect is rather abrupt, the blurred landscape in the background is easily identifiable and works to enhance the foreground subject.

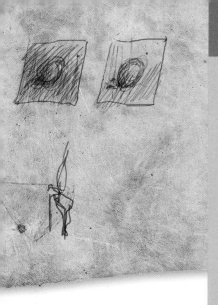

Creating Intimacy

An extreme depth of field can create intimacy between an object and the viewer because it pulls you in close and lightly whispers its detail in your ear. If the background or foreground softly drops away, you're left with a detailed and tactile portrait of the subject. In the example shown in Figure ⓰, the subject is a vine clinging to the side of a tree. The soft sun-dappled background makes you feel even closer to the sharpness in the foreground, and the strong side lighting accentuates the crisp edge and grainy texture of the central leaf.

Can I Fix the Exposure in Photoshop?

The fast answer to this question is "yes and no."

Photoshop can do amazing things to bring out detail and tonal information, but an analogy to film exposure is a fitting one. In the dark room, you can do wonders dodging or burning a final print if any detail exists on the negative to start with. If the information isn't in the negative, there's no good way to bring it out. The same is true with Photoshop, in that the digital info must be in the file before you can bring it out.

Thus, beware of highlight or shadow areas that have been clipped into the flat black or flat white of zone IX or zone I. Also remember that trying to lighten shadow areas that are severely overexposed will often yield a lot of noise, especially in the blue channel. Make sure that you expose for the shadows when photographing digitally, because there is less latitude to lighten them in Photoshop. Check your histograms as you go, and reshoot if necessary.

Another area to be mindful of is glare and brightness. Photoshop can enhance color casts and image detail, but asking Photoshop to remove glare from the sky, water, or a department store window can be a much harder task. To minimize glare, a good Polarizing filter for your camera can work wonders to reduce glare and pump up saturation in the image. Brightness is not often considered a problem for most situations, but occasionally you will have to darken an image, even when you've stopped the lens down to its smallest setting. Instead of shooting an image that's too bright, or using a shutter speed that unnaturally freezes the action, use a Neutral Density filter. ND filters darken the image without introducing a color cast, and come in a wide range of intensities for controlling the degree of darkness applied to the image.

Depth of field in a landscape situation usually means creating a deep focus range that's crisp and sharp from foreground to horizon. Keep in mind, however, that most close-up work is also shot outdoors, and close-up work has the narrowest depth of field range. Even when you're focusing on a landscape, there is still a focal range; not all landscapes benefit from the "focus to infinity" approach. Tips for controlling depth of field in the landscape include:

17 Woods III
Nikon D2H
1/200 sec, f/5.6
Focal length 330mm

18 Woods II
Nikon D2H
1/45 sec, f/4.5
Focal length 24mm

19 Untitled
Nikon D2H
1/250 sec, f/7.6
Focal length 78mm

20 Plowed Field
Nikon D2H
1/90 sec, f/12
Focal length 24mm

- Compose with an interesting object in the foreground to hold focus and interest and to emphasize a deep depth of field.

- Underexpose or stop down by 1/2 stop to a full stop to emphasize details in clouds. Underexposing the sky deepens the depth of field even more.

- Because depth of field extends quickly to infinity in a short lens, you can shut off autofocus and manually set your 50mm lens to f/8 and 6 meters for sharp focus from 3 meters to infinity.

In most cases, you want the object in sharp focus unless you're trying to abstract it or create a generalized shape. The bigger question tends to be whether you want to isolate the object from its surroundings with a shallow depth of field, or to keep the entire scene in full detail.

- Watch the background patterns of light and shadow and shift the camera angle to frame and highlight the subject in strong contrast.

- Set the focus point in the subject at the area with the highest contrast.

- Consider zooming to a tight crop on the subject to integrate the focus areas and the abstracted background.

- Set the focus point slightly *ahead* of the desired focus area to push more sharp focus into the foreground.

㉑ White Flower
Nikon D2H
1/180 sec, f/11
ISO 640
Focal length 75mm

㉒ Waterspout
Nikon D2H
1/320 sec, f/5.6
Focal length 400mm

㉓ Pienza Cheese
Nikon D2H
1/60 sec, f/4.5
Focal length 75mm

㉔ Leaf I
Nikon D2H
1/60 sec, f/4.5
Focal length 105mm

When shooting images close-up and capturing textures, an extremely narrow depth of field is inevitable. The challenge simply becomes one of how you're going to control it to ensure that you're getting the proper composition and emphasis.

- Shoot from an angled position to create a sense of depth and deep space.

- Position the lens at a 90° angle to the textured surface to maintain focus across all areas of the surface.

- Use a tripod to steady the shot and set the focus point exactly where you want it.

- Use focusing rails to make small control adjustments to the focus point and depth of field.

Woods IV
Nikon D2H
1/200 sec, f/5.6
Focal length 75mm

Green Window
Nikon D2H
1/160 sec, f/6
Focal length 75mm

Key Hole
Nikon D2H
1/80 sec, f/4.5
Focal length 75mm

Leaf II
Nikon D2H
1/100 sec, f/5
Focal length 75mm

Chapter 4

COMPOSITION

This just might be the most important chapter in this book. The fact is, if you don't have solid composition skills, you have little chance of making artistic images that have impact. Exposure and focus are important technical skills, but composition frames reality and structures the viewing experience. Without effective composition, you're left with a detached and soulless view of the world, even if it is clearly exposed and presented.

This chapter presses you to define and refine your message; asking what you're trying to express with your images while acknowledging that not everyone has the same motives and aspirations. Some of you are aiming for artistic expression, while others are simply out to show the relatives that you really were in that famous or exotic place. It's all valid, although your approach to composition will vary accordingly in each of these instances. In addition to examining intentions and ideas, this chapter considers the various compositional building blocks, including color, the rule of thirds, cropping, and depth of field. Finally, we examine a method for controlling composition using multiple exposures to optimize sharpness and exposure, as well as to create dramatic lighting effects.

❶ Façade
Nikon D2H
1/320 sec, f/9
Focal length 400mm

❷ Duomo Detail
Nikon D2H,
1/250 sec, f/8
focal length: 105mm

Composition and Style

When you take a picture, you reveal a great deal about yourself as well as the world around you. First and foremost, you reveal the things that are important to you based on your choice of subject. Some folks shoot landscapes while others shoot people or abstract images. The things that draw your attention and create the impulse to capture them tell a lot about how you see the world. They're what define your photographic style.

In addition, your approach to your subject is telling. Do you use a wide lens and keep a distance from the subject, or do you push in close and provide a more intimate view? Finally, what are your personal feelings about the scene in front of you? Do you have an emotional or passionate reaction to the subject, do you want to push the aesthetic elements and create an artistic message, or do you simply want to capture and preserve the face of someone you love?

Your answer to these questions should be your guide to how you approach image composition. Whatever your motivation, don't forget that it's all about telling a story about what you see as well as what you feel.

Compositional Building Blocks

Most people have a vague idea about what composition is, and some may even have an idea about what "good" composition is. Whatever your familiarity and comfort level may be with this subject, I'm going to encourage you to throw out any rigid, predetermined rules about what good composition is, and to adopt a more flexible, modular approach to the subject.

The problem with most formalist approaches to composition is that they're too limited and repetitive. They seldom consider the full expressive range of the subject, or assist in communicating the subtle nuance of the photographer's mes-sage. And although these definitions might produce images that are tech-nically sound, they often act as bar-riers to creating images that have real power or deliver a unique, per-sonal message.

Instead, approach good composition as an intuitive puzzle for which you need to find the right combination of tools to use on your subject to convey your message. Rather than learning a few rules about the Greek Golden Mean or the Rule of Thirds, open yourself up to new forms of expression. In addition, continue to explore ways of combining elements in new and unexpected ways.

Thinking About the Subject

What is your subject? What are you trying to capture and express? Is it a person, landscape, or even an aes-thetic element such as a texture or shape? If your subject is an object (that is, a noun), your approach to composition is going to be much more formal and direct. Compose the image in an interesting way, expose properly, and keep the sub-ject sharp. All that's left is finding a suitable frame for your Eiffel Tower picture, preferably one that matches the couch.

The one caveat to the "noun as sub-ject" axiom is when shooting people. Because people are capable of a wide range of expression and feeling, it's

③ San Gimignano Panorama
Nikon D2H
1/80 sec, f/21
ISO 640
Focal length 34mm

almost impossible to separate these emotions from the physical body. When photographing a human subject, an interesting dynamic occurs. There is a strong impulse on the part of the artist and audience to orient themselves in relation to the subject in the photo. What are they thinking or feeling? Do they see me? Are they a threat? Could I run if they attacked me? Could I reach them to provide comfort? Your goal in shooting most people-as-subject images is to get the viewer to connect with the subject in some way. If they're asking these kinds of questions, you've succeeded, and the image is likely to be compelling and memorable.

Thus, when you're shooting a person, it's important to decide how you want the viewer to interact with the subject. What is the balance between intimacy and detachment, or the overall level of identification and accessibility?

The most abstract type of subject involves trying to express an idea or concept. What if your subject is speed, or rage, or fidelity? Concepts that function as adjectives are often expressed abstractly. It's easy to imagine an abstract image that conveys speed, for example. In addition, emotional concepts are often communicated through color, whether it be the rage and passion of red, or blue's calm and serenity.

The list that follows breaks down the compositional building blocks at your disposal as you compose a picture. You should think about how to combine them in a way that best communicates your message. The subject sets the tone for the composition, which you respond to as you choose a viewpoint that orients the viewer within the scene. Finally, you make perceptual choices around light, color, or focus that reveal more or less of the subject and determine the subject's accessibility.

Orienting the Viewer

The very act of capturing an image creates a window or frame that the viewer looks through as they encounter the image. The size and

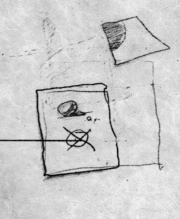

shape of the image (its *frame*), as well as the perspective and viewpoint, all conspire to orient the viewer with the subject.

Frame Geometry and Size

The standard height-to-width ratio used by your camera's viewfinder is a pleasing and flexible format that grew out of the photographer's preoccupation with the landscape. In addition, you can also turn the camera on its side and shoot a full figure, getting head and feet in the frame without too much trouble.

Think about whether you're trying to isolate your subject in full view, or whether there's a specific area within your subject that's drawing your attention. In Figure ❻, the wide-angle perspective emphasizes the overall structure and shape of the building; Figure ❼ changes to a standard focal length to bring out the detail in the stone and the steps. Think about how you want the subject to come through the window of the frame, and what sort of reaction you want the viewer to have when they see it.

One last point is to think about the size at which you will print the image. Today's large-format inkjet printers can make prints as wide as 72 inches, and dozens of feet long. Printing an image larger than life tends to abstract it and has a disorienting effect on the viewer. Conversely, small prints tend to objectify your subject, literally giving the viewer the sense that they can pick it up and put it in their pocket. Both of these approaches distance the viewer from the subject and force them to interact on more of a conceptual or technical level, rather than an emotional one.

Cropping

Although you should thoughtfully compose images in your camera's viewfinder, the fact remains that you should consider cropping any image that's worth printing and framing. *Cropping* allows you to reconsider the decisions you made while you were shooting, refining the areas of emphasis within the composition.

❻ **Shed**
Nikon D2H
1/100 sec, f/9
Focal length 12mm

❼ **Shed Detail**
Nikon D2H
1/125 sec, f/17
Focal length 22mm

8 **Duomo Facade III**
Nikon D2H
1/60 sec, f/4.5
EV -0.33
Focal length 75mm

Cropping is reductive in nature; it can only make the image smaller and take away some of the shot. As you crop, consider two main questions: Do I want to change the aspect ratio? Does the image become more clear and concise if I zoom in and eliminate areas that are superfluous or unnecessary?

The main aspect ratio options include a horizontal or vertical orientation; a panoramic, standard photo frame; and a square. Horizontal images are more narrative and communicate more of a sense of time, while vertical images tend to emphasize and isolate the subject. These are not specific measured frame sizes; they simply refer to the general shape of the

frame and how that shape effects how we view the subject. We'll touch more on these characteristics later in the chapter.

Viewpoint

As the viewer looks at the scene, is their eye level above the scene or below it? The answer to this question plays a key psychological factor in how the image is felt and perceived. Position yourself lower and shoot up at the subject or landscape to give the subject a sense of dominance or power. Shooting down on the subject can have the inverse effect, making the subject feel more accessible and perhaps even vulnerable.

Lens Perspective

Most people think about the lens they want to use only when they need to zoom in or out from their subject. But it's important to remember that the focal length determines the perspective in the scene, making things look normal or distorted.

Wide lenses with short focal lengths tend to stretch the scene at the edges of the frame, while creating a feeling of extra distance between the viewer and the subject (think of the rear-view mirror on your car, where "objects are closer than they appear"). For a more intimate look, try a telephoto or zoom lens. Although these long lenses bring

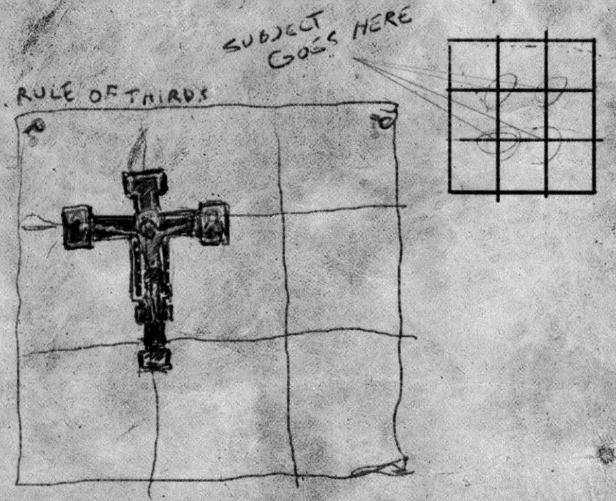

9

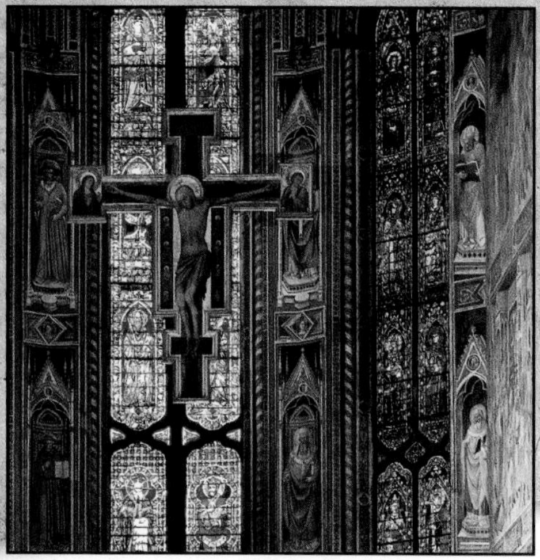

you in closer to the subject, they also flatten and compress the space, reducing the sense of depth in the image. Stick to medium lenses with focal lengths of 40mm–80mm for image perspective that looks the most natural.

Dividing the Frame

Ask most people to define image composition, and they usually describe some process of organizing the subject within the frame, perhaps alluding to geometric divisions and proportions. "Don't put the subject right in the middle," they'll say. "Make it more interesting."

In many instances, they'd be correct with this definition, but on the other hand, some of my best pictures have centered the subject right in the middle of the frame. If the right subject is combined with the proper frame proportions and message, any rule can be effectively broken. But as the old adage goes, you need to learn the rules before you can break them, so consider the list that follows as an overview of methods for arranging the picture plane.

The Rule of Thirds

The Rule of Thirds is a well-known compositional technique that divides the picture plane into a matrix that looks like a tic-tac-toe board. The idea is to place the subject or focal point at one of the four intersections of lines to create a good composition. This is an acceptable approach that achieves its purpose of keeping the subject out of the center of the frame. In Figure 9, you can see how Cimibue's massive crucifix in the church of Santa Croce is positioned along the linear divisions, with the center of the cross and the head of Christ at the upper-left intersection.

The Greek Golden Mean

The Greek Golden Mean is an analytical system for creating geometric divisions that are well proportioned and inherently pleasing. There are tons of things you could learn about

9 **Cimibue Crucifix**
Nikon D2H
1/5 sec, f/4.5
Focal length 75mm

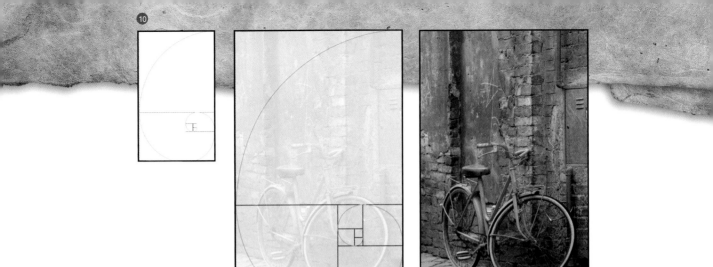

⑩ Siena Bike
Nikon D2H
1/45 sec, f/5
Focal length 130mm

this system, including its discovery by the Greek mathemetician, Eulid; the fact that it's responsible for many repeating spiral forms in nature; and that its ratio of 1:1.618 is the same basic proportion behind the faces we instinctively consider the most beautiful.

The diagram in Figure ⑩ shows the basic proportions of this principal. The geometric divisions and the resulting arc created by mapping the intersections is a familiar image to those who may have studied composition at some point in their lives. Unfortunately, few people know how to move from theory and interesting trivia to practical application. What does a nautilus shell and this diagram have to do with taking pic-

tures? Start by trying to apply the Golden Mean proportions while cropping your images. Try to work intuitively, not by calculating the formula to an infinite decimal point, but by feeling its natural balance and rhythm. Your goal should be to create a balanced geometric division that approximates the Golden Mean as you are framing shots in the viewfinder. Then, as you're reviewing your images in Photoshop, think about cropping to reflect the Golden Mean framing ratios. Draw the shapes and spend some time trying to develop an intuitive feel for the relationship: *this, next to this, feels right*. ***That*** is the basis for all good composition.

Angles and Pointers

In addition to defining geometric divisions in the image frame, objects and shapes can also serve as visual pointers to lead the viewer through the composition. A country road is an obvious path that leads the eye into a scene, although any shape can suggest a direction for the eye to follow. This concept is discussed in more detail later in this chapter, but keep it in mind as a compositional building block that's at your disposal.

Presenting the Subject

At this point, we've looked at how to orient the viewer in the scene, lead his or her eye through the

composition, and divide the frame into interesting and pleasing proportions. Although these factors contribute to the viewer's approach to the image, we still have the question of the subject itself, and how it is depicted by the composition.

How we depict the subject, or rather, how we allow the viewer to perceive the scene, has a huge impact on the emotional state of the viewer. If the lighting in the image is clear and vibrant, the viewer's reaction is likely to be positive and cheerful. Desaturated and cloudy conditions usually have an opposite effect, and dark and hazy lighting can create a sense of discomfort or fear.

Depth of Field

Depth of field was covered in some detail in the Chapter 3, "Focus and Depth of Field," and it is mentioned here as a compositional device. Used properly, depth of field can help to isolate your subject in sharp detail, while blurring unwanted distractions. The eye moves quickly past areas that are out of focus and is attracted to the areas of sharp focus and detail. As a result, you can use depth of field as a type of compositional pointer to lead the viewer through the composition.

Color

The way you use color has a tremendous impact on the overall look and feel of the image. Color can be used to set the tone for the entire image, impacting the overall quality of light in the scene. In this sense, it is the temperature of the color that often has the most impact, either through the warm light of an evening sunset or the cool light of a misty morning.

Color intensity can also play a role in image perception and compositional control. An image that is color dominant, with highly saturated colors that jump off the page, immediately takes on a graphic feel because the color intensity draws attention to the overall shapes of the objects. Conversely, when the color saturation is lower, the

⑪ Galgano Arches
Nikon D2H
1/80 sec, f/7.1
Focal length 12mm

⑫ Duomo Mosaic
Nikon D2H
1/500 sec, f/5.6
Focal length 400mm

13

tonality of the light and shadows tends to dominate, and the scene can take on a patina or nostalgic glow. Thus, in highly saturated images, the overt object shapes and edges can create directional pointers that lead the eye through the image.

Finally, think about using color contrast as a way to draw the eyes to the primary subject area. Because our eyes are immediately drawn to high-contrast areas, treat the subject with a contrasting color. If the majority of the image is primarily green, and the subject is red, the subject will demand the viewer's attention. You can contrast color areas with intensity (saturation), hue (color), or value (shades and tints).

Contrast

In the sense of presenting your subject, I'm specifically referring to tonal contrast in the scene. In general, high-contrast images sacrifice detail in the shadows in exchange for highly delineated edges and a graphic look and feel. In some cases, you might want to shift to a low-contrast emphasis so that the scene takes on a supple and sensuous feel, with tonal gradations that are subtle and soft. Contrast has a huge impact on how the image feels, and how quickly it unfolds for the viewer. In addition, think about the requisite level of detail that the shot requires; high-contrast treatments sacrifice a fair amount of information.

When to Compose

Now that your head is full of all these compositional options, you might be asking exactly how you're supposed to remember them all, or when you're supposed to deploy them. The good news is that there's no single answer for that, and if you miss applying them at the shooting phase, you can often deploy them later.

There's no question that you need to be thinking and using solid compositional strategies as you're looking through the viewfinder and taking pictures. As you look at your previews, assess how the image looks and make adjustments, reshooting if necessary. When you look at your images in Photoshop, you can apply

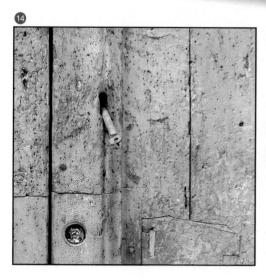

additional sharpening and focus effects while pushing the color or contrast relationships in the image. The thing to remember is that you must employ a discerning eye at all phases of the creative process; while shooting, previewing, and in Photoshop.

Documenting a Moment

One of the most basic reasons to take a picture is to capture a likeness, the essence of a place, or the power of a moment. We want to freeze it in time so that we can look back on it and remember. This is a basic motivation that most photographers have, from the most basic amateur to the seasoned professional. To move past simple snapshots and begin taking compelling photographs, we must abandon this basic impulse and expect more from the image compositions.

Depiction of a Place

How do you communicate the essence of a place? A good way to approach this is to imagine how you react to a place you're encountering for the first time. Your first reaction is likely impacted by the quality of light that's present. If it's a landscape, and there is full sunshine or a dramatic sunset, you're likely to have a much more positive response than if the same scene is cloudy or gloomy. Even if it's an interior room or enclosed space, a dark space with shadows elicits a different emotional response than if the space is well lit and clearly described. Are you looking to express the scene positively, or to convey a sense of foreboding?

We usually don't think of lighting as a compositional element unless it defines delineated shadows that create shapes or textures in the subject. But I'm not talking about that aspect of lighting at this point. I'm talking about how the lighting in the scene sets a tone that we can use as a starting point for how we approach the composition. With a basic idea of the tone you want to set, consider the variables of spatial

14 Yellow Door
Nikon D2H
1/10 sec, f/8
Focal length 75mm

15 Statue with Skull
Nikon D2H
1/250 sec, f/7.6
Focal length 340mm

15 **Monteriggioni Vineyard (uncropped)**
Nikon D2H
ISO 640
1/125 sec, f/15
Focal length 75mm

16 **Monteriggioni Vineyard**
Nikon D2H
ISO 640
1/125 sec, f/15
Focal length 75mm

depth and diagonal pointers for creating compelling images of places and landscapes.

Spatial Depth

When we look at an image of a place, we tend to analyze it and navigate through it as though we were there. Perceptually, we break the space into foreground, middle-ground, and background areas, considering the elements in each section in relation to our viewpoint within the scene.

If we see clear paths that allow us to move through the foreground and deeper into the scene, we're likely to go further and visually explore the space. Conversely, if there is little description in the foreground area, the image is less likely to hold our attention. Even worse, if the foreground elements block our path and get in our way, it's extremely difficult to engage with the scene at all. The vineyard path in Figure **16** provides a clear entrance to the scene, which is picked up by the winding road, taking us to the compositional focal point of the building in the middle ground.

When considering this principal, keep in mind that the deeper the space, the further you can stretch or compress it. If the visibility stretches deep into the landscape, you can sometimes pass over the foreground all together and introduce elements in the middle-ground that stretch to the back. Or in the case of Figure **16**, the deep horizon was cropped out to keep the viewer from exploring the distant hills, focusing instead on the house. A scene that has a deep space that's full of detail from foreground to back (as is the case in the uncropped Figure **15**) can overwhelm the viewer with too much detail and make it harder to create emphasis. Compressing or eliminating the space can be effective when you want to draw attention to other subject elements.

CASTLE WALL
↓ LEADS EYE
DOWNWARD

⑰

↗ SHADOW & HILL POINT ←
TO BLUE TARP.

Diagonal Pointers

It's important to make the distinction between physical pathways into the scene and purely visual ones. Figures ⑮ and ⑯ show a literal pathway in the vineyard that leads the viewer into the scene, but in reality, almost any diagonal line pointing in the right direction will do the trick. Figure ⑰ shows this idea: the hill, rock wall, and foreground shadow all point the viewer's gaze to the blue tarp in the lower center of the scene. These pointers, and the unique landscape in general, create a sense of mystery and drama around something as mundane and ordinary as a blue piece of plastic. In addition, notice how the wall and trees close off the background, pushing the interest to the subject.

A Sense of Time

Capturing a moment forces you to take a position with regards to time. Are you trying to convey that the scene is old and stagnant—having endured a long passage of time—or are you saying that the scene is fresh, new, and immediate? Is the scene volatile and rapidly changing, or is it steady and constant, perhaps even timeless? When you have a basic idea for how you want to communicate the scene, consider the following tips for using the angle of view to convey time, movement, or stability.

Movement, Diagonals, and Duration

Because we read from left to right, we read the visual cues in an image—as well as the progression of events—in a left-to-right fashion. Viewing image elements from left to right implies a narrative sequencing that moves you from one thing to the next.

When your gaze is pulled in the opposite direction, moving from right to left in a scene, it feels unnatural and awkward. For example, look at the image of the village of Cuna in Figure ⑱. The first image shows the scene as shot, with the sloping fields moving from left

⑰ **Blue Tarp**
Nikon D2H
ISO 640
1/200 sec, f/9
Focal length 12mm

to right, leading you up to the fortress. Figure **19** shows the same image flipped, so that the field leads you to the left, creating an uncomfortable imbalance.

As you think about the presence and direction of angles in the scene, consider how you might use contrast to create emphasis. Instead of making everything dynamic, what if you arranged one dynamic element in an otherwise static composition? Or what if all the angles moved in one direction while one element went against the grain, creating a counterpoint? In Figure **20**, the angular projection of light against the square column elements is more dramatic because of the contrast in directional elements. Consider these options and use angles to create a dynamic sense of time and movement in your image.

Symmetry, Stability, and Eternity

If angles create movement and a sense of time, then the absence of angles creates a sense of stability and timelessness. Images that are square to the viewer, with thoughtful proportions and right angles tend to offer themselves up for contemplative study. It's as if they invite the viewer to slow down and explore the object or scene being presented, rather than following pointers and angles that would lead the viewer into the space.

The cross in Figure **21** is a good example of this; the symmetry of the cross shape and the right angles in the composition keep the image plane square with the viewer, flattening the space. As a result, the viewer slows down a bit and begins to explore the shape and texture in greater detail, noticing the dappled stone surface, the drips of paint on the cross, and perhaps the subtle modulation of color.

When a composition overtly emphasizes symmetrical elements, the image can take on a classic quality in which time appears to slow down. As external references and hints at the dynamic passage of time are stripped away, you are left face to face with the subject. If this composition is done well, it distills the subject down to its essence and creates a more contemplative viewing experience.

Face to Face

From the time we're infants, we have a unique and intimate relationship with the human face. We instinctively recognize and respond to it, and are masters at reading the wide range of subtle expressions that can flash across a face during a single conversation. Although we respond quickly to faces and engage with them immediately, we look to get something back from the subject that reveals their mood, persona, or character. Perhaps this is why it's so hard to do portraits well. Instinctively we know when an expression is forced or insincere, and we're disappointed when we don't get the visual cues that we're used to.

Composing Heads

There are so many ways to depict the face and head that it's hard to come out with a finite list of do's and don'ts that you should follow. Although I do list some tips for portraits and people later in this chapter, the main thing to remember is not to be tentative while you're composing the shot. Be purposeful and emphatic with all your decisions; don't let anything look casual or accidental.

For example, if you're going to crop the top of someone's head (presumably to focus on their features), crop in tight to the point of emphasis, completely eliminating any distracting areas. For candid shooting, be your own toughest critic and throw out images that

20 **Santa Croce Sunlight**
Nikon D2H
1/10 sec, f/4.5
Focal length 75mm

21 **Cross**
Nikon D2H
1/90 sec, f/4.8
Focal length 28mm

The Speed of the Read

When you're working on a composition, it's easy to get bogged down in all the rules and options at your disposal. In the process, you can loose the forest for the trees and the design can get overworked, self-conscious, or just fall apart. If you have a design or image concept that's giving you problems, get back to basics with these compositional premises.

What's the Main Idea?

Make sure that the central emphasis is clearly stated, with no ambivalence or distractions. If the image is a portrait, present the face clearly and directly. Don't emphasize the background or create an intricate spatial division that's going to compete with it. If the image is about an overall tone or feeling, make sure that you treat the image components so that they support the central feeling.

Supporting Cast

With the central subject in view, make sure that the rest of the image supports and enhances the main idea. In some cases, this will simply mean creating a harmony with the aesthetic treatments of the main subject. It can also mean adding nuance and detail that moves the subject out of the realm of the cliché and adds a certain authentic specificity. For example, the image at the top of this sidebar is about the beautiful ornate patterning of these Tuscan frames. The oval shapes of the mirror and the lights echo the curving lines of the frame mouldings. And yet, my favorite piece of nuance is the small white price tags that dangle from some of the pieces. They

serve to take the scene out of the realm of being just an abstract composition, grounding it in the real world of a Florentine frame shop.

Contrast and Paradox

Finally, try to draw allusions to things that might be paradoxical or suggest multiple levels of meaning or connection. It might be a metaphor that is unintentionally implied by the subject, or aesthetic similarities between various image components. It doesn't have to be a major component of the design (although it could be). It just needs to create a sense of double meaning or inferred association. In the Frame Shop image, I like the way the white price tags hang down in contrast to the upward movement of the white candle lights. They act as counterpoints to each other and provide additional visual interest without distracting from the central theme.

don't quite live up to your expecta-tions. Be decisive and act fast so that you can reshoot your subject while you have the opportunity.

Shooting the Figure

As with the face, the human body is also easily recognized. A key compo-sitional aspect of the figure is that it is naturally dynamic, always moving and always implying movement, even when it's at rest. Arms and legs naturally act as visual pointers, while torsos and necks twist and bend, suggesting movement and drawing arcs through space.

Overlap these formal considera-tions with the emotional connec-tions we have with faces and figures. Our subjects will be dis-playing feelings and emotions, even as they interact with each other and their immediate envi-ronment. It's very important in these instances to use all the compositional building blocks at your disposal to direct the viewer to the main point of emphasis. Reveal the subtleties of emotion and interaction, focusing on expression, body language, or other non-verbal cues that may be present in the scene.

Controlling Compositions with Multiple Exposures

One of the great things about digital capture is the way it lets you shoot and react quickly to a scene. When you combine this feature with the ability to create and combine multi-ple exposures seamlessly, you have a powerful process for creating and controlling a composition.

The basic approach for taking multiple-exposure images is to set up the camera on a tripod to keep it stationary, and shoot multiple images without moving the camera

22 Siena Girl
Nikon D2H
1/160 sec, f/6.3
Focal length 400mm

23 Horse Trainer
Nikon D2H
1/80 sec, f/4.5
Focal length 80mm

24 **Background Exposure**
Nikon D2H
1/60 sec, f/9.0
Focal length 48mm

25 **Bottle Exposure**
Nikon D2H
1/160 sec, f/9.0
Focal length 48mm

26 **Bottle Composite**

position. By varying the exposure, lighting, or compositional vehicles, you can create and combine multiple versions of the same scene, with much greater control.

The Basic Approach

After setting up the tripod and framing the scene, I shot Figure **24** to expose for the background and Figure **25** to bring out some glow in the bottles.

I opened both images in Photoshop, copied and pasted the files into one master file, and aligned the two layers. I added a mask to the top layer by clicking the

Mask button in the Layers palette. I painted in the mask with a brush set to a black or white foreground color to reveal the glow of the bottles. The result of blending these two images is shown in Figure **26**.

Options and Variables

This multiple-exposure approach can be applied in a number of ways. The example of the bottles shows an outdoor candid setup, which allows you to control focus and exposure. You could also shoot a sunset, exposing for the foreground area first, waiting with the camera in place, and exposing the saturated sky areas later as they intensify. In Figure **27**, I set up my camera in

Siena's main square and captured several images, capturing people walking through different areas of the square.

I brought each image into Photoshop as a separate layer. Because the images were shot on a tripod, I didn't have to make any adjustments to align the layers, I simply copied and pasted them into the composite image. I added a layer mask to each image and revealed or concealed the various figures using a transparent mask.

Painting in Shadows and Light

One of the most dramatic applications for using multiple exposures is in the studio. In Figure 28, my intention was to create a soft, warm image that would support the overall ambiance of the lit candles.

With the camera set up, I took a series of shots from the same vantage point, using a cable release and tripod. After exposing for the foreground area, I moved the lights to the front to light the rectangular copper plate behind the bowl and changed the exposure to bring out the detail there. I moved the lights again to backlight the vase, and shot another exposure to bring out the details in the glass. Finally, I lit the candles and shot two exposures, one

to clearly delineate the flames, and another to capture the glow coming off the candles.

I opened each image in Photoshop, selected it, and copied each into a single file as multiple layers. I added a layer mask to each layer by clicking the Mask icon at the bottom of the Layers palette. In some cases where I only wanted to add a small section of the layer, I added a mask that concealed the entire layer by holding down the Option key (Alt in Windows) as I clicked the Mask icon. This action generates a mask filled with black, which conceals the entire layer. This makes it easy to select a brush with white as the foreground color to paint in nothing but the desired area.

Using this approach, I blended the candle flames, candles, copper plate, and vase areas together with masks, and I added a Curves adjustment layer to even out the warm yellow light effect I was after. I set the Curves options to

- **RGB channel:** Input: 190, Output: 195, Input: 50, Output: 38
- **Red channel:** Input: 123, Output: 135
- **Green channel:** Input: 187, Output: 172, Input: 93, Output: 87
- **Blue channel:** Input: 121, Output: 97

27 **Campo Time Lapse**

28 **Tuscan Still Life**

127

We've all seen our share of poorly composed landscapes, with centered subjects and cliché points of view. Follow the steps below to make your landscape compositions more interesting.

- Don't center the horizon vertically; experiment with high and low horizon placement.

- Use compelling foreground objects that draw the viewer into the scene.

- Consider the direction of the shadows and use them as pointers to lead the eye through the composition.

- Use the correct focal length to express the expansive grandeur of the scene or to capture close-up, intimate details.

29 Vineyard Sunset
Nikon D2H
1/125 sec, f/5
Focal length 125mm

30 Ripa d'Orcia
Nikon D2H
1/160 sec, f/13
Focal length 24mm

31 Treeline
Nikon D2H
1/200 sec, f/7.1
Focal length 46mm

32 Olive Trees
Nikon D2H
1/125 sec, f/7.1
Focal length 105mm

33 Hay Bales
Nikon D2H
1/350 sec, f/10
Focal length 75mm

Objects can be composed in a wide number of ways. Consider whether your intent is to feature the object itself, or just use it as an element of the overall composition.

34 Marconi Statue
Nikon D2H
1/250 sec, f/7.6
Focal length 400mm

35 Duomo Face
Nikon D2H
1/640 sec, f/4.8
Focal length 75mm

36 Duomo Minstrels
Nikon D2H
1/500 sec, f/4.5
Focal length 75mm

37 Bronze Statue
Nikon D2H (Image Flipped)
1/160 sec, f/6.3
Focal length 105mm

- Use a symmetrical, centered composition to spotlight the object.

- Cropping the object partially out of the frame immediately draws attention to object details and texture, de-emphasizing the object as a whole.

- Use depth of field to present the object in sharp detail, blurring any background or foreground elements that might be distracting.

Close-up photography is abstract by nature because we're generally not used to the shallow depth of field and enlarged textural images. This fact narrows our compositional options, although there are still some basic compositional tips you should keep in mind.

38 Fresco Detail
Nikon D2H
1/6 sec, f/4.5
Focal length 75mm

39 Two Trees
Nikon D2H
1/400 sec, f/6.3
Focal length 75mm

40 Tree Bark
Nikon D2H
1/60 sec, f/4.5
Focal length 60mm

41 Key Hole II
Nikon D2H
1/60 sec, f/4.5
Focal length 75mm

- Use color to your advantage because color often becomes the dominant aesthetic attribute in close-up compositions.

- Find an interesting angle and use the depth of field and focus plane to enhance it. Remember that the focal plane can be a diagonal pointer.

- Look for interesting textural pattern and variation, and frame the composition to emphasize it. Use the Rule of Thirds, offset center, or other composition techniques to guide your explorations as necessary.

41

People are very compelling subjects to whom everyone can relate. This makes shooting people and portraits both difficult and rewarding.

42 Siena Girl I
Nikon D2H
1/200 sec, f/7.1
Focal length 400mm

43 Siena Girl II
Nikon D2H
1/200 sec, f/7.1
Focal length 250mm

44 Palio Procession
Nikon D2H
1/100 sec, f/5
Focal length 75mm

45 Palio Boy
Nikon D2H
1/80 sec, f/4.5
Focal length 80mm

- Structure the composition to harmonize the body language, expression, and lighting within the geometry of the frame.

- Crop the body to emphasize clothing, texture, or specific limbs. Crop on a face to emphasize features such as skin, eyes, or mouth.

- Avoid casually framing a face straight on. Turn the subject's face a quarter turn to create depth and to articulate the form of the face and features.

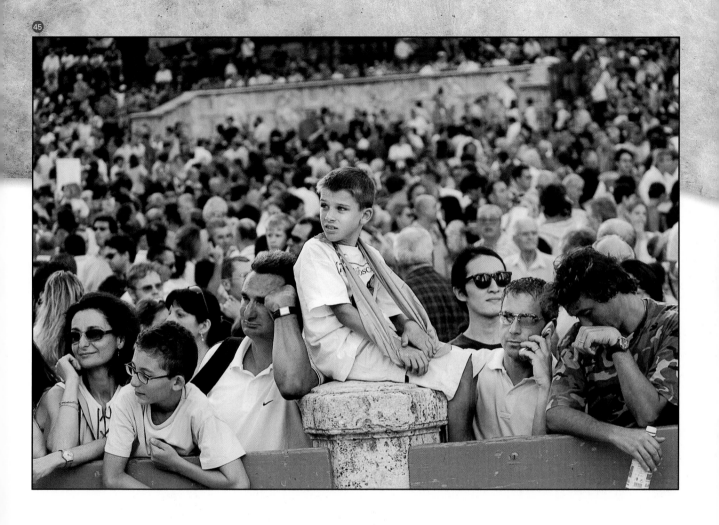

ESPLORAZIONI

Part 2
PHOTOSHOP EXPLORATIONS

Digital photography is notorious for generating tons of raw material; it's unfortunate that most people never move past the **My Photos** folders that act like digital shoeboxes, crammed full of snapshots that are stored out of sight. The chapters in this part provide ample ammunition for what to do next.

Chapter 5, "Photo Explorations," considers ways to manipulate photos while maintaining a final result that still looks like a photo. Darkroom and optimization explorations maintain a look that is still photographic while adding a more expressive element. Chapter 6, "Artistic Explorations," gets even more expressive as it delves into drawing and painting. You'll need a digital tablet for many of these effects, but the results are well worth the effort it may take to get one.

Chapter 5

PHOTO EXPLORATIONS

This chapter looks at ways to enhance photos while maintaining their photographic quality. It considers effects that simulate alternative and antique photo processes, making image panoramas, and hand coloring, among others. The main idea is that the effects that used to require hours in the darkroom, toxic chemistry, and a fortune in specialized materials can now be replicated on your computer and inkjet printer. I know that purists will argue that using Photoshop to create these darkroom effects is not perfect or exactly the same, and that people who love the process of hand crafting will still take the methodical route. But for those looking to broaden their visual photographic range and be more expressive in their work, these explorations can suggest a range of options.

DRAMATIC SHADOWS

Dried Roses
Nikon D2H
1/60 sec, f/4.5
Focal length 60mm

You should think about adding dramatic shadows to a photo when you want to create an emotional edge or emphasize a specific area or feature of the subject. You might want to create deep shadows that obscure certain details in darkness, or create pools of light that spotlight an area. When adding dramatic shadows, it's also likely that you'll sharpen or blur certain areas in conjunction with the lightness and darkness.

Throughout the process, you'll find that you're making decisions about what's important in the image. What's the main message and focus? How does the composition lead the eye to various areas of the image? These are things you could take into consideration as you start to make revisions. If the image already has an area of focus and emphasis, the task is one of emphasizing and accenting what's already there. Remember that you can also create an effective composition out of a mundane image by simply adding shadows and highlights in the right places.

This exploration is good for things such as picking a person out of a crowd, shining a spotlight on an object, or creating a dramatic landscape. Make sure that you have an image with adequate detail and image quality so that it stands up to scrutiny when you draw attention to a specific area.

About the Original Image

The original image for this effect was a photo called *Dried Roses*, shot at the abbey of Santa Anna in southern Tuscany. I love the texture on the top petals of the central rose, as well as some of the spotting on the right side. I wanted to bring that out more by sharpening the detail in those areas.

I also wanted to remove some of the extra details that were distracting from what I wanted to set up as the focal area. The blurred background had a number of shapes and colors in it that created a busy pattern while adding nothing to the image. My plan was to darken down the entire background and pull focus to the top of the center rose.

Building the Effect

① *Selecting the background.*

② *Darkening the background.*

③ *Redefining the edges.*

Simplification was my goal with the *Dried Roses* image because the undulating stalks, red color, and high contrast of the background created lots of unwanted detail and distracted from the main focal point of the top petals on the central rose.

I selected the Magic Wand tool and made sure that the Anti-alias and Contiguous check boxes were enabled in the Options bar. I clicked in the blue background area while entering various Tolerance values in the Options bar. I found that a value of 22 was a great Tolerance setting that allowed me to select large background sections without impinging on the roses in the foreground. I held down the Shift key and selected various sections of the background until the entire background was selected, creating a silhouette around the central rose (Figure **①** shows the selected area, which has been enhanced for clarity).

With the selection still active, I chose Select, Save Selection; in the Save Selection dialog box that appeared, I typed *Sharp* in the Name field to name the selection. After clicking OK, I chose Select, Feather, entered a feather value of 100 pixels , and clicked OK to feather the selection. This command created a soft-edged selection that would work well to smooth out the background without leaving a harsh edge around the flower.

Darken the Background

To adjust the tones in the current selection, I selected Curves from the Adjustment Layer pull-down menu in the Layers palette to create a Curves adjustment layer above the main image layer. I set the Input/Output points to Input: 155, Output: 73. The result of this Curves adjustment is shown in Figure **②** . To redefine some of the edges on the rose, I highlighted the Background layer, chose Select, Load Selection, and reloaded the Sharp selection. I copied the selection,

pasted it above the Curves adjustment layer, and Option-clicked (Alt-clicked in Windows) the Add Layer Mask icon in the Layers palette to add a layer mask filled with black, obscuring the entire layer. I selected the Brush tool with a feathered brush and a white foreground color and painted in the central rose and the partial flower, focusing on the edges and highlights. This brightened the flower slightly and brought back some of the edge details.

To add more contrast in the highlight areas of the rose, I created an additional Curves adjustment layer with Input/Output points of Input: 78, Output: 8, and Input: 221, Output: 250. Although this adjustment deepened the shadows, it also oversaturated the color. To compensate I selected Hue Saturation from the Adjustment Layer pull-down menu in the Layers palette to create a new adjustment layer, and set the Saturation slider to -47 (see Figure **③**) .

④ *Creating a selection around the blur.*　　④ *Adding detail to the blur.*　　⑥ *Blending modes finish the effect.*

Fix the Blur

I liked where things were going but there was a big out-of-focus area right in the middle of the flower. I knew that I couldn't restore sharp focus to an area that was this soft, but I wanted to try to bring out a bit more contrast. To do this, I selected the Pen tool and chose the Path mode from the Options menu instead of using the default Shapes mode. I then drew a path that defined the edges of the petals in the blurry area, clicking to add anchor points that would define the area. I used the Option key (Alt in Windows) to switch from smooth to angled corners, and the ⌘ key (Ctrl in Windows) to convert to the Direct Selection tool to manipulate the points and handles. After closing the path, I opened the Paths palette, made sure that the path was highlighted, and selected Make Selection from the palette menu (see Figure ④).

I used the Dodge and Burn tools to deepen the shadows and brighten the highlights in the blurred area. In the Options bar, I set the range for the Burn tool to Midtones or Shadows as needed, and painted into the shadow areas of the petals to darken and sharpen. I set the range for the Dodge tool to Highlights and went back over the edges of the petals, bringing out the highlights and creating a deeper illusion of space. I kept the Exposure settings for all these adjustments between 6% and 12%. With the selection still active, I selected the Clone Stamp tool with a 30-pixel brush, and added detail into the light areas of the petals. I Option-clicked (Alt-clicked in Windows) the source point on areas where the lines and textures flowed in the same direction, and added these details sparingly so that the effect did not appear artificial or plastic (see Figure ⑤).

Apply Global Sharpening

Finally, I decided to add some global sharpening using the High Pass filter. I chose Select, All to select the entire image and then chose Edit, Copy Merged to copy all visible layers. I then selected Edit, Paste to paste the composite design as a single layer. I selected Filter, Other, High Pass, set the Radius slider to 4.2 pixels, and clicked OK to apply the effect.

With the new filtered layer at the top of the stack, I experimented with blending modes for the High Pass filter layer. Hard Light sharpened the petals on the left, while Vivid Light created additional separation on the right. To apply both blending modes, I duplicated the High Pass layer, set one layer's blending mode to Hard Light, Option-clicked (Alt-clicked in Windows) the Add Layer Mask icon in the layers palette to hide the layer, and painted with white to reveal just the petals on the upper-left of the central flower. I set the other layer's blending mode to Vivid Light and followed the same process to reveal the details in the spotted petal on the right (see Figure ⑥).

CUSTOM BLACK AND WHITE CONVERSIONS

Photoshop offers lots of options for converting photos from color to black and white. For example, you can use the Desaturate, the Convert to Grayscale, or the Hue/Saturation command to create a black-and-white image, but these options by themselves offer very little control over how the colors in the image are converted to black and white.

Hue, saturation, and tone combine to determine the resulting shades of gray when Photoshop converts an image to black and white. If you can control these variables as you're converting an image—as I'll show with the Channel Mixer and Hue/Saturation controls—you can control the tone in a specific area as well as the tonal relationships between different areas. You can also create solid results if you can map specific shades of gray to the colors in an image using the gradient map adjustment layer.

This exploration combines these two approaches into a single exercise. Sometimes you can use the Channel Mixer and Hue/Saturation controls on their own; with other images, you'll want to use the gradient map approach. I like the first method when I'm going for a subtle photographic effect that doesn't stretch the tonal mapping in an image. If I'm trying to create more dynamic range and contrast, I like the gradient map method, or even a combination of the two, as shown in this example.

Siena Madonna
Nikon D2H
1/125 sec, f/5.3
Focal length 60mm

About the Original Image

The winding streets in the hill towns of Tuscany are adorned with small statues representing patron saints. These idols are associated with a given neighborhood (or the entire town if it's a small one). The statues sit in small niches high in the building walls, embedded within the social fiber of the community just as surely as they're embedded within the stone walls themselves.

This photo stood out to me for the texture and patina of the wall and the sculpture, as well as the way the space was divided compositionally. The wire that runs vertically is an interesting division of space, and the shutter anchors the upper-left corner as an effective counterpoint to the main subject.

The goal of this exploration was to create contrast in the brick wall while enhancing the texture of the Madonna statue. It was a challenge to do this while still maintaining a wide tonal range in the Madonna, but it's ultimately what set this image apart as a successful exploration.

Building the Effect

① *Desaturate with Channel Mixer.*

② *Define tones with color channels.*

③ *Control detail in the alcove area.*

The first step in converting to grayscale is to desaturate by adding a Channel Mixer adjustment layer. Select it from the Adjustment Layer pull-down menu in the Layers palette. Enter the following values in the dialog box that appears: Red +20%, Green +70%, Blue +10%. Enable the Monochrome check box and click OK to create a grayscale image (see Figure ①). These are the default settings Photoshop uses when you desaturate an image.

Adjusting Tone with Hue/Saturation

Select the Background layer in the Layers palette and select Hue/Saturation from the Adjustment Layer pull-down menu. This command places the new adjustment layer below the Channel Mixer layer and above the Background layer.

In the Hue/Saturation dialog box that appears, click the Edit pop-up menu and select a color area to make modifications to that specific color within

the image. The choices are Reds, Yellows, Greens, Cyans, Blues, and Magentas. Selecting a color restricts the edits to only that color range, which is represented in the color spectrum at the bottom of the dialog box.

For this image, I adjusted the sliders within each color space as follows: **Reds**: Hue: +1, Saturation: -91, Lightness: -100; **Yellows:** no change; **Greens**: Hue: -1, Saturation: 0, Lightness: -99; **Cyans:** Hue: 0, Saturation: 0, Lightness: -100; **Blues:** Hue: -1, Saturation: -100, Lightness: 0; **Magentas:** no change (see Figure ②).

Advanced Adjustments

The two-step process described thus far is the standard approach for using the Channel Mixer and Hue/ Saturation adjustment layers to desaturate an image. These instructions will suffice for most of the images you work with, but if you want to bring out more details, consider the additional steps in this exploration. While

making global corrections in the previous steps, I lost the opportunity to bring out additional detail in the teal alcove behind the statue. To bring it back, I added a second Hue/Saturation layer above the first, but still below the Channel Mixer layer.

For the second Hue/Saturation layer, I adjusted the sliders within each color space as follows: I clicked in the teal section of the primary image layer (behind the Madonna) with the Eyedropper tool and set the sliders to **Reds:** Hue: 0, Saturation: +100, Lightness: 0; **Yellows:** no change; **Greens:** no change; **Cyans:** no change; **Blues:** no change; **Magentas**: Hue: 0, Saturation: +100, Lightness: 0. As a final step, I selected Master from the Edit Menu and modified the global settings to Hue: +98, Saturation: +100, Lightness: 0 (see Figure ③).

To restrict the effect to only the teal alcove, I concealed the rest of the effect with a mask. I also made one

④ *Mask the adjustment layer.*

⑤ *Add a gradient map adjustment layer.*

⑥ *Add highlight details.*

final adjustment to the Channel Mixer settings. I double-clicked that layer in the Layers palette and set the sliders as follows: Red: +32%, Green: +48%, Blue: +26%, and Constant: +6% (see Figure ④). This change adjusted the global grayscale corrections, which brightened the highlight areas a bit more.

Gradient Map Adjustments

At this point, I felt that the Madonna figure was very striking and the rest of the image was a bit flat in comparison. To bring out just a bit more detail in the rest of the image, I added a gradient map adjustment layer to the top of the layer stack. This approach also works great as a standalone technique for converting to grayscale.

After selecting Gradient Map from the Adjustment Layer pull-down menu in the Layers palette, I clicked the gradient strip in the Gradient Map dialog box, launching the Gradient Editor. I double-clicked the left color stop and selected black from the

Color Picker, and clicked OK . In like manner, I set the far-right color stop and set it to white to create a black-to-white gradient.

To set a middle-gray color in the proper spot, I clicked just next to the color midpoint diamond along the gradient strip in the Gradient Editor to create a new color stop in the middle of the gradient. The color of the stop was white, based on the previous selection, but I positioned the mouse pointer in the gradient strip above the right midpoint diamond and clicked to set the new color stop, which should approximate middle gray. I set one more color stop at the color midpoint diamond between middle gray and white, selecting the color in the gradient strip just above the far right midpoint diamond (the quartertones). If you want to be exact, you can double-click each color stop and set each RGB value to 128 for the middle-gray color and to 64 for the quartertones.

Thus far we've replicated the default tonal range, with midtones and quartertones properly placed. The next step is to adjust the midpoint diamonds to tweak the tonal transitions between the color stops without altering the overall tonal mapping as dictated by the color stops. To stretch the highlights, I highlighted the white color stop and dragged the associated color midpoint diamond location to 20% (see Figure ⑤).

This correction opened up the details in the wall, but washed out some detail in the Madonna, so I added a layer mask to bring back the detail in the statue. I also wanted to brighten a few highlights in the brick wall at the bottom of the image. With the Background layer selected, I selected the Dodge tool with a 200-pixel brush, set the range to Highlights in the Options bar, and the Exposure to 11%. I painted in a few more highlights at the bottom to complete the image (see Figure ⑥).

SHIFT DEPTH OF FIELD

Red Bike
Nikon D2H
1/160 sec, f/6.3
Focal length 28mm

There was a time when creating extreme depth of field effects was a task reserved for view cameras with ground-glass viewing backs that could tilt and swivel to throw various sections of the image out of focus. This was important because controlling focus (or the lack thereof) was a great way to emphasize objects or specific sections of the frame.

Photoshop makes fast and easy work of depth-of-field effects, especially if you set up the image properly and understand how the camera interprets focus and detail. Much of the theory is covered in Chapter 2, "Digital Exposure," but the practical application is to understand that the focus point is actually plotted along a plane that runs through the composition. It's usually parallel with the camera's film plane, although the view camera's shifting film back goes against this axiom, and is exactly how it achieves its control over extreme focus.

With this in mind, I like to run the focus plane slightly askew from traditional linear perspective where things just get softer as they move away from the camera. Instead I throw things out of focus at a slight angle. In this exploration, the blurred background creeps up the wall on the left in a way that suggests that the focus plane is running slightly parallel with the wall. Don't get too technical or scientific as you make these decisions, but be aware of how the traditional tools achieve their effects if you want a convincing result.

About the Original Image

A red bicycle in front of the town hall in Pienza is the subject for this exploration. Considering the dominant gray stonework in most Tuscan towns, a bright spot of color is pretty irresistible. I chose a low point of view and did my best to emphasize the perspective that ran along the wall, anchoring the back of the composition with the café in the background.

When selecting an image for this exploration, be sure to find one that has detail in the full focus range, from foreground to middle ground, to background. For example, landscapes where everything is in the distance don't work well. This image had detail in the street, in the middle ground steps, and in the background café. I could control the degree of focus at each of these points, as dictated by the composition.

Building the Effect

① *The arrangement of layers.*

② *The Extreme Blur layer.*

③ *Mask to show the Extreme Blur layer.*

I began by creating three layers of the main image. One layer has everything is in sharp focus; the second is blurred slightly and is used to represent the blur in the middleground. The third layer has a more extreme blur effect and represents the background focus level.

To keep the layer contents straight as I'm working, I double-clicked each layer name to highlight it and renamed them Focus Layer, Slight Blur, and Extreme Blur. Finally, I arranged the layer sequence from top to bottom: Focus Layer, Slight Blur, Extreme Blur (see Figure ①).

Using Lens Blur

For this exploration, I decided to use the Lens Blur filter instead of the Gaussian Blur filter. Lens Blur is supposed to emulate the look of camera optics, including the impact of iris shapes, iris blade curvature, and iris rotation. I'm not sure if the wealth of controls actually delivers a superior result, or if you can really tell the dif-

ference between a blur with a six-blade iris as opposed to an eight-blade iris, but the filter *does* produce an excellent result.

I clicked the Slight Blur layer in the Layers palette and selected Filter, Blur, Lens Blur. In the dialog box that appeared, I focused all my attention on the Iris section, ignoring the other options. I set the iris shape to an 8-sided iris by selecting Octagon (8) from the Shape pop-up menu; I set the Blade Curvature to 21, and Rotation to 65. The main control for the effect is Radius, which I set to 42 to create the blur effect I was looking for in the middleground area. I clicked OK to apply the effect. I then selected the Extreme Blur layer and relaunched the Lens Blur dialog box. I left all other settings the same as before, and adjusted the Radius slider to 78 (see Figure ②).

I clicked the visibility icon for the Slight Blur layer to temporarily hide it, and then selected the Focus Layer. I clicked the Add Layer Mask icon at the

bottom of the Layers palette to add a mask, and selected the Gradient tool from the toolbox. I set the foreground colors to black and white, clicked the Gradient Picker in the Options bar, and selected the Foreground to Background preset swatch. After selecting the Linear Gradient option in the Options bar, I dragged a gradient from the upper right to the middle of the image, masking the Focus Layer so that the Extreme Blur layer was visible in the upper-right half of the image, and the Focus Layer dominated the lower-left half.

To adjust the orange building in the background, I added a Hue/Saturation adjustment layer above the Extreme Blur layer and set the Saturation to -56 and the Lightness to +22 to tone down the bright orange (see Figure ③).

To add the moderate blur to the middle ground, I turned on visibility for the Slight Blur layer and added another layer mask. I selected the Gradient tool with the same settings as before and

④ *Mask the Slight Blur layer.*　　⑤ *Bring back the bike detail.*　　⑥ *Brighten the bike.*

drew a gradient starting in the extreme upper-right corner to the top of the central steps. This gradient created a mask for the upper-right corner, through which the Extreme Blur layer was still visible (see Figure ④).

Selecting the Bike

I wanted to bring back the color and sharpness for the entire bike, and the easiest way to do this was to create a path around the entire object, which I could convert to a selection repeatedly as needed. By selecting the Path tool with the Paths option selected in the Options bar, I started drawing the shape of the bike. I converted corner points from curved to angled by Option-dragging (Alt-dragging in Windows) on the point itself. The ⌘ key (Ctrl key in Windows) changed the Pen tool into the Direct Selection tool so that I could select handles and alternate points, and the Spacebar changed the pointer to the Grabber so that I could reposition the composition.

I closed the outside shape of the bike and then created smaller path shapes

for the negative space areas around the seat and handlebars. When the paths were complete, I double-clicked the work path tile in the Paths palette and named the path Bike. With the Bike path active (pun intended), I chose Make Selection from the Paths palette menu. In the Make Selection dialog box that appeared, I left the Feather Radius set to 0, enabled the Anti-aliased check box, and chose New Selection in the Operation section. I clicked OK to create the selection.

With the selection active, I highlighted the Mask icon for the Focus Layer in the Layers palette, set the background color to white, and pressed Delete. This action removed the mask from the bike shape, hiding the blurred layers (see Figure ⑤).

A Brighter Red

The final step in this exploration was to brighten the bike a bit. It was such a great red, and that blue bag on the

back of it really popped against the gray stone. The blue bag also resonated with the two patches of blue in the background.

I added a Curves adjustment layer to the top of the layer stack to bring out the colors, selecting Curves from the Adjustment Layer pull-down menu in the Layers palette. I created an S-shaped curve, with data points of Input: 43, Output: 33, and Input: 150, Output: 201. Clicking OK applied the curve to the entire image. To restrict the curve to just the bike, I opened the Paths palette and selected the path of the bike shape. I chose Make Selection from the Paths palette menu and clicked OK, using the same settings as before.

I chose Select, Inverse and selected the Mask thumbnail for the Curves adjustment layer. With black as the foreground color, I selected the Paintbucket tool and clicked to fill the selection with black, restricting the curve effect to only the bike (see Figure ⑥).

IMAGE PANORAMAS

Great panoramas in Photoshop start with great source images. The rolling hills and azure skies of Tuscany just scream for an image that extends horizontally, taking in the full field of vision.

Although you can spend thousands of dollars on a panoramic camera with an extended format that will capture a wide field of vision, you can stitch together a series of images taken with a standard camera using Photoshop's Photomerge command. The general process involves shooting a series of sequential images horizontally or vertically and then combining them in Photoshop to create a single seamless image.

Using Photomerge doesn't necessarily mean that you have to keep the camera perfectly level and use special equipment, although Panoramic tripod heads are definitely a plus if you're serious about this discipline. The process does mean that your camera's auto metering and auto white balancing should be turned off while shooting. If you leave them on, each image will shift in color and exposure, making them much harder to stitch together. The other thing to keep in mind is to leave lots of overlap between frames, allowing about a third of the images to overlap.

About the Original Images

In this exploration, there are ten original photos, shot in a sequence, from which I assembled the final image. I had spent the day in the hills northwest of Siena, shooting in and around San Gimignano, but the crowded and touristy streets of the walled city were wearing thin on me. There was nothing very interesting to see, and the plethora of bad restaurants and currency conversion storefronts obliterated whatever charm might have been left in the city.

So I got in the car and began to drive. The late afternoon sun made everything glow, and the winding roads and softly rolling hills soon made me forget the tourist-choked streets of San Gimignano. As I rounded a bend in the road, there was a grove of birch trees on my left, backlit by the setting sun. I pulled over, set up my gear and shot this panorama sequence. The photos represent a 180-degree field of vision; the sun is at your back as you face the sunlit hill on the right.

Panorama sources
Nikon D2H
1/200 sec, f/4.5
Focal length 42mm

Building the Effect

① *Selecting the files to merge.*

② *Photomerge's first attempt at merging.*

③ *Manually adding photos to the panorama.*

After sharpening all the source images with Unsharp Mask, I placed them in a single folder for easy access. To begin stitching the images together, I opened Photoshop and selected File, Automate, Photomerge. In the Photomerge dialog box that appeared, I set the Use menu to Folder and clicked Browse. I navigated to the target folder of images and clicked the Choose button. All the images in the selected folder appeared in the Photomerge dialog box, and I clicked OK to start the Photomerge process (see Figure **①**).

Alternatively, you can set the Use menu to Files and then browse to select each file separately. The Shift key allows you to select multiple sequential files, while the ⌘ key (the Ctrl key in Windows) lets you select multiple files not in sequence.

The Initial Merge

When you click OK, Photomerge automatically opens each target file

and attempts to combine all the pieces into a cohesive panorama, within the Photomerge interface. Initially, it tries to match images using sequential file names and then by looking for repetition in edge patterns. Matched files are assembled in the work area of the dialog box, using the program's best guess at what goes together. If it cannot make a match, it leaves the unused files as thumbnails in the upper gallery of the Photomerge dialog box (see Figure **②**).

After Photomerge makes its best attempt at merging all the files you selected, automation starts to fall away and the alchemy starts. If a file was left out or not matched, I dragged its thumbnail into the compositing area and positioned it manually. If the edges were not properly aligned, I dragged them into proper position, turning off the Snap To Image option on the right side of the dialog box as necessary for more pinpoint control.

The preview image was quite small because I used ten source images. Dragging the Zoom slider in the Navigator section to the right enlarged the preview, allowing me to switch the view from detailed to global as needed. Before clicking OK, I enabled the Keep as Layers and Advanced Blending check boxes to smooth the transitions and provide more control in the next steps (see Figure **③**).

Tweaking the Alignment

Remember that Photomerge is only a starting point. After it assembles the images into a single frame, you usually need to apply some post-Photomerge correction. Having preserved each layer separately, I used the Move tool to tweak and adjust layer alignment. I like to zoom to 100% or even 200% in some cases to make sure that things are aligned. Be sure to use the Navigator palette (select Window, Navigator) to move between the frame edges, dragging the red active window box to define the visible area.

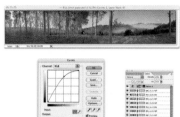

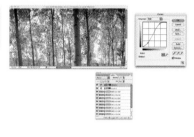

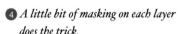

❹ *A little bit of masking on each layer does the trick.*

❺ *Correcting exposure problems.*

❻ *Lightening up the birch trees.*

In most cases, you'll need to compensate for perspectival distortion that throws the edges out of alignment. I like to use layer masks to align the edges between frames, concealing or revealing the top overlapping layer. To add a mask, click the Add Layer Mask icon in the Layers palette and paint with the Brush tool, varying the brush feather and opacity to create the mask. Remember, black conceals the current layer and white reveals it. Leaving significant overlap between frames pays dividends during this step in particular because you have a larger area to blend the overlapping images. It's a bit tedious, but I worked my way through all nine layer transitions, adding a mask to each layer and aligning them so that the transitions were seamless (see Figure **❹**).

Exposure Adjustments

Correcting exposure differences was the next step, and it was a bit tricky. This particular image represents a 180-degree field of vision; the birch trees on the left are actually at your back as you look towards the sunny hill. When I shot the source photos, I exposed for the deep blue sky; as a result, the rest of the image went a bit dark. To compensate, I added a Curves adjustment layer by selecting Curves from the Adjustment Layer pull-down menu in the Layers palette. I added a single data point with a value of Input: 134, Output: 206, which lightened the image. Because the sky was now *over*exposed, I selected the layer mask for the Curves adjustment layer, selected the Brush tool with black as the foreground color, and painted a mask into the sky to maintain its original tone (see Figure **❺**).

I wanted to try to express more of the brilliant light that was breaking through the birch trees as I took these photos. I added a second Curves adjustment layer, this time with two data points forming a slight S curve. The point values were Input:

53, Output: 41 and Input: 183, Output: 239 (see Figure **❻**). This slight adjustment did wonders for the trees, but blew out the entire right side of the image. So I added a mask to this layer as well, only this time I selected the Gradient tool and set the foreground and background colors to black and white. In the Options bar, I selected the Linear Gradient icon with the Foreground-to-Background gradient preset and drew the gradient from left to right. (Don't forget that if you hover over a gradient swatch in the Options bar, its name appears as a ToolTip.)

Finally, because I was combining multiple images taken from different angles, the chances of having the image edges line up as a perfect rectangle are pretty slim. To square things off, I selected the Crop tool, drew a marquee to define the rectangle for the image, and clicked to crop the image.

DAGUERREOTYPE
EFFECTS

The daguerreotype was invented by Louis Jacques Mande Daguerre and patented in 1839 as the first successful method for capturing and fixing a photographic image. The original process involved chemically sensitizing a copper plate with bitumen of Judea, exposing it through a camera obscura, and developing the image using vapor of mercury.

As the process was perfected, the copper plate was coated with a thin layer of silver, making the surface highly reflective and giving it the appearance of a mirror. These images were sometimes colored using pigments, and the copper sometimes tarnished with age, creating other areas of discoloration. Because the image was so reflective, it can appear as both a negative and positive image, depending on the angle from which it's viewed. The handmade nature of the plates often created spots and blemishes resulting from dust, brushstrokes created when coating the plates, and unevenness in applying the emulsions.

When I simulate daguerreotypes, I like to embrace these imperfections and include them as graphic texture and detail. Remember that each image was unique and reflected a true spirit of experimentation. Focus and detail was sometimes elusive, and depth of field was often very shallow. Vary the use of dust spots and discoloration as you wish and remember that the final design is more important than being faithful to the replication of the process.

Pod in Landscape
Nikon D2H
1/400 sec, f/10
Focal length 75mm

About the Original Image

I was driving south of Siena on a rolling country road when I stopped to shoot the landscape (as I did a few dozen times a day). In this instance, I looked down to see a seed pod growing next to the road. Initially, I was drawn to its detail and texture, but after taking a few shots I decided to shoot it from a low angle so that I could capture the landscape in the background. I still wanted the detail in the plant, knowing that this would shift the background landscape way out of focus. My idea was to *imply* the landscape through shape and color without losing the emphasis on the main subject.

Building the Effect

❶ *Mask to create a bright center.*

❷ *Desaturate with a gradient map.*

❸ *Add color and highlight.*

The first step is to add shadows and depth to the image. You tend to see light fall off at the edges and around the corners of the image. The brightest areas are often the center of the frame.

I duplicated the Background layer and applied a curve to darken the entire layer. I selected Image, Adjustments, Curves and created a single data point with a value of Input: 150, Output: 96, and clicked OK to apply the effect. I then clicked the Add Layer Mask icon and painted the center of the duplicate layer with a 300-pixel feathered brush with black as the foreground color. This mask brightened the center of the image, leaving the corners and edges dark (see Figure ❶).

Removing the Color

The next step was to replace the color in the image with a toned sepia color, simulating the look of an aged photograph. I selected Gradient Map from the Adjustment Layer pull-down menu in the Layers palette and clicked the gradient strip in the dialog box that appeared, launching the Gradient Editor.

I double-clicked the color stop on the left end of the gradient and elected pure white in the Color Picker I set the color stop on the right side to black, following

the same procedure. I then clicked below the gradient to add two additional color stops. I set the first stop to location 35% with an RGB value of R203, G193, B146. I set the second stop to location 68% with an RGB value of R105, G90, B75. I clicked OK to close all the dialog boxes to apply the gradient to the image (see Figure ❷). The important thing to focus on in this step is to select a tan color for the quartertones and a darker brown for the shadows. Exact placement of the color stops will vary from image to image.

Adding Metallic Patina and Lowering Contrast

I added two more gradient map adjustment layers to complete the toning process. The first introduced a red-and-teal color gradient that simulated the metallic patina that is often found in daguerreotype images. The second toned everything to more of a neutral black and white while lightening the blacks to create a faded look. For the first gradient, I followed the same procedure as before to launch the Gradient Editor and created a gradient with six color stops, with values as follows: **Stop 1:** Location 0, RGB value R255, G255, B255. **Stop 2:** Location 24%, RGB value R50, G81, B243. **Stop 3:** Location 40%, RGB value R108, G135,

B168. **Stop 4:** Location 61%, RGB value R201, G193, B153. **Stop 5:** Location 80%, RGB value R105, G90, B75. **Stop 6:** Location 100%, RGB value R0, G0, B0. Again, these settings will vary from image to image; the key is to create the color transitions and position the color stops so that they appear in the desired areas of the image.

After creating this first gradient, I set its blending mode to Pin Light and added a layer mask, painting out the plant section and a bit of the upper-left corner. The gradient added the blue accents to some of the highlight areas without dominating the entire image.

Finally I added a gray-to-white gradient map, creating a simple two-stop gradient. I set the first stop to location 0% with an RGB value of R255, G255, B255. I set the second stop to location 100% with an RGB value of R98, G96, B96. Finally, I set the layer opacity for this second gradient to 42% to lighten the effect (see Figure ❸).

Blurring the Details

Now the image looked too sharp and crisp to be a convincing daguerreotype; it reflected the high-quality Nikon optics that were unavailable circa 1839. I duplicated the Background layer and

④ *Blur and lighten the image.*

⑤ *Simulate dust specks.*

⑥ *Fine-tuning the dust specks.*

positioned it above the Curves adjustment layer and beneath the gradient map layers. I selected the Blur tool from the toolbox, specified a 200-pixel brush, and set the Strength at 50% in the Options bar. I painted the center of the seed pod that had the most detail, applying the blur directly to that area.

I duplicated the Background layer a second time, positioned it above the previous blur layer, and chose Filter, Blur, Motion Blur. I set the Angle to 0° and the Distance slider to 19 pixels and clicked OK to blur the background slightly. Finally, I clicked the Add New Layer icon to create a third blur layer above the motion blur, and selected the Brush tool with a 200-pixel brush set to 14% Opacity. I Option-clicked (Alt-clicked in Windows) the highlight areas of the image to sample the global highlight color and painted in the area in the lower-left area of the seed pod to blur and lighten it slightly (see Figure ④).

Add the Dust Specks

The final step was to add the dust specks indicative of many daguerreotypes. I added a fairly dense dot pattern because I liked what it did to this image, but you can vary the density based on your image and preference. I used a scan of paint

splatters on white paper for the original pattern, similar to the ones used in Chapter 12, "Molecola Sogni," and Chapter 14, "Parte Interna."

I opened the scan and used the Magic Wand tool to select one of the droplets; then I chose Select, Similar to select all the droplets. I copied the selections and pasted them into the composite image; then I selected Edit, Free Transform and repositioned the droplets by dragging the corner handles to set the right proportion. Then I duplicated the droplet layer by dragging it to the Create New Layer icon in the Layers palette. I selected Image, Transform, Flip Horizontal to flip the duplicate droplet layer, and then selected Image, Transform, Flip Vertical to flip it upside down, concealing some of the symmetry. I used the Move tool to drag the copied layer to the right. I held down the Shift key and clicked both droplet layers in the Layers palette to select both layers and then chose New Group from Layers from the Layers palette menu. I added a mask to the layer group and masked out any mirrored specks to conceal any last traces of the symmetry (see Figure ⑤).

I selected both layers in the new group and selected Merge Layers from the

Layers palette menu. I selected Outer Glow from the Add Layer Style icon at the bottom of the Layers palette and double-clicked the Glow Color swatch, selecting an RGB color of R233, G227, B187, and leaving all other settings at their defaults. I then dragged the merged layer to the Add New Layer icon to duplicate it. With the topmost droplet layer selected, I chose Filter, Blur, Gaussian Blur and set the Radius Slider to 1.6 pixels to create a blurred halo around each of the specks.

To make some of the specks white instead of black, I added a Curves adjustment layer to the layer group above the blurred dots layer, and inverted the tonality, setting the 0 point at 255 and the 255 point to 0. I highlighted the Curves layer mask, selected the Paintbucket tool with black as the foreground color, and clicked in the image area to create a mask filled with black, obscuring the adjustment layer. Then, with a small feathered brush set to white, I painted back any spots I wanted to appear as lighter specks. Finally, I created a new layer and painted in the tiny white flecks that sometimes appear in the center of the dust specks (see Figure ⑥).

INFRARED EFFECTS

The infrared photography process uses special film that is sensitive to infrared light rays that exist outside the visual spectrum, in addition to visual light frequencies. Although the visual light spectrum records to the film in a standard way, the light in the infrared spectrum also records to the film, augmenting the final image design.

Although infrared films exist in both color and black-and-white formats, this exploration focuses on replicating a black-and-white infrared effect. The black-and-white infrared films create a dramatic graphic effect that works well, especially given the graphic nature of black-and-white photography as a whole. Specifically, the infrared process for black-and-white images makes greens (such as grass and leaves on a tree) look abnormally brighter, while making blue skies look much darker.

Infrared levels are stronger in the morning and evening, when the sun is lower in the sky. As a result, evening skies may appear almost black in the image, and in very high contrast against white tree leaves or grass. Thus, you might want to adjust and compensate for these variables as you're modifying the source image. Remember that the ultimate criterion is whether you're satisfied with the final result, not whether you're adhering to the characteristics of the infrared process.

Cuna Tree
Nikon D2H
1/320 sec, f/6.7
Focal length 120mm

About the Original Image

There are many ways to achieve an infrared effect, although they all share a common approach of selecting the green and sky areas of an image and modifying them for the way they appear in the infrared process. The approach described here is especially effective in that it keeps each color area separate, allowing you to tweak all variables in a non-linear fashion, fine-turning the relationships between the various tonal areas.

The photo I started with is a singular tree near the fortress of Cuna, just outside of Siena. The area was lush and green, with sloping hills covered with trees and foliage. The late afternoon sun was just beginning to stretch the shadows a bit while creating a warm diffuse glow over the landscape. The strong greens and visible blue sky make it a perfect source image for this effect.

Building the Effect

① *Select the greens in the grass.*

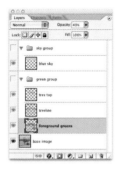

② *Group the layers.*

③ *Convert to black and white.*

The first step is to define and isolate the local areas you want to change. These areas usually include the green grass and trees, as well as the blue of the sky. The Select Color Range command is perfect for isolating areas of color because it allows you to sample a color within the image, set the tolerance for the exact color range desired, and click OK to create the selection.

With the image open, choose Select, Color Range to launch the Color Range dialog box. Enable the Selection radio button (it's located below the image preview section) and move the mouse pointer into the image. Click in a representative area of the grass for the foreground shade of green. Adjust the Fuzziness slider as needed, making sure to select at least some of the tones in the shadow areas (see Figure ①).

Click OK to complete the color-based selection.

With the selection active, Copy and Paste the green information to its own layer. Because I wanted to treat some of the green tones differently, I repeated this process for the green tones in the distant tree line and for the top of the main tree. After pasting each separate green selection, I clicked the new layer titles and renamed them Foreground Greens, Treeline, and Treetop. In addition, I made a color selection for the entire sky area, which I pasted into its own layer and named Blue Sky.

I Shift-clicked the green layers in the Layers palette to select them all and chose New Group From Layers in the Layers palette menu. I named the group Green Group in the dialog box that appeared and clicked OK to group the layers. I high-

lighted the Blue Sky layer and repeated the process to create a group to control the tones in the sky, which I named Sky Group (see Figure ②).

Converting to Grayscale

The next step was to convert the color image to black and white. Again, there are many ways to accomplish this, but for replicating an infrared effect, it's best to use a gradient map adjustment layer. This approach maps the colors in a gradient to the tonal and color ranges of an existing image.

With the foreground and background colors set to black and white, select Gradient Map from the Adjustment Layer pull-down menu in the Layers palette. In the dialog box that appears, click the gradient strip to launch the Gradient Editor and select the

④ *Brighten the foreground and tree-line.*

⑤ *Darken the sky and lighten the tree.*

⑥ *Adjust the source tonality.*

Foreground to Background preset (hover the mouse over the preset swatches to see their names). Click OK and drag the new adjustment layer to the top of the layer stack, if necessary, to convert the image to black and white (see Figure ③).

Adjust the Blues and Greens

To turn the green areas white (as they'd be in a real infrared photo), I selected Curves from the Adjustment Layer pull-down menu in the Layers palette. I positioned the adjustment layer below the Treetop layer and above the Treeline and Foreground Greens layers, and added two curve points: Input: 25, Output: 15 and Input: 124, Output: 245. This arrangement increased the brightness of the greens throughout the image, from front to back (see Figure ④). The next step

was to create a focal point with the greens at the top of the tree (which is why I created a separate layer for this area, and left it above the previous adjustment layer).

I added a second Curves adjustment layer above the Treetop layer, with a single curve point of Input: 35, Output: 138. To restrict this curve adjustment to just the Treetop layer, I created a clipping mask with the Treetop layer as the base. To do this, I held down the Option key (the Alt key in Windows) and clicked the line between the adjustment layer and the Treetop layer (the mouse pointer changes to a mask icon as you do this). This action adds the bright, hazy-white effect to the top of the tree, which is central to a good infrared image.

I followed the same process for the Blue Sky layer, adding a Curves

adjustment layer to make the blues darker, creating a clipping mask to restrict it to just the Blue Sky layer. The curve for the Blue Sky layer in this image had a single point: Input: 206, Output: 31 (see Figure ⑤).

With separate groups for the greens and blues and a master gradient map controlling the grayscale, you can control most of the variables and make adjustments to get the tones to blend seamlessly. My final step was to add a Curves adjustment layer just above the Base Image layer to darken down the center of the image and expand the contrast in the middleground. I added a single point to the curve: Input: 111, Output: 35 (see Figure ⑥).

Simulate Twilight

The idea for this exploration is a painting by French surrealist Rene Magritte, depicting the front façade of a house at twilight. The front of the house is bathed in shadows, with a porch light illuminating the doorway. The dynamic thing about the painting is the sky. It's bright and illuminated, as if it were the middle of the day.

Each time I look at Magritte's painting, and even now as I recall it in my mind, I'm undecided as to whether this is a true distortion of reality or merely a depiction of that elusive moment where daylight slips into night. Whether or not the sky is really that light when shadows fall, there's no denying that it makes for an evocative image.

The keys to making the effect convincing are an understanding of how light is cast on various surfaces, an interesting sky area, and an interesting overall composition.

Siena Backstreet
Nikon D2H
1/125 sec, f/5.6
Focal length 42mm

About the Original Image

The original photo is a picture of the rooftops of Siena, looking towards the cathedral. At first look, it's not much of a photograph...the primary landmarks are all but hidden and obscured, and the main buildings are pretty scruffy and beat up. We have antennae, satellite dishes, and an overall absence of a primary focal point.

And yet, for this exploration, this photo is a great choice. First of all, the sky is very solid, filling the top half of the image with rich color and puffy clouds. And the irregular tile shapes that jut up into the sky create an interesting pattern that's far better than if it were simply a flat straight skyline. And although the buildings appear a bit rough, the geometry of planes and shapes is quite interesting, and as you'll see, we're going to create our own dynamic focal point.

Building the Effect

❶ *Creating the warm color tones.* ❷ *Creating the dark building tones.* ❸ *Lightening only the sky.*

To approach this exploration, I needed to think about the different lighting zones within the image and isolate the tonal values for those zones in separate layers. I needed to create a lighting value for the sky, as well as for the deep shadows in the buildings, and another for the illuminated areas within the buildings. The trick when separating the lighting areas is to visualize the relationship between these tonal areas holistically, and be able to articulate exactly the right tone for a given area without being distracted by other areas that might be way off.

Defining Lighting Zones

For example, my first tonal area was the building illumination areas, which I wanted to have a warm, incandescent glow. I selected Curves from the Adjustment Layer pull-down menu in the Layers palette, and modified the curve as follows: I selected Blue from the Channel pull-down menu and added a single curve point with a value of Input: 139, Output: 91, which increased the amount of yellow in the

image. I then selected the Red channel and added a single curve point with a value of Input: 112, Output: 142, which added a bit of red. Finally, I reset the Channel pull-down menu to RGB and added two curve points—Input: 18, Output: 41, and Input: 137, Output: 217—which brightened the image overall (see Figure ❶).

To create the dark tones of the buildings, I dragged the Background layer to the Create New Layer icon in the Layers palette to duplicate it, and then dragged the new layer to the top of the layer stack. I chose Image, Adjustments, Curves and modified the new image layer by adding three curve points: Input: 59, Output: 12; Input: 105, Output: 50; and Input: 181, Output: 158. Because this was a duplicate layer and I wanted to keep the layer stack concise, I clicked OK, applying the Curves correction directly to the layer, which I named Dark Bldgs (see Figure ❷).

Creating the Bright Sky

I duplicated the Background layer a third time so that I could create a

lighter layer for the bright sky. After positioning it as the uppermost layer in the layer stack, I applied a curve directly to the duplicate sky layer which had two data points—Input: 61, Output: 115 and Input: 203, Output: 238. I named this third layer Bright Sky, and with it still active, I set about the rather tedious task of selecting the skyline so that I could mask the lower half of the layer. I started by selecting the Magic Wand tool from the toolbox and attempting to select the sky area. If I could do this, I could then simply invert the sky selection to select the buildings.

In the Options bar, I set the Tolerance to 44 and began selecting the sky, Shift-clicking to add areas to the selection. After the large areas were filled in, I selected the Lasso tool and circled the smaller islands that were left over, making sure to hold down the Shift key throughout the process to add each section to the global selection area.

In the process of selecting the sky, I inadvertently selected areas of the

④ *Adding the illuminated buildings.*

⑤ *Darkening the buildings.*

⑥ *Adding the light bulb.*

tower as well as the blue dome. In addition, many of the detail areas, such as the cross and statues at the tops of the buildings had been absorbed into the sky selection. To clean up these details, I entered Quick Mask mode by clicking the Quick Mask icon (the lower-right corner of the toolbox, beneath the background color swatch). This action placed a mask over the unselected areas, leaving the selected area clear (you can reverse this by double-clicking the Quick Mask icon and choosing Selected Areas from the Color Indicates section).

I selected the Brush tool with a small brush size and the foreground color set to black. I painted in the mask to subtract from the selected area, using the Zoom tool as necessary to see all necessary details. Finally, I clicked the Standard Mode icon (to the left of the Quick Mask icon), to exit Quick Mask mode and apply the selection to the sky. I then clicked the Add Layer Mask icon in the Layers palette to mask the lower buildings, revealing the Dark Bldgs in the lower layer against the bright sky (see Figure ③).

Illuminating the Buildings

With the dark buildings and the sky working together, it was time to introduce the building illumination tones I'd created earlier. I highlighted the Dark Bldgs layer in the Layers palette and added a layer mask. I wanted to add a glowing light bulb to the center of the building area, illuminating the dark niche. I selected the edges of the building that would define where the light would fall, faithfully tracing the edges of the tile roofs and edges of the buildings and satellite dish. I also selected the area on the right in the same way. Then I selected the Brush tool with a 300-pixel brush and black as the foreground color. I also set the Opacity in the Options bar to 23%, and began lightly painting the mask in the building areas. I varied the Opacity further and gently feathered the mask to create a subtle lighting effect (see Figure ④).

Now that I had illuminated some of the buildings, I wanted to darken the surrounding buildings a bit more to

add a additional contrast. I added a Curves adjustment layer above the Dark Bldgs layer, with two curve points— Input: 38, Output: 25, and Input: 221, Output: 163. This adjustment darkened the light areas in the dome and tower, although it also flattened the shadows. I added a layer mask and painted the mask into the shadows to make them a bit brighter (see Figure ⑤).

The final step was to add the light bulb in the lower building area. I clicked the Create New Layer icon in the Layers palette to add a new layer above the Background layer and highlighted the layer name, renaming it Light. I selected a large feathered brush and sampled a yellow orange color from the illuminated wall area. With the Brush opacity set to 11%, I lightly painted in the glow with a single click. I gradually made the brush smaller and the foreground color brighter, clicking in the same spot repeatedly. Because I was working in a separate layer, I selected the Move tool and repositioned the "light bulb" to find the proper placement (see Figure ⑥).

Hand Coloring

Palio Procession
Nikon D2H
1/100 sec, f/5
+0.67 EV
Focal length 75mm

There was a time when all photographs were monochromatic, and the only way to add color was to paint them with a transparent dye, in a process called hand coloring. Photo retouchers would sit hunched over a black-and-white print with a small sable brush and painstakingly apply thin transparent coats of Marshall's Retouching Oils. Marshall's Oils are still available today, and people still hand color their images to replicate the nostalgic style and patina of this hand-crafted process. Photoshop replicates the hand-colored effect quite well, making it easier to erase your mistakes and start over without having to go back to the darkroom to make extra prints.

When you select an image to hand color, you must first consider how the photo will look in black and white. Keep in mind that the color additions will fade and desaturate the colors slightly to simulate the look and feel of hand coloring. Does the print have high contrast and sharp detail? Are its color areas clear and well defined? If so, it's a good candidate for this process.

If necessary, pump up the contrast or improve the tonal range with the Curves or Levels command. In general, the image should be a touch lighter than normal, with an extended tonal range in the highlights and midtones. The easiest way to achieve this is to use Curves, set the white and black points accordingly, and then place a single point on the curve with an input value of around 160 and drag the point straight up. This action opens up the tonality while having a minimal effect on the blacks and the shadows.

About the Original Image

The photo I selected for this effect is a flag bearer from the Palio festival in Siena. His colorful costume provides ample opportunity to use the hand-colored effects to their fullest, while providing broad areas of flat color that should fill in pretty easily.

In addition, I like to use a hand-colored effect with faces, especially close-ups like the one in this photo. Faces permit me to simulate the old-fashioned hand-colored look by using multicolored flesh tones; selecting a peach-colored tint for the base with a deeper red for the apples of the cheeks.

As you'll see, I decided to leave the background in black and white to emphasize the hand-colored effect, although you can certainly fill it in if you're going for a subtler effect that's not quite as obvious.

Building the Effect

① *Creating a palette of color swatches.*

② *Reducing the image to black and white.*

③ *Painting the hat green.*

The first step in the process is to build a color palette that will define the number of colors used while you're painting. Keep in mind that the tonality of the image will come from the black-and-white image we're about to create. The key thing in selecting colors is to select a limited number of hues that are representative of the image as a whole.

These colors will be stored in the Swatches palette. By default, the Swatches palette is loaded with a bunch of distracting color presets that seldom relate to the image I'm working on. As a result, I usually start by deleting the presets so that I can build my palette from scratch. To delete the presets, go to the Presets Manager by choosing Edit, Preset Manager and then select Swatches from the Preset Type menu. Shift-click to select all the presets and press Delete to remove them. Click Done to close the Preset Manager.

To sample the palette colors, select the Eyedropper tool from the toolbox

and click within the image to set the selected color as the foreground color. Then open the Swatches palette by choosing Window, Swatches and move the mouse pointer into the palette. As you move the pointer over a blank space in the palette (which at this point is just about any portion of it), the pointer changes to a paint bucket. Click the mouse, and the foreground color you just sampled is loaded as a swatch. A Color Swatch Name dialog box appears as well, asking you to name the color, which you should absolutely do before clicking OK (see Figure **①**). For example, I started by sampling the green in the flag bearer's hat, clicking in the Swatches palette and naming the swatch *green hat*. I created a total of nine swatches for this image: green hat, yellow hat, pink vest, face base, cheeks, lips, eyes, gold chain, and feather.

Reduce to Black and White

There are numerous ways to convert an image to black and white, and any of them will work for this process. In

this instance, I used a gradient map adjustment layer so that I could maintain the flexibility of future editing options as I worked through the coloring process.

I began by clicking the Foreground color default button in the toolbox to set black as the foreground and white as the background colors. In the Layers palette, I selected Gradient Map from the Adjustment Layer drop-down menu. In the dialog box that appeared, I clicked the gradient strip to launch the Gradient Editor. Then I clicked one of the color stops—clicking either color stop activates the color midpoint diamond. You can drag the diamond left or right to lighten or darken the image (see Figure **②**). (If you accidentally miss and click an empty space, a new color stop is created. Click and drag it off the gradient strip or press Delete to remove it.)

Add the First Color

There are many ways to go about adding color, depending on your style

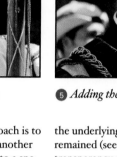

④ *Adding the colored feather.*

⑤ *Adding the gold trim to the hat.*

⑥ *Leave the background uncolored for style.*

and temperament. One approach is to devote a layer to each color; another approach is to devote a layer to a specific object or area. I prefer this second approach because it allows me to combine colors within a narrow range while still keeping areas separate.

I added a new layer to the top of the layer stack by clicking the Add New Layer button in the Layers palette. When the layer appears in the palette, double-click it and type a layer name. Set the Layers palette blending mode to Color for this layer. If possible, use a graphics tablet for the painting, to ensure full control.

Because the green area in the hat was so well defined, it was easy to select it with the Magic Wand tool. (Selecting the area I wanted to paint limited my brushstrokes to just the selected area.) To paint the image, I choose a brush, set the Opacity to 68% in the Options bar, clicked in the Swatches palette to select a color, and began painting. The color was applied, but

the underlying tones of the photo still remained (see Figure ③). By using transparency and a feathered brush, I can vary the color density to create a hand-painted feel.

Add Additional Layers

I continued to add layers for the various areas I wanted to color, slightly modifying the technique along the way. In the second layer, I painted the feather as a brightly saturated orange, and used the Dodge tool with the range set to Highlights and Exposure at 22% to create additional color variation (see Figure ④).

After painting a layer, you can select Image, Adjust, Hue/Saturation to open the Hue/Saturation dialog box. Drag the Hue slider to change the color on the layer. This approach is effective if you've missampled the color area, or you want to deviate from the original color you've applied.

For the gold braid and the gold medallion on the hat, I painted the

gold in at 100%, and then used an eraser with its Opacity setting of 46% to lighten the color and imply a gold finish (see Figure ⑤).

The face looks complicated but was really pretty simple. I started by painting the lighter color that I named Face Base on its own layer. I then used a 300-pixel, feathered brush set to 11% Opacity, and lightly painted the cheeks in the same layer, using the darker red color I named Cheeks. I used a smaller brush to add the lips and eye color. I did all this coloring on a single layer, but you could also create separate layers for each face part if you want to play it safe.

To finish the effect and accent the hand-colored patina, I intentionally left the background in black and white. In addition to the stylized effect, the uncolored background also created an emphatic sense of space and depth, making the figure seem closer to the viewer (see Figure ⑥).

CYANOTYPES

The cyanotype is an early photographic process with a distinctive look that lends itself to graphic design treatments and fine art applications. The process, which was invented in 1842 by Sir John Hirschel, uses potassium ferricyanide as an emulsion base. This simple and inexpensive technique was used extensively throughout the nineteenth century, especially for the reproduction of architectural drawings.

Many books suggest that replication of a cyanotype involves nothing more than simulating a bluish tone, effectively creating a duotone effect. Although it's necessary to do this, it's important to keep in mind that a cyanotype is a photograph, and must adhere to photographic aesthetics. In other words, you must make sure that the blue tonality maps well to the source image, accurately describing the image. This is especially true in the shadow areas, where things tend to get dull and muddy. In addition, I find that having a singular bright highlight area helps establish the tonal range and create a compositional emphasis.

Whenever I create cyanotypes, I spend most of my time dodging and burning the image, just as I would if I were in a darkroom. It helps to separate dodge and burn stages into separate layers so that you can revert to various stages in the process and compare image states and iterations.

Ochre Alley
Nikon D2H
1/40 sec, f/4.5
Focal length 75mm

About the Original Image

Montepulciano is a hill town in southern Tuscany with winding streets that ascend to the cathedral at the highest point of the city. The alleyways slope and dip off the main streets like rivulets, with arched passageways that give them the feeling of caves.

I initially took this shot because of the color; specifically the way the blue shadows compliment the warm orange and ochre tones of the building. But for a cyanotype, I liked the fact that this photo had a bright focal point to which I could map the highlights, and tons of detail in the shadow areas.

Building the Effect

1 *Apply a blue gradient map.*

2 *Lighten the shadows.*

3 *Burning in the shadows.*

The first step in creating a cyanotype effect is to generate a gradient map layer that will simulate the signature Prussian blue color range. It's important to do this step first so that you can evaluate all subsequent edits through this blue filter.

After selecting Gradient Map from the Adjustment Layer pull-down menu in the Layers palette, I clicked the gradient strip to launch the Gradient Editor.

I double-clicked the color stop on the left end of the gradient and selected a color with the RGB values R0, G11, B48 in the Color Picker that appeared. I set the color stop on the right side to white, following the same procedure. I then clicked below the gradient to add an additional color stop. I dragged the new stop to location 25% and assigned it an RGB value of R3, G71, B172. To adjust the blend between the center and right color stops, I dragged their shared color midpoint diamond to location 36%. Similarly, I adjusted the midpoint diamond between the center

and left color stops to location 62% (see Figure **1**).

Adding a Tone Curve

I wanted there to be a bright concentration of light at the top of the stairs as opposed to the general diffuse brightness that was currently in the center of the image. I chose Layer, New Adjustment Layer, Curves to create a Curves adjustment layer, and added three data points — Input: 114, Output: 88; Input: 185, Output: 159; and Input: 225, Output: 232. I clicked OK to close the dialog box and create the adjustment layer.

Dodge and Burn

Although this curve forced the light into the upper area as I wanted, it flattened out the rest of the image a bit, especially the shadows. To correct this, I duplicated the Background layer and selected the Dodge tool from the toolbox with a 480-pixel feathered brush. I set the Range value to Midtones and the Exposure to 11% and began dodging the shadows. I

started with the wall on the left near the lower railing and lightly dodged to create more contrast and detail. I then switched to a smaller 65-pixel brush and set the Range menu to Highlights so that I could brighten the upper-steps area and the bright wall at the top of the stairs (see Figure **2**).

In areas where you want to create contrast, you can lighten the image using the Dodge tool and then go back over the same areas with the Burn tool to deepen the shadows. To do this, set the Range for the Burn tool to Highlights or Midtones in the first pass, and then change to Shadows for the second pass. That's what I did here: I set the Range for the Burn tool to Shadows and went back over some of the same areas I'd dodged to deepen only the shadows, creating contrast and adding detail.

I also deepened the shadows in the center wall, around the steps, and at the base or the left wall where it meets the ground (see Figure **3**).

④ *Add details in the railing and steps.*   ⑤ *Emphasize the top of the stairs.*   ⑥ *Eliminate distracting text on doors.*

I wanted more drama and detail in the steps. This is a delicate moment however, because you can easily overwork an image with the Dodge and Burn tools and end up with something that looks forced and unnatural. I started by duplicating the current layer by dragging it to the Create a New Layer icon in the Layers palette.

I switched to smaller brushes, in the 13- to 65-pixel range, and began dodging in the area around the steps in an effort to bring out additional tonality and detail. As I worked, I moved into the center wall as well as the railing on the left.

To bring out the railing detail, I used a 13-pixel brush that approximated the width of the railing itself. Because the area I was dodging was a straight line, I clicked once at one end of the railing, repositioned the brush at the other end, and Shift-clicked, which action drew a straight line between the two clicks with the current tool (in this case, the Dodge tool). I Shift-clicked from end to end with an Exposure setting of 8%, gradually building the effect for all the railings.

I also lightened the bricks at the base of the stairs using a 300-pixel brush, lightly tapping to create the right level of contrast. In this case, I applied the Dodge tool several times until I finally got what I was after. I used the History pallet to retrace my steps when necessary, undoing a series of Dodge edits so that I could try again (see Figure ④).

The lower area was coming together, but I wanted more from the bright spot at the top of the stairs. I started by selecting the Magic Wand tool with a Tolerance setting of 44, and with the Contiguous and Anti-Alias options enabled in the Options bar. I clicked the area at the top of the steps to define the general area above the steps and to the right of the railing. I reduced the Tolerance setting to 22 and Shift-clicked to add to the selection, finally switching to the Lasso tool to encircle any "island" shapes that were still eluding my selection attempts.

With the area selected, I added a new layer by clicking the Add New Layer icon in the Layers palette. I selected a 200-pixel Brush with white as the foreground color and 18% Opacity. I lightly tapped in the white color, building up brightness and obscuring some of the detail (see Figure ⑤).

Cloning to Finish

The image was starting to feel right. It had an air of timeless antiquity, especially the steps, well-worn and eroded from hundreds of years of use. This view could almost have been from any time or era—*except* for the word *Gas* that was stamped all over the access doors in the center right of the image. With the aim of obliterating these letters, I selected the Clone Stamp tool with a 13-pixel brush. I set the Options menu to Sample All Layers, enabled the Aligned check box, and set Opacity to 100%. I Option-clicked (Alt-clicked in Windows) around the text to set the sample points as necessary, painting out the words to complete the image (see Figure ⑥).

Chapter 6

ARTISTIC
EXPLORATIONS

In this chapter of artistic explorations, our experiments will become more painterly and expressive. Instead of looking at ways to create different photographic styles, these explorations look at options that are much more graphic and linear. They look to flatten graduated tones into flat shapes, smooth transitions into dappled textures, and transform tonal edges into drawn lines. A few of these effects require a certain amount of drawing skill and a digitizing tablet, but if nothing else they provide examples of what's possible in the realm of artistic expression within Photoshop.

PRINTMAKING EFFECTS

The interesting thing about printmaking effects is that they rely heavily on texture and color. There is also a strong graphic feeling to a print that supersedes the sense of photographic realism. This exploration looks at one way of achieving a graphic effect, although it is certainly not the only way. Image subject matter as well as color and texture variances will dictate modifications of the procedure.

The key things to keep in mind are the aforementioned points of texture, color, and graphic composition. As you work, look for ways to articulate and emphasize texture in your images. In this case, I created an etched look that creates unique texture in the foreground as well as detailed markings in the other field areas. The process of converting photographic areas to textured markings is central to the process. By pushing the contrast and saturation, I moved the print out of the photographic space, which also emphasizes the marks and textures.

Finally, be thoughtful about your photo choice to ensure that you've selected an image that lends itself to this type of conversion. Some images will lead you to emphasize one characteristic over another, pushing the compositional elements, for example, at the expense of color. Remember that these are just guidelines; explore these variables and don't feel constrained by the image or the process.

Layered Landscape
Nikon D2H
1/320 sec, f/9
Focal length 200mm

About the Original Image

I liked this shot from southern Tuscany because of the layers that formed as the landscape receded in space. The foreground is one stripe, the middleground is a strong contrasting area, and so on, all the way back to the atmospheric horizon.

In addition to the graphic division of the frame, I also liked the variety of textures in the image. The rough texture of the freshly plowed field in the foreground contrasts with the harvested field with tire tracks and markings, which is differentiated further by the granular texture in the middle section. Colors, textures, and graphic elements combine to create an interesting and diverse landscape image.

Building the Effect

❶ *Multiple filters applied.*

❷ *The Color blending mode applied.*

❸ *Restore detail in the distance.*

When following a process such as this, I always create and modify duplicates of the background image, leaving the background layer clean and unchanged. Thus, I started by duplicating the Background layer by dragging it to the Add New Layer icon in the Layers palette. I double-clicked the duplicated layer name and renamed it Filter Layer. I selected Filter, Blur, Smart Blur to launch the Smart Blur dialog box. I like the Smart Blur filter for this process because it maintains and emphasizes the edges of objects while blurring smaller details. This is the first step in creating a graphic feel for the image. I set the Radius to 8.3 and the Threshold to 40.4, left all other settings at their defaults, and clicked OK to apply the effect.

Filter Gallery Combinations

To further the graphic feel, I launched the Filter Gallery and applied a combination of filters. Filter Gallery allows you to experiment

with multiple filter combinations in a single dialog box, combining their application order and individual settings in countless combinations, all before committing a single modification.

After selecting Filter, Filter Gallery, I opened the Artistic filter grouping in the center column and selected the Fresco filter. I set the Brush Size to 2, Brush Detail to 8, and Texture to 1. I then clicked the New Effect Layer icon at the bottom-right of the dialog box and selected the Poster Edges filter, which is also in the Artistic filter grouping. I set the Edge Thickness to 2, Edge Intensity to 1, and Posterization to 2. I repeated the process to add a third filter: I selected Diffuse Glow from the Distort filter grouping, set the Graininess to 6, Glow Amount to 1, and Clear Amount to 19. Remember that you can drag the filter tiles in the lower-right area of the dialog box to change their order, and turn them on and off using the visibility icons. I tried many combinations

and this is the final configuration I settled on, clicking OK to apply the effect.

The graphic texture of high-contrast, sharp-edged grain detail was working pretty well at this point, although the tonal density and color was a bit flat. To address this, I selected Image, Adjustments, Hue/Saturation. In the dialog box that appeared, I set the Hue slider to -10, Saturation to -40, and lightness to +4. I then selected Image, Adjustments, Curves and created a curve with two data points of Input: 29, Output: 28, and Input: 167, Output: 223 (see Figure **❶**).

Blending Mode Revisions

Now that the tonal relationships were starting to work, I wanted to bring back a bit of color saturation. To do this, I duplicated the Background layer again and dragged the duplicated layer to the top of the layer stack, above the Filter layer. I set the blending mode in the Layers palette to Color, which directly applied the colors of the upper

④ *Even more detail in the distance.*

⑤ *Fading out the very top edge.*

⑥ *The final "print."*

layer to the lower layer, without changing any tonal detail (see Figure **②**).

Working the Background

I really liked the lower part of the image, but wanted to bring back some detail in the upper portion, which was currently reduced to almost pure white. I duplicated the Background layer, dragged it to the top of the stack, named it Distance, and applied the Smart Blur filter to it, using the same settings I used in the previous application. After softening the image with the Smart Blur filter, I applied the same Filter Gallery settings to the Distance layer as I had to the original Filter Layer. (It's convenient in this context that the Filter Gallery retains the filter groupings and settings from the last time it was used; it was easy to choose Filter, Filter Gallery and click OK to quickly reapply the same settings to the new layer.)

I then highlighted the Filter Layer in the Layers palette and selected the Magic Wand tool from the toolbox; I set the Tolerance setting to 22 in the Options bar. I clicked in the white sky area to cleanly select the white section only. I then activated the Distance layer again and clicked the Add Layer Mask icon to mask out everything in the Distance layer except for the selected area. The result shows additional detail at the top of the image (see Figure **③**).

To add a bit more texture to the Distance layer, I duplicated the Background layer yet again and named it Distance B. I applied the Filter Gallery settings again, this time without applying the Smart Blur filter. This choice added a bit more texture to the result. With the Distance B layer positioned above the Distance layer in the Layers palette, I Option-dragged (Alt-dragged in Windows) the mask thumbnail from the Distance layer to the Distance B layer to duplicate the mask. As a final

modification, I set the Opacity of the Distance B layer to 50% (see Figure **④**).

To add a bit of atmospheric perspective, I created a new layer by clicking the Create New Layer icon in the Layers palette. I selected a feathered 300-pixel brush with white as the foreground color and 17% Opacity selected in the Options bar. I lightly painted the top edge of the image to lighten the far distance slightly (see Figure **⑤**).

To complete the effect, I decided to pump up the color saturation a bit and lighten the image overall. I selected Hue/Saturation from the Adjustment Layer pull-down menu in the Layers palette to add an adjustment layer to the top of the layer stack. I left Hue at 0, set the Saturation slider to +58, and set Lightness to +13. Even though it reduced the overall shadow density, the Lightness setting made the image feel more like a graphic and less like a photo (see Figure **⑥**).

Painterly Illustration

Painterly illustration effects differ from printmaking effects in the sense that there is more evidence of the artist's hand. Where printmaking is more of a mechanical transfer of ink from plate to substrate, illustrational effects typically reveal evidence of drawing or painting.

Although you can set up a lot of the effect using filters or Photoshop effects, at some point you'll have to create a blank layer and start drawing. Working on a separate layer allows you to erase and redraw as many times as necessary without changing the underlying marks or lines. This freedom should allow you to draw more expressively, knowing that you have a reliable safety net. On the other hand, it should also make you more discerning. Don't be easily satisfied with your first few attempts unless you've really nailed it. In fact, even if you think it's perfect on the first try, create a few additional layered attempts and compare the results.

It's pretty hard to create any meaningful results without a digitizing tablet and stylus. The movement of the mouse is too unnatural and doesn't offer adequate control. Use the mouse to follow along and get the general idea of how to achieve the effect, but don't expect your best results with this effect until you've invested in a drawing tablet.

Ghiberti Head
Nikon D2H
1/180 sec, f/5.6
Focal length 400mm

About the Original Image

Michelangelo described Ghiberti's massive carved doors as "the Gates of Paradise." The immense doors that adorn Saint John's Baptistry in Florence are covered with numerous relief sculptures depicting biblical scenes and figurative details. The photo I'm starting with is of a small decorative adornment on the right side of the south doors, roughly six inches high. Although some of the sculpted heads are significant—including a Ghiberti self-portrait—I'm not sure exactly who this might be. I do know that it's an example of the excessively beautiful and detailed ornamentation that fills every corner and side street of Florence.

Building the Effect

① *Fresco, Poster Edges, and Diffuse Glow.*

② *Lighten the image.*

③ *Settings for the second filter layer.*

This effect starts by using the same Filter Gallery settings I used in the "Printmaking Effects" exploration. It's a good example of how one idea or direction can open up other possibilities. I started by dragging the Background layer to the Create New Layer icon in the Layers palette to create a duplicate image layer. I then selected Filter, Filter Gallery, opened the Artistic filter grouping in the center column, and selected the Fresco filter. I set the Brush Size to 2, Brush Detail to 8, and Texture to 1. I then clicked the New Effect Layer icon at the bottom-right of the dialog box and chose the Poster Edges filter, which is also in the Artistic filter grouping. I set the Edge Thickness to 2, Edge Intensity to 1, and Posterization to 2. I repeated the process to add a third filter: I selected Diffuse Glow from the Distort filter grouping, set the Graininess to 6, Glow Amount to 1, and Clear Amount to 19.

After clicking OK to apply the filter effects, I double-clicked the new layer in the Layers palette to highlight it. I renamed it DG PE F as sequential shorthand for the filters I'd applied to the layer (see Figure **①**).

I liked the grain that resulted in the left side, in the area with the green vertical stripes. But in this case, I felt that the dark and heavy modulations were filling in the shadows with a dull, flat gray. The color felt a bit heavy around the face, which worked against the delicate and ornate details.

To lighten things up, I started by setting the filtered layer's opacity to 75% and its blending mode to Overlay. From there, I selected Curves from the Adjustment Layer pull-down menu to create a Curves adjustment layer and dragged a single Input/Output point to Input: 41, Output: 76 (see Figure **②**).

Adding a Graphic Effect to the Face

Because the green striped area on the left was working so well, I decided to try to infuse that graphic effect on the right side. I dragged the Background layer to the Create New Layer icon to create another duplicate image layer and positioned it at the top of the layer stack, above the Curves adjustment layer.

I then selected Filter, Filter Gallery, to relaunch the Filter Gallery dialog box. It opened with the Diffuse Glow, Poster Edges, and Fresco filters already active and set to their previous settings. I clicked the New Effect Layer icon to create a new filter effect. To add the bright bleached effect, I selected Note Paper from the Sketch filter grouping and dragged the filter tile to the bottom of the effects stack on the right. I set the Image Balance slider for this effect to 17, Graininess to 8, and Relief to 0. I then clicked the New

④ *Mask the filter layer for facial detail.*

⑤ *Draw lines to define the edges.*

⑥ *Add color to the eyes.*

Effect Layer icon a second time and selected Torn Edges, which is also in the Sketch filter grouping. I set the Image Balance to 37, Smoothness to 11, and Contrast to 23. I then selected the Diffuse Glow tile in the lower-right area of the dialog box to modify its settings: I increased Graininess to 10, increased Glow Amount to 17, and set Clear Amount to 12.

After clicking OK to apply the filter effects (see Figure ③) I double-clicked the new layer in the Layers palette to highlight it. I renamed it DG PE F TE NP as sequential short-hand for the filters applied to the layer.

To integrate the filter effect with the composite image, I highlighted the second filter layer in the Layers palette and selected Pin Light from the Blending Modes menu. This blending mode retained only the white areas on the selected layer, leaving the green stripes on the right and some of the facial features. To bring back more of the face details, I high-

lighted the DG PE F TE NP layer and clicked the Add Layer Mask icon in the Layers palette. I selected a 35-pixel bush, set the foreground color to a middle gray, and set Opacity in the Options bar to 27%. Because black in a mask conceals the current layer and white reveals it, a middle gray will reveal the underlying image as a transparency (see Figure ④).

Drawing Additional Detail

Now it was time to add the drawing. I created a new layer by clicking the Create New Layer icon in the Layers palette, and dragged it to the top of the stack. Using my digitizing tablet, I selected the Brush tool with a 9-pixel hard-edged brush. I held down the Option key (the Alt key in Windows), momentarily turning the Brush icon into the Eyedropper tool, and sampled a medium orange from the fringe at the edge of the black texture around the face.

I drew outlines to define the neck and turban, as well as a series of

hatched lines to articulate the cheek and eye socket. To clean up some of the marks, I switched to the Eraser tool with the same brush tip and erased line ends or edges to make them feel more fluid and natural. Remember that you can also run the eraser across a line to create a dotted-line effect, as I did in the line defining the turban above the figure's left eye (see Figure ⑤).

About the Eyes

I finished the piece by adding details around the eyes and nose. Because these details overlapped other marks, I created new layers to isolate the activity: I created a new layer to draw in reflected light details around the nose and lip, erasing and modifying the marks until I achieved the right balance. For the eyes, I created an additional layer and drew in the blue coloring, and then added yet another layer just for the highlights (see Figure ⑥).

LINE ENGRAVING

Mike's Tomb
Nikon D2H
1/160 sec, f/6.3
Focal length 28mm

The idea behind the line engraving effect is to simulate the engraved-print look you see in currency or nineteenth-century print reproductions. The challenge in producing this effect is that, in most cases, you wouldn't take the time to hand-engrave a complex image. I wanted to find a way to simulate the look of an engraving without spending hours crafting the entire illustration. Although some of you might be accomplished illustrators with the training to make such a time investment pay off, I acknowledge that many more of you are photographers and enthusiasts who would not even think of creating this sort of effect by hand.

What follows is a simpler way of creating an etched effect by combining a stipple layer and a halftone layer, which have been modified to take on a graphic look and feel. As you'll see, there's a bit more to it than that, but the effect is achievable by a wider audience than is the hand etching approach, and the emphasis is on Photoshop technique rather than drawing and rendering.

About the Original Image

This serene and contemplative statue adorns the final resting place of Michelangelo. The tomb is located in the church of Santa Croce in Florence, in a dark, somewhat secluded corner of a vast and ornate interior. Although this work is not necessarily up to Mike's immortal status, it's still a powerful, contemplative statement.

I like how the putty-colored statue conveys a ton of detail without washing out to pure white. The bright and detailed statue contrasts well with the dark, textured marble in the background.

Building the Effect

① *Fresco, Poster Edges, and Diffuse Glow.*

② *Apply a Curves adjustment.*

③ *Blend the stipple layers.*

I started creating the line drawing effect by dragging the Background layer to the Create New Layer icon to create a duplicate image layer, which I named Stipple Base. I then selected Filter, Filter Gallery. Starting with a single filter layer, I opened the Artistic filter grouping in the center column and selected the Fresco filter. I set the Brush Size to 2, the Brush Detail to 8, and the Texture to 1. I then clicked the New Effect Layer icon at the bottom right of the dialog box and selected the Poster Edges filter, which is also in the Artistic filter grouping. I set the Edge Thickness to 2, Edge Intensity to 1, and Posterization to 2. I repeated the process to add a third filter: I selected Diffuse Glow from the Distort filter grouping, set the Graininess to 10, Glow Amount to 8, and Clear Amount to 0 (see Figure ①).

The result of this filter group is a very light stipple image that's pretty hard to see. The good news is that there is plenty of color and tonal information that can be emphasized. To start this process, I chose Image, Adjustments, Curves to launch the Curves dialog box. I added a single data point with the coordinates Input: 217, Output: 47, and clicked OK to apply the effect (see Figure ②).

Adding a Stipple Texture

I wanted to create a pair of layers that rendered the same source image with different stipple densities. I wanted one to have more detail and a tighter dot pattern, and the other to be more loose and textural.

I dragged the Stipple Base layer to the Create New Layer icon in the Layers palette twice to create two

additional layers. I highlighted the top layer in the stack and selected Image, Adjustments, Threshold. I dragged the Threshold slider to 48 and clicked OK to apply the effect. I repeated the process for the second layer, selecting a Threshold setting of 201. Finally, I double-clicked each layer name and renamed the top layer Threshold 48, and the second Threshold 201. To blend the two layers together, I highlighted the Threshold 48 layer, set the Opacity slider to 48%, and set the blending mode to Dissolve. These settings created a stipple effect that smoothed the blending of the two layers. Notice that moving the Opacity slider creates a dot pattern of different densities (see Figure ③).

After the balance between the two layers was set, I chose Select, All, to select the entire image, and Edit, Copy Merged to copy all the layers

④ *Apply the Halftone filter.*

⑤ *Resaturate the color.*

⑥ *Let the highlights show through.*

as a single merged layer. I then pasted a copy of the composite image at the top of the layer stack by choosing Edit, Paste. After naming the new merged layer Stipple Composite, I chose Filter, Sketch, Halftone Pattern to launch the Halftone dialog box in the Filter Gallery. I set the Size slider at 2, Contrast at 8, selected Circle from the Pattern Type pull-down menu, and clicked OK to apply the effect (see Figure ④). Depending on the size of the image and the desired line weight, adjust the Size slider to fit the needs of the image. Just remember that the larger the halftone Size value, the more you'll sacrifice image detail.

Adding More Color

To create additional color in the image, I duplicated the original photo (which was preserved as the Background layer), and renamed it Color Source. After dragging the new layer to the top of the layer stack, I set the blending mode to Color, applying only the color to the lower textured layers. I then selected Hue/Saturation from the Adjustment Layer drop-down menu in the Layers palette, moved the Saturation slider to +62, and clicked OK to apply the effect and create the adjustment layer (see Figure ⑤).

To create additional detail in the image, I started by turning off all layers except Threshold 201, Stipple Composite, Color Source, and the Hue/Saturation adjustment layer. The final step was to mask out part of the Stipple Composite layer and let some of the Threshold 201 layer show through. I wanted to add some detail and nuance, especially in the highlight areas.

I selected the Stipple Composite layer and clicked the Add Layer Mask icon to add the mask. I started with a large 150-pixel feathered brush and black as the foreground color. I painted the main highlight areas of the central figure and then switched to a smaller 13-pixel brush to articulate the details of the mask around the arm, hand, and face (see Figure ⑥).

PAINTED CANVAS

Simulating painted canvas is tricky on a number of fronts; you need to display a convincing texture, show just enough depth to convey the feeling of canvas and paint, and still render a realistic result. You walk a fine line to retain the critical photographic aspects of the image, and still portray a graphic and painterly look and feel.

Realistically, you should try to simulate more of a graphic look than a true painterly result. Other programs can help you achieve faux oil-paint textures better than Photoshop can. What I was looking for here was a convincing texture and interpretive color similar to what you might find in a painting. In this result, the color is more dramatic and expressive, and the texture does a nice job of removing the image from the realm of the photographic.

In the end, I liked the way the color worked in the image. Specifically, the golden-orange hues in the shadows were reminiscent of romantic illustrations of the early twentieth century (think Maxfield Parrish) and images from the Arts and Crafts movement. The result had a golden, luminous glow, as well as a painterly texture and overall graphic feel.

Orcia Tree
Nikon D2H
1/250 sec, f/8
Focal length 105mm

About the Original Image

I never got tired of shooting these patches of open hillside, anchored by a lone tree in the center. This one is in the Orcia valley in southern Tuscany. The biggest challenge in creating a pleasing effect was in dealing with the large areas of foliage that tended to flatten out and loose their detail. By pushing the subtle ochre accents into the shadows, I hoped to add a bit of drama to these flat areas.

Building the Effect

① *A woven textile pattern.*

② *Emphasize the teal "canvas" fibers.*

③ *Use fiber texture to displace photo.*

In an attempt to simulate the look of woven canvas, I started by dragging the Background layer to the Create New Layer icon in the Layers palette to create a duplicate. I repeated this process a second time for a total of three duplicate layers.

Create a Woven Texture

I clicked the foreground color swatch and set the RGB color values to R172, G199, B165. Then I clicked the background color swatch and set the RGB color values to R249, G227, B178. I highlighted the top layer and chose Filter, Render, Fibers to launch the Fibers dialog box. I set the Variance value to 16 and the Strength value to 4 and clicked OK to apply the effect. I highlighted the second duplicate layer and chose Image, Rotate Canvas, 90° CCW to turn the entire image on its side. I applied the Fibers filter a second time using the same settings, which applied the effect horizontally instead of vertically. I then selected Image, Rotate Canvas, 90° CW to return the image to its proper orientation.

I double-clicked the name of the top layer and renamed it Vert Fibers; I renamed the second layer Horiz Fibers.

To blend the two layers, I highlighted Vert Layers and selected Multiply from the blending mode, creating a woven textile pattern (see Figure ①).

Adding Depth to Texture

To give the pattern the dimensional texture of woven canvas, I chose Select, All, to select the entire image. Then I chose Edit, Copy Merged to copy the combined layers; I pasted the merged layers into a single layer by choosing Edit, Paste. To select only the teal color, I chose Select, Color Range. In the dialog box that appeared, I selected the darker area of the teal color, set the Fuzziness slider to 182, and clicked OK to make the selection. After copying the selection, I chose Edit, Paste to paste the teal fiber pattern into its own layer. To add depth to the teal fiber layer, I selected Bevel & Emboss from the Add Layer Style pop-up menu, chose Inner Bevel from the Style pop-up menu, Smooth from the Technique pop-up, and set the Depth slider to 191%. I left all the other settings at their defaults. Finally, I turned off the visibility in the new pasted teal fiber layer and set the layer's Opacity slider at 29% to blend and combine the layers (see Figure ②).

Displacing the Original Photo

I wanted to apply a Displace filter to the photo to warp it slightly, making it conform to the canvas texture. Displace always needs an external file to base its warp effect on, and it applies its warp offset based on the tonal values of the external file. Black & White pixels displace the image more, while gray pixels create less of a warp effect. Since I wanted the displacement warp to conform to the canvas texture, I decided to use the canvas texture I had just created as the external file.

I selected the entire canvas image and chose Edit, Copy Merged to copy the beveled and multiplied result. I pasted this into a new layer and then selected Duplicate Layer from the Layers palette menu. In the resulting dialog box, I selected New from the Document pull-down menu and clicked OK to copy the merged layer as a new image file. Finally, I closed the new file, saved it as a .psd, and named it Canvas Displace.

To apply the displacement to the original photo, I dragged the

4 *Blend original photo into composite.*

5 *Brighten image with Lighting Effects.*

6 *The final painted canvas.*

Background layer (the original photo, not the canvas texture) to the Create New Layer icon to copy it. I positioned the copy at the top of the layer stack. I selected Filter, Distort, Displace filter, and selected the Canvas Displace.psd file from the dialog box that appeared. I then set both of the Vertical Scale values to 10, and clicked OK without modifying any of the other controls. I double-clicked the title of this new layer to highlight it and renamed it Displace.

To blend the displaced layer with the texture layers, I set the Displace layer blending mode to Difference and set Opacity to 67% (see Figure **3**).

I duplicated the Background image layer once again and dragged it to the top of the layer stack. To create a linear graphic effect and flatten the shadows, I selected Filter, Stylize, Find Edges (this command applies the effect without any dialog box intervention). I set the blending mode of the resultant filtered layer to Overlay and its Opacity to 74%.

At this point, the blending mode for the Vert Fibers layer was set to Multiply to allow the two fiber layers

to overlap, but the blending mode for the Horiz Fibers layer was still set to Normal, obscuring the Background image photo. I set the blending mode for the Horiz Fibers layer to Multiply to add back the green foliage color and integrate the original photo into the composite (see Figure **4**).

Revitalizing the Color

The color was looking good, but things still felt kind of dull and flat. To add additional contrast and deepen the shadows, I selected Curves from the Adjustment Layer pull-down menu in the Layers palette. In the Curves dialog box, I set three curve points— Input: 47, Output: 44; Input: 117, Output: 145; and Input: 197, Output: 225.

I decided to add additional texture using some directional lighting effects. I chose Select, All to select the entire image. Then I chose Edit, Copy Merged and Edit, Paste to paste a copy of the combined layers into a single layer. I selected Filter, Render, Lighting Effects to launch the Lighting Effects dialog box. I set the controls as follows: Light Type Omni, Intensity 35, Focus 69,

Gloss -87, Material -6, Exposure 16, Ambiance 20, Texture Channel Blue, Check White is High, Height Slider 86. I dragged the light in the thumbnail preview to the left of the tree and clicked OK to apply the filter.

I liked the result of this filter except for the sky, which felt too textural and unnatural. I selected the Magic Wand tool from the toolbox and set the Tolerance in the Options bar to 22. I clicked once in the sky to select the area, and Option-clicked (Alt-clicked in Windows) the Add Layer Mask icon in the Layers palette to hide the selected sky area with a mask, allowing the color from the lower layer to show through (see Figure **5**).

For the last step, I wanted to eliminate some of the white highlight noise in the tree areas. I duplicated the Background layer one last time and dragged it to the top of the layer stack. I set the blending mode for this duplicated layer to Pin Light to tone down some of the bright spots and complete the effect (see Figure **6**).

Conté Crayon Drawing

Conté Crayons are hardened and compressed pieces of chalk that have been used by artists for centuries. They typically come in shades of sienna and umber, as well as black, white, and gray. Artists often apply them to colored or toned paper so that they can use white to draw in highlights, leaving the paper as the midtone.

I confess that I hesitated to include this exploration for primarily two reasons: The first is that this is a photography book, and discussing chalk drawings seems somewhat divergent. Second, this effect takes a certain degree of skill. It's not just a follow-the-steps-and-get-these-results kind of task. You must be able to draw at least a little bit to get decent results. The good news is that you can undo each stroke if necessary to get it right; multiple layers allow you to protect the parts that look good, allowing you to draw with confidence, without fear of messing things up.

However, this book is also about Tuscany, which abounds with old master chalk drawings on faded and yellowed paper. I decided that the Conté Crayon effect did indeed fit with the subject matter and techniques offered in this book. Ultimately, even if you have drawing skills, you should still follow a process to translate those skills to the digital realm. This exploration provides a solid process for getting the most out of your current skills or developing new ones. As I've mentioned with other tasks in this chapter, you really need a digitizing tablet to make this work; this effect is impossible to achieve with a mouse.

Marconi Statue
Nikon D2H
1/350 sec, f/9.5
Focal length 80mm

Handmade Paper
Scanned paper image

About the Original Images

I love this statue. It stands in Marconi square in Siena, off to one side, looking somewhat innocuous amid the splendor of this old and beautiful city. I was supposed to meet a tour guide in the square to gain access to the Palio race, and the guide was following the time-honored Italian tradition of not honoring time. I sat in the square for an hour and a half before the guide showed up, which gave me plenty of time to study and photo-graph this immovable muse.

In addition, I also used a scanned piece of handmade paper to use as the ground for the drawing. Technically, it's not an original "image," but it *is* an external source, so I'm listing it here nonetheless.

Building the Effect

❶ *Loosely outline the figure.*

❷ *Block in areas of tone and shadow.*

❸ *Define the dark end of the tonal range.*

The first step in creating the drawing was to create two custom bushes that would simulate the texture and marks of Conté crayons. You can draw a line with a Conté crayon for detail work, but you can also turn it on its side to block-in broad tonal areas.

Build the Right Brush

To create a brush to simulate the detail and line effect, I opened the Brushes palette by selecting Window, Brushes; I then selected the Brush tool in the toolbox to activate the palette's contents. I selected Brush Tip Shape from the list on the left and set the Diameter slider to 28, leaving all other settings at their defaults. Still in the Brushes palette, I enabled the Shape Dynamics check box and set the Size Jitter slider to 23%; because I was using a digitizing pen, I selected Pen Pressure from the Control menu. I set Minimum Diameter at 1% and Angle Jitter at 23%, and selected Pen Pressure from the Control menu. I set Roundness Jitter to 29% with no Control menu setting, and set Minimum Roundness

to 25%. Setting Pen Pressure as a control means that the pressure of the pen determines how the variable is applied. More pressure in this case would mean a larger brush size with more scattering of marks.

Then I went through the other sections in the Brushes palette and made adjustments to the settings. In the Scattering section, I set Scatter to 91%, set Control equal to Pen Pressure, enabled the Both Axes check box, and set Count to 2. In the Texture section, I selected the Wrinkles tile, set Scale to 112%, enabled the Texture Each Tip check box, set the Blending Mode to Hard Mix, and left all the other settings at their defaults. In the Other Dynamics section, I set Opacity Jitter to 100% and set its Control menu equal to Pen Pressure; I set Flow Jitter to 100% and set its Control menu equal to Pen Pressure also. Finally, I enabled the Noise check box, selected New Brush Preset, and named the brush Small Conte.

For the broad brush effect, I started with the previous settings and went

through the sections in the Brushes palette and made adjustments to their variables. In the Texture section, I selected the Wrinkles tile, set Scale to 112%, enabled the Texture Each Tip check box, set the Blending Mode to Linear Burn, and left all other settings at their defaults. In the Other Dynamics section, I set Opacity Jitter to 55% and set its Control menu to Pen Pressure; I set Flow Jitter to 16% and its Control men to Pen Pressure also. Finally, I enabled the Noise check box, selected New Brush Preset, and named the brush Broad Conte.

Drawing in Layers

To start the drawing, I loaded the statue photo above the scanned paper layer and set the blending mode for the photo layer to Luminosity and its Opacity to 40%. I created a new layer by clicking the Create New Layer icon, double-clicking the layer name, and titling it Rough In. I double-clicked the foreground color and selected a rust-orange color with RGB values of R127, G60, B24.

④ Add the highlights.

⑤ Add facial detail.

⑥ Subtle details in the raised arm.

I clicked the Brush tool in the toolbox and selected the Small Conte brush from the Brushes Presets section of the Brushes palette, and loosely traced the figure. The goal at this stage was simply to capture the proportions and globally map out the drawing (see Figure ①).

I created a new layer, which I titled Block Shading, and turned off the photo layer in an effort to draw the areas rather than simply tracing them. I began blocking in large areas of tone and shadow using the Broad Conte brush, filling in areas defined by the Rough In layer (see Figure ②).

At this point, I was creating multiple layers right and left. My goal was to define the dark end of the tonal range, and I did so using four different layers. Throughout this process, I was turning the photo layer on periodically to check for general accuracy, while still letting the drawing remain loose and fluid. I repositioned the photo layer higher in the layer stack as needed to maintain visibility relative to the drawing layers as they were created. As you

work, create a new layer to preserve any section that's starting to come together. When you're drawing, you don't always know that you'll want to revert or go back to a previous state until much later, after you see the drawing coming together. Layers protect your work and provide high flexibility (see Figure ③).

To balance the darks, I created a single layer for the white marks. After selecting white as the foreground color, I began working the white color into the various areas (see Figure ④). As you're doing this, try to resist the urge to simply trace the photo layer. I like to open the photo in a separate file and keep it next to the drawing file so that I can compare the images. It's okay to turn on the photo layer to check your work and proportions, but don't draw over the actual photo, or your image will take on a traced look.

Adding the Details

From here on in, it was painstaking work to polish the details in the face as well as the lower-leg area. I created a layer for the face and another for the

figure as a whole. Throughout the process, I had been adjusting the Diameter slider in the Brush Tip Shape section of the Brushes palette to set the appropriate brush size for the task at hand. In the face area, I worked with a 5- to 8-pixel brush; I also erased liberally until I got the exact marks I was after (see Figure ⑤).

I finished with a step that would be very hard to do with a conventional drawing. I was unhappy with the shadow area beneath the shield—it was too dark and muddled. With the Brush tool active, I Option-clicked (Alt-clicked in Windows) in the paper area to sample the paper color. I then used the Small Conte brush to draw into the arm and shield with the cream color of the paper. It lightened things up and visually worked to clean up the area (see Figure ⑥).

The entire drawing process for this image took me a little more than four hours. For best results, approach the Conté Crayon drawing task with patience, and practice as much as possible.

GRAPHIC EFFECTS WITH BLENDING MODES

Marconi Drawing

Photoshop's blending modes allow you to combine multiple sources of pixel data for a wide variety of graphic effects. The two data sources can be adjacent layers in the Layers palette, the pixel value in a brush as it paints on a target layer, or even the result of a filter effect in comparison to the previous state of the image. As a result, blending modes are every-where—on the Layers palette, on the Options bar for paint tools, and in the Fade command under the Edit menu, just to name a few locations.

Blending modes compare the information being applied (such as a brush stroke, an upper layer, or a new filter effect) with the target data (such as a layer or a previous unfiltered state). Based on the comparison and the criterion of the blending mode, Photoshop makes judgments about which pixel value it displays—the new value or the previous value. The general effect categories allow you to lighten, darken, combine, or apply a specific aspect of the pixel information—such as the luminosity, color, or hue. For example, the Lighten blending modes look at the two pixel values and display the one that's lighter; the Overlay blending modes combine and average the pixel values. You don't need to understand how each mode works, the key is to jump in and experiment. The modes are arranged in logical groups; everything in the Lighten group creates a lighter result, everything in the Darken group darkens.

In this example, we'll look at the range of results that can be generated by modifying just a couple of layers along with the full spectrum of mode options. Rather than progressing through a linear sequence that results in a single effect, this exploration shows the wide range of options you can create.

About the Original Image

For this exploration, the perfect starting point is the completed drawing from the previous exploration. It has a photo and graphics we can combine, and the paper scan can be added or subtracted to create additional variety. I know it's not a source photo *per se*, but it does contain multiple sets of pixel data with which we can experiment. Besides, you should be very familiar with its construction at this point!

Building the Effects

❶ *The Color blending mode.*   ❷ *The Vivid Light blending mode.*   ❸ *Adjusting Hue/Saturation.*

The first step in this exploration is to drag the photo of the Marconi Statue drawing to the top of the layer stack. We'll be applying several blending modes to this image to alter the drawing in the lower layers. With the photo layer active at the top of the layer stack, I selected Color from the blending mode pull-down menu in the Layers palette. This effect applies the color values from the photo to the lower pixel values without altering the drawing marks. The photo information is sublimated in favor of the drawing.

Because the photo source does not extend to the edges of the image frame, strips of cream-colored paper appeared vertically along the sides. To fix this, I selected the Paintbucket tool and Option-clicked (Alt-clicked in Windows) in the gray background behind the statue. The mouse pointer changed to an Eyedropper, and the background color became active. I then clicked once on either side of the image to fill in the strips with the

gray color, which smoothed the background to a solid gray, completing this iteration (see Figure ❶).

The Vivid Light Blending Mode

Because the shadow area in the shield was such a prominent part of the original image, I wanted to create a version that had an extremely high-contrast feeling, with dark, solid shadows. I started by highlighting the photo layer and selected Vivid Light from the blending mode menu in the Layers palette. This overlay effect creates bright whites, high contrast, and highly saturated areas of color around the edges of objects. In this case, it blew out the highlights to a flat white, while creating a red-and-ochre cast from the underlying scan of the paper layer (see Figure ❷).

To tone down the color a bit, I highlighted the photo layer and selected Hue/Saturation from the Adjustment Layer pull-down menu, adding the new layer above the photo layer. I set

the Hue slider to -13, the Saturation slider to -58, and the Lightness slider to -1. To focus the attention more on the figure, I cropped the image to eliminate a lot of the white space: I used the Crop tool to draw a rectangular selection horizontally around the figure, to the edges of the stone-wall texture. The crop clipped the figure vertically just above the left knee and at the top of the shield, completing this second version (see Figure ❸).

The Soft Light Blending Mode

This next version results in another drawing effect that feels significantly different than the result of the Conté Crayon exploration. It starts by setting the blending mode on the photo layer to Soft Light, which creates a very soft and subtle effect. When this blending mode is used, the target layer of information almost always dominates, while the information being applied is muted and diminished. As you can see in Figure ❹, the target layers of the drawing are

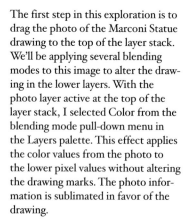

④ *The Soft Light blending mode.*

⑤ *Making the background white.*

⑥ *The final image.*

prominent, while the photo information is muted. Although muted, the photo data is still important because it's providing depth and contrast to the shadow areas, especially in the shield.

Turning Off Image Layers

To push the image further, I turned off the visibility icon for the paper scan layer, eliminating the cream-colored background and reverting the background to pure white. I felt that the cream color was distracting from the marks of the drawing, making things a bit muddy and inarticulate. After I'd reduced the background to pure white, it felt wrong to leave the white layer in the drawing active. When I shut it off, the drawing felt more direct and immediate. I also shut off the detail layers in the face and leg, which were added in the final steps of the Conté Crayon exploration. Although the resulting face was rounder and less detailed, I liked the way the white of the paper moved from the chest to the face and

through the hair. The drawing felt more cohesive (see Figure ⑤).

A Final Color Shift

The last iteration is not so much a blending mode effect as it is the pointed application of the Hue/Saturation controls. At this point, my blending mode iterations had turned the figure white, green, and several shades of ochre; a logical conclusion to the process was to convert the figure to a more natural flesh color. To do this, I set the photo layer's blending mode to Color, applying the colors from the photo to the underlying drawing.

The Hue/Saturation adjustment layer I had created earlier was turned off and sitting at the top of the layer stack. To shift the colors, I turned the adjustment layer back on and began looking for the proper Hue setting to simulate a flesh color for the skin areas of the figure. I ended up moving the Hue slider to -118. I also set Saturation at +55 and Lightness at -1. These settings created a pretty good

skin tone, although there was a distracting magenta tone in the shadows of the shield and around the folds of some of the fabric.

The easiest way to fix this was with a layer mask. With the Hue/Saturation adjustment layer still active, I clicked the Add Layer Mask icon to add a layer. With a 300-pixel brush and a foreground color of black, I painted the mask into the shield and fabric areas. This action hid the latest Hue/Saturation effect and allowed the Color blending mode from the photo layer to come through.

Finally, I turned back on the Whites layer (the layer with the crayoned highlights that I had turned off when I changed the paper to white), shut off the Rough-in layer (the first crayoned layer that outlined the statue) to let the color and texture dominate, and reactivated the details in the face. The result of this final iteration looks like a watercolor sketch (see Figure ⑥).

78

CARTELLA

Part 3
GALLERY

The images presented in the following chapters represent my own personal explorations, based on my Tuscan experiences. You'll find that I used some of the same techniques described in Part 2, "Photoshop Explorations," and full image-capture information is provided for all source photos. Each image includes a brief introduction and a complete description of how it was created. No red-tiled roofs and blue skies in this bunch, but hey, sometimes emotional responses stray off the path of the standard travel brochure.

CHAPTER 7

ABBAZIA

FINDING
TRANSCENDENT SPIRIT

The abbey (abbazia) at Monte Olivetto di Maggiore provided the key source file as well as the inspiration for this contemplative image. My drive to the abbey took several hours and was prompted by my desire to see the early fresco cycle of Sienese painter Il Sodoma (Giovanni Antonio Bazzi). After parking, walking to the abbey, waiting in an admission line, and making my way through the winding hallways, I was finally face to face with these murals. My gate slowed to "museum pace," hands behind my back; I began to take it all in.

It was at this point that the guard approached and informed me that the abbey would be closing in 15 minutes and would not reopen for three hours. As I looked around for something to hold my attention, I realized that the real attraction was the wooded walking paths that surrounded the abbey, illuminated by crisp, direct lighting that was nothing short of transcendent. Even at midday, the light sparkled through the trees, pooled on the paths, and brought out a wealth of detail and texture. There were signs on the walking paths that encouraged visitors to respect that this was a place of prayer and worship, and to meditate on the beauty and completeness of creation, as well as the creator.

This image reflects the transcendent spirit of that special place, emphasizing that the true spirit of Tuscany does not lie in cliché images of tiled roofs, cathedrals, and ancient frescoes. These human constructs are byproducts created by those fortunate to live in this amazing place—a place defined by geography, climate, and timeless serenity. I had been racing for hours to get in front of some old pigmented panels created by some guy that was 500 years dead. I was fortunate that circumstances forced me to slow down and take in a timeless subject as stunning now as it was 500 years ago.

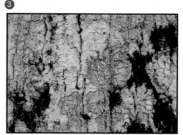

Two Trees

This photo was captured on the grounds of Monte Olivetto di Maggiore. The light in the woods created texture, detail, and drama as it moved from surface to surface; slipping from highlight to deep shadow, in a concurrent gesture of revealing and hiding.

Tree Bark

This close-up of tree bark was a handheld image shot in the same wooded area as the *Two Trees* photo at Monte Olivetto di Maggiore.

Assumption of the Virgin

Entitled *The Assumption of the Virgin*, this altarpiece from the Cathedral in Montepulciano was painted by Sienese master Taddeo di Bartolo from 1398 to 1401. It was named for a popular Sienese festival, which originated when the Hospital, glutted with requests from plague victims, purchased what was supposed to be a piece of the virgin's girdle which she let fall as she ascended into heaven (as reflected in the painter's elaborate handling of the virgin's skirt).

❶ Two Trees
Nikon D2H
1/400 sec, f/6.3
Focal length 75mm

❷ Birch Panorama
Nikon D2H
1/200 sec, f/4.5
Focal length 28mm

❸ Tree Bark
Nikon D2H
1/40 sec, f/4.5
+0.33 EV
Focal length 75mm

❹ Assumption of the Virgin
Nikon D2H
1/40 sec, f/4.5
+0.33 EV
Focal length 75mm

Birch Panorama

This photo is a segment from a larger panorama image that I captured near San Gimignano. The sun was breaking through a grove of birch trees to my left and it fell over rolling hills to the right.

⑤ *Primary image: Two Trees.*

⑥ *Add texture.*

⑦ *Convert to grayscale.*

Building the Image

The spotlight and subtle gradations were what originally drew me to the *Two Trees* photo, as well as the strong vertical divisions which imposed structure and order to the composition (see Figure ⑤).

Adding Tree Bark

As I began building images for the Tuscany suite for this book, I decided to focus on designs that were more square in proportion. As a result, I began thinking about adding a lower horizontal section to the image to square it off. Thus I added more canvas, increasing the entire image size from 2354 × 1578 pixels to 2354 × 2513 pixels.

The thing that jumps out from the top *Two Trees* photo is the clarity and detail in the bark texture, so I decided to go with that and explore the patterning that comes from bark textures. I opened the second *Tree Bark* photo and pasted it into the image. With the Tree Bark layer active, I created a selection and clicked the Add Layer Mask button in

the Layers palette to restrict the layer only to the lower rectangle. By default, layer masks are linked to the original layer when they are created. I clicked the chain link icon between the image and mask thumbnail in the Layers palette to deactivate the link, separating the mask and image information. This allowed me to click the Tree Bark thumbnail and reposition it with the Move tool, dragging the bark texture within the lower rectangle until I found a crop that worked for the composition (see Figure ⑥).

Going Grayscale

At this point, the texture juxtapositions were working well, but I felt that the color was distracting. The pale green of the bark texture was overt and just way too dominant. In addition, the entire color palette was very close in value, with the grays, greens, and browns of the upper layer running so close together. Adding the greenish yellow bark texture to the bottom felt divergent and even more disconnected.

My first move to address this problem was to reduce the top region of the composite to black and white in an

effort to let the texture and detail of the Two Trees layer stand on its own. After setting black as the foreground color and white as the background, I added a Gradient Map adjustment layer by selecting Gradient Map from the Adjustment Layer icon in the Layers palette. When you do this, a dialog box appears showing a gradient using the current foreground and background color set—which in this case converted the image to black and white. I clicked OK in the dialog box to apply the gradient.

Because adjustment layers apply their effects to everything beneath them in the Layers palette, I needed to restrict this effect to only the larger *Two Trees* layer. I created a clipping mask by holding down the Option key (the Alt key in Windows) and clicking the line in the Layers palette between the Two Trees layer and the adjustment layer itself. (You can also do this by selecting Layer, Create Clipping Mask from the menu bar.) Figure ⑦ shows the results of applying the gradient adjustment layer to just the Two Trees layer.

⑧ *Add motion blur.*

⑨ *Blending the texture.*

⑩ *The Gradient Map dialog box.*

Blurring the Bark

Part of the problem with the bark section was that it was just too much of a two-dimensional surface. It was flat and didn't have much depth. To address this deficiency, I duplicated the layer by dragging the Tree Bark layer to the New Layer icon in the Layers palette. With the mask link still deselected, I used the Move tool to drag the bark image within the lower rectangle until I found a complimentary section of texture.

With the new layer still active, I selected Filter, Blur, Motion blur to open the Motion Blur dialog box. I set the Angle to 0° and moved the distance slider to 560 pixels to create an extreme horizontal blur. To combine it with the lower layer, I set the blurred layer's opacity to 78% and selected Difference from the Blending Mode drop-down menu in the Layers palette (see Figure **⑧**).

More Landscape

The piece was feeling more cohesive, but it felt like the message was getting lost. I started thinking about combining a more expansive landscape image with the bottom bark texture, exploring the extremes of close-up photography and normative landscape images and how they communicate the sense of place in different ways.

I added the *Birch Panorama* photo across the bottom of the composition, scaling it to fit the horizontal image using the Free Transform tool. To make it work with the monochromatic palette of that portion of the image, I applied another gradient map by selecting Image, Adjustments, Gradient Map. This time I selected black and a pale green/yellow that keyed off the color of the bark texture in the Tree Bark layer. By selecting Gradient Map from the Image, Adjustments menu, the effect is applied directly to the layer rather than in a separate adjustment layer. I dragged the Birch Panorama layer between the bark and blur layers and set the opacity to 78% to combine the three layers.

This left additional vertical space around the Birch Panorama layer. Rather than creating distortion by stretching the entire image up, I selected the Clone Stamp tool and cloned parts of the Birch Panorama layer, extending the vertical of the central birch tree and adding a top to the group of trees on the left. The resulting combination lets the landscape combine effectively with the Tree Bark Blur layer, inferring strong motion and interesting coloration. The bark texture fills in the gap at the top right where the lower rectangle meets the Two Trees layer (see Figure **⑨**).

Adding a Mocha Gradient

I have to confess that at this point I got stuck. It's easy to sit here after the fact and show you how everything came together, but in the actual flow of the design, this point was a problem. I tried countless combinations of images and effects, but nothing seemed to pull it together. The move that finally pushed it over the top was the

⑪ *The result of the gradient map.*

⑫ *The pattern selection.*

⑬ *The final result.*

addition of a peculiar inverted gradient map that ranged from a mocha coffee color to black.

I created a Gradient Map adjustment layer just as I had before when converting the *Two Trees* layer to black and white. The difference in this case is that I clicked the gradient strip in the Gradient Map dialog box to launch the Gradient Editor (shown in Figure ⑩).

The Gradient Editor allows you to create custom gradients by adding additional colors and controlling the blending range as the colors flow together. The gradient bar that runs along the bottom of the Gradient Editor represents the new gradient. Clicking anywhere beneath the gradient bar inserts a square with an arrow called a *color stop*. Double-clicking a stop launches the Color Picker so that you can select the color for that stop.

After exploring various monochromatic options, I settled on a smooth two-color gradient that ranged from mocha to black. Remember that in

the Gradient Editor, the color stop on the left maps to the blacks in the image and the color stop on the right maps to the whites. Thus, by double-clicking the color stop on the left and selecting a color with an RGB value of R106, G96, B79, I converted the deepest blacks in the image to a pale mocha brown. I then double-clicked the right color stop and selected black as the color, pushing black into the brightest whites area (see Figures ⑩ and ⑪).

Adding the Virgin's Skirt

The final elements that completed the image are the star-like circular shapes that seem to float around the upper-left region of the image. These shapes echo the textures and shapes in the tree bark, while adding a dynamic accent that carries an innate specificity and attention to detail, without being overtly realistic or referential.

They were pulled directly from the skirt in the *Assumption of the Virgin* photo I took in the Montepulciano Cathedral (see Figure ⑫). I opened

the file and selected a single dot from the skirt pattern, using the Magic Wand with the Tolerance set to 7. With a single dot selected, I chose Select, Similar to select the remaining dots from the skirt. I copied the resulting selection and pasted it into a new file.

The resulting pattern had some artifacts and fringe details from other parts of the skirt, so I deleted those using the Eraser tool until only the dots remained. When the pattern was sufficiently cleaned up, I copied the image and pasted it into the composition, dragging it into position in the upper-right corner.

The final step was to add a layer mask to the dot pattern layer and fade some of the dot circles. To do this, I selected a brush with black as the foreground color, and set the opacity in the toolbar to 59%. I painted various sections of the pattern layer to achieve the final atmospheric effect, completing the image (see Figure ⑬).

**The Layers
Palette**

1. Open the *Two Trees* file.

2. Select Image, Canvas Size. In the dialog box that appears, click the top center anchor box and change the height dimension from 1578 to 2513. Click OK to increase canvas size.

3. Open the *Tree Bark* file and copy and paste it into the composite image.

4. Select Image, Canvas Size. In the dialog box that appears, change the vertical dimension to 2513 pixels, click to place the anchor box at the top center, and click OK to add canvas to the bottom of the frame.

5. Create a selection in the lower rectangle with new canvas and click the Add Layer Mask button in the Layers palette.

6. Click the chain link icon between the image and the mask thumbnail in the Layers palette to deactivate it. Drag the image with the Move tool to position the bark texture within the rectangle.

7. Click the foreground color swatch and select black from the Color Picker. Click the background color swatch and set the background color to white.

8. Click the Adjustment Layer icon in the Layers palette and choose Gradient Map from the drop-down menu. Name the layer B&W Gradient Map and click OK in the dialog box that appears to apply the gradient.

9. Hold down the Option key (Alt key in Windows) and click the line between the Two Trees layer and the adjustment layer to create a clipping mask, restricting the gradient to the Two Trees layer.

10. Click the Tree Bark layer in the Layers palette and drag it to the New Layer icon at the bottom of the palette to duplicate the layer. Name the new layer Tree Bark Blur.

11. With the mask link still deactivated, select the Move tool and recompose the Tree Bark Blur layer within the lower rectangle.

12. Choose Filter, Blur, Motion Blur. In the dialog box that appears, set the Angle to 0° and move the distance slider to 560 pixels. Click OK.

13. Set the Tree Bark Blur layer's opacity to 78% and select Difference from the Blending Mode drop-down menu at the top of the Layers palette.

14. Open the *Birch Panorama* file and copy and paste it into the composite.

15. Choose Image, Free Transform. Press the Shift key and drag a corner handle to reduce the width to the same size as the composite. Drag the Birch Panorama layer to the bottom of the composite and double-click to apply the transformation.

16. Click the foreground color swatch and select black from the Color Picker. Click the background color swatch, move the cursor into the bark texture area, and click to sample a pale yellow color.

17. With the Birch Panorama layer still active, choose Image, Adjustment, Gradient Map. Click OK in the dialog box that appears to apply the gradient map directly to the active layer.

18. In the Layers palette, drag the Birch Panorama layer between the bark and blur layers and set the opacity of that layer to 78%.

19. Select the Clone Stamp tool and Option-click to set the reference point on the central tree in the lower image area. Paint to extend the tree up to the Two Trees area. Reset the reference point and paint in the tops of the trees on the left side of the lower image area.

20. Select Gradient Map from the Adjustment Layer icon in the Layers palette. Click the gradient strip in the Gradient Map dialog box to launch the Gradient Editor.

21. Double-click the color stop on the left side of the gradient bar and enter the RGB values R106, G96, B79 in the dialog box that appears. Double-click the right color stop and select black as the color to replace the highlights. Name this layer Mocha Gradient Map and click OK.

22. Open the *Assumption of the Virgin* photo.

23. Select a single dot in the skirt pattern, using the Magic Wand tool with the Tolerance value set to 7. Choose Select, Similar to select the remaining dots in the pattern. Copy the resulting selection and paste it into a new file.

24. Select the Eraser tool and erase any unwanted pixels from the pattern as necessary.

25. Copy the image and paste it into the composition, dragging it into position in the upper-right corner. Rename the layer Assumption o/t Virgin.

26. Click the Add a Mask icon in the Layers palette to add a mask to the Assumption layer.

27. Select a brush with black as the foreground color, and set the Opacity value in the toolbar to 59%. Paint various sections on the Assumption layer mask to achieve the final atmospheric effect and complete the image.

Passagio Scuro

PASSAGIO SCURO

REVEALING
SHADOWED VITALITY

I was visiting the abbey of Santa Anna in Camprena when I found the inspiration for this image. The abbey was at the end of a long, winding dirt road—the kind that constantly makes you question whether you're going in the right direction. No cars passed me, and it didn't look as though any had been on this dusty, quiet road for some time. I pressed on in spite of the nagging voice in my head that wondered just how lost an English-speaking American can get on the back roads of Tuscany. At the same time, I resisted asking whether there had ever been an Italian version of the movie Deliverance.

After 45 minutes, I finally reached the top of the hill and began to explore the abbey. It was just about sunset, and although the building and grounds were open, the entire place seemed deserted. I explored inside and around the grounds and didn't see a single person. Around back I discovered a small, quiet, and slightly disheveled garden, with olive trees, wildflowers, and cypress trees.

As the shadows began to deepen, I found two pale orange roses. They were fading fast, sagging under their own weight, with wrinkles and blemishes that almost looked like age spots. The light and context of place gave these dying flowers a sense of warmth and beauty; and yet in another day, perhaps two, they would be lifeless and discarded. Passagio Scuro means Dark Passage, and it explores the tangible point where momentum and vitality slip away, and living things become entropic objects.

① **Dried Roses**
   Nikon D2H
   1/60 sec, f/4.5
   Focal length 60mm

② **Frame Shop**
   Nikon D2H
   1/160 sec, f/6
   Focal length 75mm

①

Dried Roses

In a small garden on the grounds of the abbey of Santa Anna, these roses seem to glow in the late afternoon sunlight. I was drawn to the intricate and compelling textures and the patterning on the leaves and petals.

②

Frame Shop

This photo is all about the patterning and intricate scroll work created by this collection of hand-carved frames in a Tuscan frame shop. The light is interesting as well because it echoes the direction and soft shadowplay created by the setting sun in the first image.

❸ *Dried Roses, cropped and optimized.* ❹ *Apply the first gradient map.* ❺ *Mask the gradient map.*

Building the Image

I started with the *Dried Roses* photo. I wanted to crop them to emphasize the detail and texture, without objectifying one flower as the central subject. After opening the image, I used the Crop tool to reduce it to a square and tweaked the contrast a bit with Curves: I applied a standard S-curve with the curve points of Input: 53, Output: 59, and Input: 185, Output: 205. This adjustment lightened the image overall, bumping up the contrast and bringing out a hint of detail in the shadow areas (see Figure ❸).

Adding Gradient Maps

From here on in for the development of the final image, I played with a series of tonal adjustments using Gradient Maps and Curves and added a complex pattern for good measure. As you look back at the result of this design, you may ask why I used three Gradient Map and two Curves adjustment layers when I might have been able to do everything with just one or two

adjustment layers. The key thing to understand is that, at the time, I wasn't sure what the final result was going to be; with such subtle gradations of tone, I needed to work in small increments. Small variations of tone and lots of adjustment layers gave me full flexibility to make subtle revisions.

The first gradient map (the Gradient Map 1 layer) reduced the highlights to pink and left the shadows black. Instead of mapping to white, I mapped the highlights to a peach color with the RGB values of R198, G183, B157. (You'll soon see that I copied and pasted this black-to-pink gradient two more times.) After creating the adjustment layer, I added a layer mask and painted on the layer mask with a soft gray brush to let some of the underlying layer's color show through, including the bottom of the flower and the background (see Figures ❹ and ❺).

Then I selected the Gradient Map 1 layer and dragged it to the New Layer icon in the Layers palette to

duplicate the layer (this action automatically named the new layer Gradient Map Copy 2). I then dragged the mask icon from this duplicated layer to the trash to delete the mask from the duplicate layer. This action darkened the image even further.

Using Pattern Maker

As I was working with the evocative romanticism of the rose imagery, I was reminded of the illuminated scrollwork from the photo I shot at a frame shop in Florence.

Pattern Maker is a Photoshop filter that generates random patterned tiles from rectangular images or selections. The results of this filter are seamless tiles that are evocative of their original sources, while presenting a geometric abstraction that recalls the cubist paintings of Braque and Picasso. In this instance, I was trying to create a pattern that captured the light and shadow of the original photo, along with the flowing scrollwork from the frame sections.

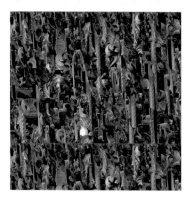
⑥ *Frames pattern.*

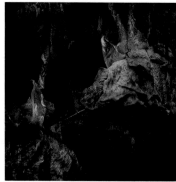
⑦ *Blended frames pattern.*

⑧ *More tonal adjustments.*

I opened the *Frame Shop* photo and selected a vertical marquee portion of the scrollwork area to serve as the source I would use to generate a pattern using the Pattern Maker filter.

I copied the selection and launched the Pattern Maker dialog box (Filter, Pattern Maker). I selected the Use Clipboard as Sample option in the Tile Generation section and clicked the Generate and Generate Again buttons to create a series of repeating pattern tiles. I scrolled through the Tile History viewer to select the pattern I was after and clicked OK to apply the pattern (*Note:* The tile generator in Pattern Maker is random and nonrepeatable. Do not expect to re-create the exact same tile result.) I copied and pasted the repeating pattern into the composite and closed the source image without saving it (see Figure ⑥).

I repositioned the pattern layer within the composite, dragging the new layer with the Move tool. To position the layer, I started by lowering the opacity to get a sense of how the graphic elements would align with the rest of the composition. When I was satisfied with its location, I set the opacity

back to 100% and began to apply blending modes to integrate it with the lower rose layers. I set the blending mode in the Layers palette for the Frames Pattern layer to Overlay, which combined the pattern with the darker areas quite nicely—although it was at the expense of all of that rose detail I had just labored over. To bring the rose back, I added a layer mask and painted the mask to hide the pattern in the center, letting the rose show through (see Figure ⑦).

More Tone Adjustments

With the blended pattern in place, I decided that any presence of color was going to work against the shadowy black shadow areas I had been developing. To reduce the color further, I added a couple more tone adjustment layers to desaturate the image and add contrast.

The first adjustment layer was another gradient map layer, which I created by copying the Gradient Map 1 layer a third time and dragging it above the Frames Pattern layer in the layer stack. This new layer was automatically named Gradient Map 1 Copy 3.

You may wonder why I would add a gradient map layer on top of an existing gradient map layer, considering that the color-stop selections of the top gradient map would overwrite the color selections of the gradient maps beneath it in the stack. At first glance, the topmost gradient map in the layer stack appears to cancel out the lower ones. Although the color information is indeed lost, the *tonality* of the lower gradient maps show through, thus allowing deep controls for contrast and tonal range.

Although the shadows were getting more subtle and evocative with this newest gradient map adjustment, the highlights suffered, so I added a Curves adjustment layer, with data points set to Input: 30, Output: 46, and Input: 112, Output: 235. I named this layer Curves 1, and it did a nice job of opening up the highlight areas and bringing back some of the details that were lost in the shadows (see Figure ⑧).

Copy Merged

I chose Select, All to select the entire image and Edit, Copy Merged, to copy the composite. I pasted the result at the top of the layer stack and named the

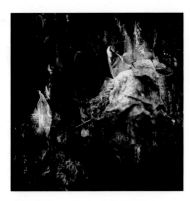

❾ *Lighten and mask the image.*   **❿** *Copy and flip the subject.*   **⓫** *The final image.*

layer Copy Merge, Dodge, Mask. I then selected the Dodge tool with a 300-pixel brush and dodged around the main rose area to lighten the center of the image. Because the Dodge tool modifies only a single layer at a time, I had to use the Copy Merged command to reduce the composite to a single layer.

Then I added a layer mask to the Copy Merge, Dodge Mask layer and masked out the outer edges and lower-right corner so that the lower areas showed through in these spots. The new mask allowed the lightened copy/merge layer to show through in the center, while the darker edges of the image remained intact (see Figure **❾**).

Adding a Mirror Image

In an effort to extend the image beyond its current boundaries, I added 675 pixels of extra canvas to the right side of the image. I then drew a rectangular selection around the main rose image in the composite and turned off visibility for all layers except the Dried Roses, Gradient Map 1, and Gradient Map 1 Copy 2 layers. This action eliminated almost all the abstract patterning and presented

more of a clear photographic rendering of the rose.

I chose Edit, Copy Merged to duplicate the visible layers and then pasted them into the composite above the Copy Merge, Dodge, Mask layer. Holding down the Shift key, I dragged the new image layer into the space where I had created the new canvas (the Shift key constrained my movement to the horizontal direction, maintaining vertical alignment). By choosing Edit, Transform, Flip Horizontal, I flipped the pasted image to create a mirror image, and named the layer Mirror Image (see Figure **❿**).

Cropping and Lightening

At this point, I figured out what this image was about. I had the predominant rose image on the right side serving as the central image, while the darker, more ominous mirror image on the left provided an evocative counterpart. The remaining areas on the far left were superfluous and distracting. I selected the Crop tool, pressed the Shift key, and drew a new square crop shape around the mirrored images, excluding the ancillary information on

the left. I double-clicked within the crop area to apply it.

To complete the design, I made one last adjustment: There was a bright swirl pattern from the Frames Pattern layer on the left side, just above the rose area. It was so bright and distinctive that it was distracting from the sensuous rose-petal detail just beneath it. I added one last layer called Swirl Adjustment, just above the Mirror Image layer, by clicking the New Layer icon in the Layers palette. I then chose the Clone Stamp tool, set Opacity to 68%, enabled the Sample All Layers check box, and selected a 147-pixel brush. I Option-clicked (Alt-clicked in Windows) in the shadows to set the reference point, and painted over the swirl area to mask the brightness and deemphasize the patterned area.

After pulling some test proofs, I decided that the overall contrast was too low, and that the shadows were filling in too much. To address this problem, I added one final Curves adjustment layer to the top of the layer stack with data points set to Input: 38, Output: 53, and Input: 169, Output: 219 to complete the image (see Figure **⓫**).

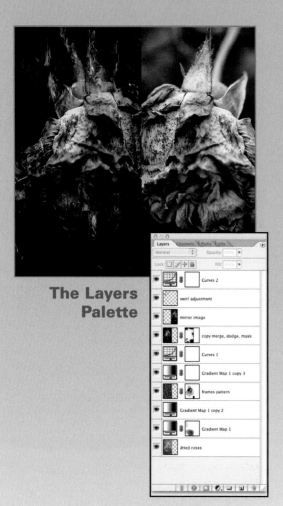

The Layers Palette

1. Open the *Dried Roses* file.

2. Choose the Crop tool and crop the image to 1630 × 1630 pixels.

3. Choose Image, Adjustments, Curves. Set curve points to Input: 53, Output: 59, and Input: 185, Output: 205.

4. Select Gradient Map from the Adjustment Layer menu in the Layers palette. In the dialog box that appears, click the gradient strip to launch the Gradient Editor.

5. Double-click the white color stop on the right, below the gradient. In the Color Picker that appears, specify an RGB "pink" color of R198, G183, B157.

6. Select the Brush tool with a 200-pixel brush; set black as the foreground color and Opacity to 36% in the Options bar.

7. Paint a transparent mask in the background and lower part of the flower.

8. Select the Gradient Map 1 layer in the Layers palette and drag it to the New Layer icon at the bottom of the Layers palette to duplicate the layer. Double-click the layer name to select it and rename it Gradient Map Copy 2.

9. Select the Layer Mask thumbnail for Gradient Map 1 Copy 2 and drag it to the trash, clicking the Discard button and closing the dialog that appears.

10. Open the *Frame Shop* file.

11. Select the Rectangular Marquee tool and drag a vertical marquee in the center of the frame image.

12. Choose Edit, Copy.

13. Choose Filter, Pattern Maker.

14. Enable the Use Clipboard as Sample check box in the Tile Generation section of the Pattern Maker window and click the Generate button to create a random pattern.

15. Click the Generate Again button repeatedly to create additional sample patterns as needed.

16. Click the Forward and Back buttons in the Tile History section to scroll through the tiles and select the desired pattern. Click OK to apply the pattern.

17. Choose Select, All.

18. Choose Edit, Copy.

19. Choose File, Close and click the Don't Save button to close the Frame Shop file without saving the pattern.

20. Activate the image composite and choose Edit, Paste to paste the pattern. Double-click the name in the Layers palette to select the new layer and name the layer Frames Pattern.

21. In the Layers palette, set the Opacity slider to 25% for the Frames Pattern layer, select the Move tool, and reposition the pattern. Reset the Opacity slider to 100%.

22. For the Frames Pattern layer, set the blending mode in the Layers palette to Overlay.

23. Click the Add Layer Mask button in the Layers palette to add a mask. Select the Brush tool and specify a 200-pixel brush and an Opacity value of 27%. Paint a transparent mask in the center of image.

24. Select the Gradient Map Copy 2 layer and drag it to the New Layer icon in the Layers palette to duplicate the layer.

25. Select Curves from the Adjustment Layer menu in the Layers palette. Set the data points to input: 30, output: 46, and input: 112, output: 235.

26. Choose Select, All.

27. Choose Edit, Copy Merged.

28. Choose Edit, Paste to paste the merged layer.

29. Select the Dodge tool with a 300-pixel brush and dodge the central area of the merged layer.

30. Click the Add Layer Mask icon in Layers palette menu to add a mask.

31. Select the Brush tool with a 200-pixel brush and set black as foreground color. Paint the mask into the lower-right corner and outer edges of the image.

32. Choose Image, Canvas Size. Change the width from 1630 to 2305, select the left-middle anchor square, and click OK to add canvas to the right side of the image.

33. Select the Rectangular Marquee tool and draw a vertical selection around the central rose image.

34. In the Layers palette, turn off the visibility icon on all layers except Dried Roses, Gradient Map 1, and Gradient Map 1 Copy 2.

35. Choose Edit, Copy Merged and Edit, Paste to paste the merged selection as a new layer. Double-click the layer title and name the new layer Mirror Image.

36. Press the Shift key and drag the Mirror Image layer to the right, aligning it with the area of new canvas.

37. Choose Edit, Transform, Flip Horizontal to flip the layer.

38. Select the Crop tool and drag a crop selection from the upper-right to the lower-left, pressing the Shift key to constrain the selection to a square. Double-click in the selection to crop the image.

39. Click the New Layer icon in the Layers palette to create a new layer. Double-click the layer title and name the new layer Swirl Adjustment.

40. Select the Clone Stamp tool, set Opacity to 68%, enable the Sample All Layers check box, and choose a 167-pixel brush.

41. Option-click (Alt-click in Windows) in the shadow areas and paint out the bright swirl shape in the upper-left center of the image.

42. Choose Curves from the Adjustment Layer menu in the Layers palette and set the curve data points to Input: 38, Output: 53, and Input: 169, Output: 219.

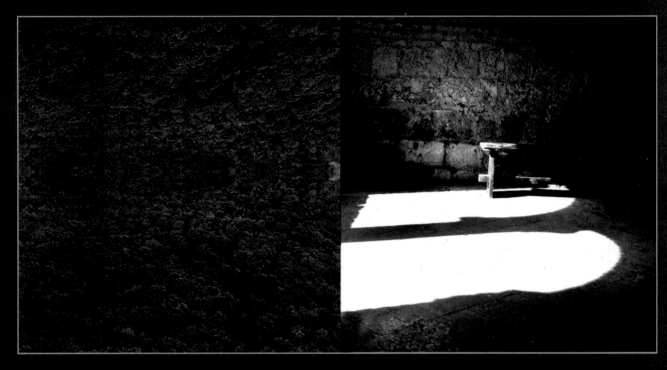

Punto

PUNTO

EXPLORING RELATIVE FUNDAMENTALISM

You can't appreciate the power of being anchored until you've experienced the disorientation of being set adrift. Punto contrasts these two extremes, as it explores the concepts of relativism, reality, and absolute truth. It's a fair question to ask how such simple and humble objects can have such heady aspirations.

The repetitive and circular pattern on the left side conveys enough detail and specificity to keep you looking and exploring. The symmetry is evident to the point that you keep looking for more, trying to piece together clues to completely define the pattern. And yet the complete logic of the system is elusive, remaining just out of reach.

On the other side of the image, the bench is solid and absolute. It provides a visual counterpoint to the texture because it is easily recognizable as a object and is solidly presented in full contrast. In addition, the bench is an obvious place to sit and orient one's self with the surroundings in the room. There is also the streaming light, a metaphor for enlightenment, that attends the anchored point of orientation.

By definition, relativism implies a lack of anchor. Absolute truth suggests that there are immovable, solid facts, and that what we know informs what we don't understand. These two polarities, presented in tandem, represent the current age of postmodern fundamentalism. Punto means "point" and suggests that a point can be both fixed and fluid, informative and useless.

CHAPTER 9

❶ Galgano Bench
 Nikon D2H
 1/80 sec, f/11
 Focal length 24mm

❷ Orcia Landscape
 Nikon D2H
 1/200 sec, f/7.1
 -1.3 EV
 Focal length 46mm

Galgano Bench

In a small chapel on the grounds of San Galgano, this bench sits against a stone wall as the only piece of furniture. The sun was streaming through open arched windows, creating strong contrast and deep shadows. In planning the exposure of this scene, I chose to reveal detail in the shadow areas at the expense of detail in the sunlight area.

Orcia Landscape

This was the scene that greeted me each morning as I looked out the window of my hotel in the Val d'Orcia in southern Tuscany. I liked the way this photo came together, with the broad compositional divisions of foreground trees, middleground house, and background sky, along with the pinpoint accent of the white house.

❸ *Orcia Landscape.*

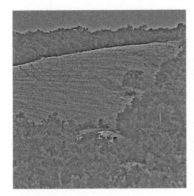

❹ *Use High Pass to sharpen.*

❺ *Crop the image.*

Building the Image

Punto was the first image in this series that began to explore the compositional duality of the diptych. A *diptych* is an artwork that consists of two panels placed side by side, and it dates back to ancient times when scrolls or religious panels were hinged together as a free-standing folding screen or as a book. In the Middle Ages, early Christian icons were created as diptychs that contained basic images to remind the illiterate of fundamental spiritual truths.

The photographic diptychs I created as part of the Tuscany series are presented as two large, separate images mounted on panels and hung together to create the finished piece. Although contemporary art diptychs don't serve a utilitarian purpose in the same way their religious counterparts did, the nature of these artworks is to impart some deeper meaning through the juxtaposition of two elements in a comparative or contrasting study. If these images succeed, it will be in the way they convey essential or fundamental messages by comparing or contrasting the two panels.

As a result, you'll find that much of the work in creating a diptych is in exploring a wide range of subject matter to find a transcendent combination. When I say "transcendent," I'm not talking so much about a deep spiritual experience per se; I'm referring to a sort of visual alchemy in which a combination of two images conveys a unique and cohesive message that goes beyond the impact of the individual images.

Cropping and Optimizing

The first image I began working with was the *Orcia Landscape* photo (see Figure ❸). I liked its composition and the feeling of place. I wanted to work with classic images of the Tuscan landscape, and this shot with the hills and olive trees seemed to fit the bill. Even though the final iteration of this panel didn't even remotely resemble this sun-drenched hillside, it was still a valid impetus for getting started. As an old art teacher used to say to me, "A diving board is good for getting you started, but you can't bring it into the pool with you." *Orcia Landscape* was my diving board.

After opening the image, I did some sharpening to bring out the details in specific areas. Although you could use the Unsharp Mask filter or Sharpen tool to sharpen, one of the best ways to sharpen an image is with the High Pass filter. To do this, I dragged the Background layer to the New Layer icon in the Layers palette to create a copy. I then selected Filter, Other, High Pass to launch the High Pass dialog box. High Pass converts the entire image to neutral gray except for the highest-contrast edges. The Radius slider determines how much contrast is applied to the edge areas; a lower value means less contrast, which translates to less sharpening in the next step. A higher value means more sharpening. In the case of the *Orcia Landscape* photo, I set the slider to 3.6 pixels and clicked OK to apply the effect (see Figure ❹).

When doing this technique, explore the Soft Light, Overlay, and Hard Light blending modes for progressively higher degrees of sharpening. After applying the filter, I set the blending mode for the Background Copy layer to Overlay to complete the sharpening effect. When the sharpen and crop steps were completed, I chose Merge Down from the Layers

⑥ *Flip the landscape.*

⑦ *Desaturate the texture.*

⑧ *The final image.*

palette menu to simplify the layer stack. To complete the effect, I cropped the image's vertical orientation to a square (see Figure ⑤).

Building a Texture

As I began working with the cropped *Orcia Landscape* image, I was drawn to how the predominant tree textures were minimalistic yet still very specific.

I started by duplicating the landscape by dragging the Default Background layer to the New Layer icon in the Layers palette, creating a new layer called Layer Copy. I renamed the new layer Flipped Landscape by double-clicking the title text to highlight it and retyping the new name. With the layer still active, I selected Edit, Transform, Flip Vertical to flip the layer upside down, placing the sky area at the bottom of the square (see Figure ⑥).

To complete the pattern effect, I highlighted the Flipped Landscape layer, selected the Move tool, and moved the layer 130 pixels higher to set up the symmetrical design. I then selected Darken as the blending mode for the Flipped Landscape layer, which

hid the sky and created the all-over texture.

I liked the texture effect, but as I started exploring the diptych format, I found that the green color worked against some of the images I wanted to integrate with the composition. Initially I tried adding a Hue/Saturation adjustment layer and lowering the Saturation slider all the way to 0. Although this approach got rid of the color, it also made the resulting gray a touch too dark.

As an alternative, I created a new layer by clicking the New Layer icon in the Layers palette (I named the new layer Black). I selected the Paintbucket from the toolbox, set black as the foreground color, and clicked within the composition window to paint the layer black, obscuring the entire image. With a neutral black filling the entire layer, I then selected the Color blending mode for the Black layer to apply the color (or lack thereof) to all the lower layers. This method opened up the highlight details, making the texture more articulate and less muddy (see Figure ⑦).

Adding the Bench Image

Adding the *Galgano Bench* photo was both simple and complex. It was complex from the standpoint that I reviewed image after image to find the right aesthetic fit for the composition. I narrowed things down to a short list of candidates which then began to impose their own will on the design (see the "Variations" section on the next page). I added images, broke up the symmetry, pushed things around, and in the end resolved things back to the simple symmetry of the dual-square design.

The simplicity of adding the bench image was on the technical side. I found the *Galgano Bench* photo and cropped it to the square format so it would fit with the composition. After doubling the canvas size in the main image to create the horizontal format, I copied the cropped bench image and pasted it into the composition, dragging it to the right side of the composite. I then set the Bench layer's blending mode to Hard Light, which created the deep shadows and high contrast of the final image (see Figure ⑧).

Variations on *Punto*

In the process of creating *Punto*, a number of variations sprang up. Although I don't consider these images secondary or inferior to the featured *Punto* image, they're just not a cohesive fit with the suite of Tuscany images featured in this Gallery of Images.

Textures

In this variation (see Figure ❾), I superimposed a close-up of tree bark with a duplicate of the foliage texture from the left side of the diptych. Setting the Tree Bark layer's blending mode to Color Dodge merges the two images on the right side, and allows for strong color saturation within the texture.

Minimalist Variation.

Additional Elements

In this next variation (see Figure ❿), I used a graphic image of tree trunks and grass on the left, in place of the foliage texture. After placing this image, I decided to break up the strong center division by running a third image to join the two areas. I placed a detail from Ghiberti's Baptistry doors in Florence, and masked the edges to combine the images.

Additional Elements Variation.

Brushstroke

In this final version (see Figure ⓫), I moved away from the figurative representation of the previous variations and added a single slashing brushstroke. Although this composition looks simple and basic, the development of the brushstroke itself was a result of extended trial and error. It was created with a drawing tablet that mapped opacity to pressure sensitivity, fading both ends of the stroke.

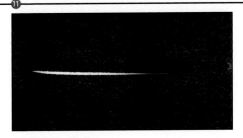

Brushstroke Variation.

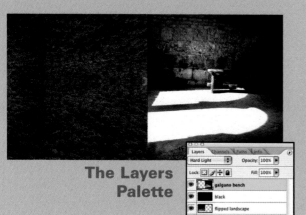

The Layers Palette

1. Open the *Orcio Landscape* file.

2. Double-click background layer and rename it Landscape.

3. Drag the Landscape layer to the New Layer icon in the Layers palette to duplicate the landscape layer.

4. Choose Filter, Other, High Pass to launch the High Pass dialog box.

5. Set the Radius slider to 3.6 pixels and click OK to apply the effect.

6. Set the blending mode for the Landscape Copy layer to Overlay.

7. Select Merge Down from the Layers palette menu to merge the two layers.

8. Select the Crop tool and Shift-drag the tool to draw a square cropping area in the lower-center of the image. Double-click within the crop selection to apply the crop.

9. Drag the Landscape layer to the New Layer icon in Layers palette to duplicate landscape layer.

10. Double-click the Landscape Copy layer title and give the new layer the name Flipped Landscape.

11. Choose Image, Transform, Flip Vertical to flip the layer.

12. Select the Move tool, press the Shift key to constrain horizontal movement, and drag the Flipped Landscape layer 130 pixels higher in the composition.

13. Select the Darken blending mode from the Layers palette for the Flipped Landscape layer to complete the foliage texture layers.

14. With the Flipped Landscape layer still active, click the New layer icon in the Layers palette. In the dialog box that appears, name the new, empty layer Black.

15. Select the Paintbucket from the toolbox, set Black as the foreground color, and click in the image to fill the new, empty layer with black.

16. Select Color from the Blending Mode pull-down menu in the Layers palette to desaturate the image.

17. Select Image, Canvas Size. In the dialog box that appears, set the Width value to 3,210, and set the Anchor box to the upper-left corner. Click OK to enlarge the canvas.

18. Open the *Galgano Bench* file.

19. Select the Crop tool and Shift-drag to draw a square cropping area around the center of the image. Double-click within the crop selection to apply the crop.

20. Choose Select, All.

21. Choose Edit Copy, activate the image composite and choose Edit Paste.

22. Select the Move tool from the Toolbox and drag the new layer to the blank canvas area on the right.

23. Double-click the layer name in the Layers palette and rename it Galgano Bench.

24. Select Hard Light from the Blending Mode pull-down menu in the Layers palette for the Galgano Bench layer to complete the image.

Santissima Addolorata

©2004 Daniel Giordan

CHAPTER 10

SANTISSIMA ADDOLORATA

EXPERIENCING BLIND FAITH

There is an evocative sculpture that stands in the corner of a small church in Montepulciano, just south of Siena. It commemorates a feast called Our Lady of Sorrows, which is dedicated to the spiritual martyrdom of Mary, whose heart was pierced with swords of sorrow. In Italy, the title of Our Lady of Sorrows is Maria Santissima Addolorata.

I didn't know any of this as I stood before this lifelike statue. All I knew was that this was a powerful and evocative statement made even more intense as I stood in this small quiet chapel, surrounded by centuries of dust and artifacts. I was in another place...experiencing the passion and pathos of an artisan whose work was a direct outworking of his faith. The belief and intensity of the long-dead sculptor who created this work still resonated in this tiny chapel. This was no Michelangelo, to be sure. In fact, the sculpture had to work to be considered second rate. And yet its charm and compelling allure was the intensity and blind faith imbued into it by its creator.

Is blind faith enough, or does faith need to be focused on the truth? You have to wonder whether the artist's passionate outpouring ultimately made a difference. It certainly made a difference when the artist was alive, enough so that he created this passionate statement. And now the artist is gone. The statue is blind...and what has become of the faith?

SOURCE PHOTOS

1 Madonna
Nikon D2H
1/30 sec, f/4.5
ISO 640
Focal length 135mm

2 Assumption of the Virgin
Nikon D2H
1/160 sec, f/4.5
Focal length 75mm

Madonna

This image captures a beautiful and evocative sculpture of a Madonna in a church in Montepulciano. I was struck by the graphic and violent representation of her pain, as well as the beautiful crafts-manship of the sculpture. The paint on the face, the gilding, and the sculptural details were captivating. I tried to empha-size these features in the image by com-posing the figure to the right, using the swords and the line of the wall as compo-sitional elements.

Assumption of the Virgin

This image shows a small corner of a massive altar piece titled *The Assumption of the Virgin*. This altar-piece from the cathedral in Montepulciano was painted by Sienese master Taddeo di Bartolo from 1398 to 1401. It was named for a popular Sienese festival, which origi-nated when the hospital, glutted with requests from plague victims, pur-chased what was supposed to be a piece of the virgin's girdle which she let fall as she ascended into heaven. This section shows a self-portrait of the artist in the lower-right corner, looking straight at the viewer with a cocked eyebrow.

③ *Cropped Madonna.*

④ *A Curves adjustment layer.*

⑤ *The tonally optimized image.*

Building the Image

After opening the *Madonna* photo, I wanted to crop the image to further emphasize the dramatic nature of the swords and her ensuing pain. The most dynamic elements were the swords, the direction of Mary's gaze, and the diagonal line in the wall behind the statue. The wall line and the swords all directed themselves to her heart in the lower right, and her pained gaze provided a counterpoint as it looked to the left. I cropped the image tightly on these components, pushing the drama right in the face of the viewer (see Figure ③).

To add a sense of mystery to the image, I added a Curves adjustment layer by selecting Curves from the Adjustment Layer pull-down menu at the bottom of the Layers palette. I set the points to Input: 72, Output: 0; Input: 121, Output: 24; and Input: 207, Output: 130. With this Curves layer active in the Layers palette, I highlighted the layer mask icon associated with the Curves Adjustment layer to select it. I then selected a 200-pixel brush, set the foreground color to black, set opacity to 35%, and painted in the mask to lighten the face from the original Curves adjustment (see Figure ④).

I liked how the Curves layer darkened the image, especially with how it added saturation and contrast to the scrolled handles of the swords. Having said that, I knew the subject was still a bit obscured, and that some of the color shifts were somewhat distracting.

To address these issues, I did a fair amount of experimentation in an attempt to strike the right balance between contrast and detail. I finally ended up creating a separate layer group (formerly called a layer set) that arranged several adjustment layers over a duplicate of the original Madonna layer. As you know, layer order, blending modes, and clipping groups create different tonal results depending on their arrangement, and I found that the following constellation of elements worked best for the image.

I selected New Layer Group from the Layers palette menu and named this new layer group Tone Adjustment Set. By creating a layer mask for the entire group and masking the background, I could use this group to lighten the midtones and adjust the color balance around the face. I pressed the Option key (Alt key in Windows) and dragged the Madonna layer to the layer group, creating a duplicate layer. I then added a Curves adjustment layer with a single point set to Input: 187, Output: 134 to deepen the shadows. I gave this layer its own layer mask and painted a light gray mask over the face to keep it light and preserve details. To cool the warm tones in the face, I created a Color Balance adjustment layer and added a bit of blue and cyan with the following settings: Shadows -6, +5, +10; Midtones -4, +6, 0; and Highlights +23, +8, -6.

Finally, I highlighted the Tone Adjustment Set in the Layers palette and Option-clicked (Alt-clicked in Windows) the Create Layer Mask icon to create a mask filled with black, concealing the entire contents of the layer set. To add back the effects, I selected a large feathered brush with white as the foreground color and an opacity of 18%. I painted to erase the mask around the face, building more density while seamlessly adding the effect (see Figure ⑤).

⑥ *Correcting the perspective.*   ⑦ *Pasting in a new image.*   ⑧ *Adding the red layer.*

Seeing Red

Next I opened the *Assumption of the Virgin* photo and corrected the distortion in perspective. Because this is such a huge painting, these was no way to shoot it without pointing the camera up at a strong angle, forcing the vertical perspective lines to converge at the top, making the image tilt away from the viewer. I selected View, Show, Grid to turn on the grid overlay, and then I double-clicked the background layer of the *Assumption* photo and clicked OK in the resulting dialog box to convert it from a Background layer to a standard layer. I then pressed ⌘-A (Ctrl-A in Windows) to select the entire image.

I used the Warp tool to correct the distortion, selecting Edit, Transform, Warp to launch the Warp dialog box. Warp overlays the image with a mesh and allows you to drag the intersecting points to adjust distortions. You can also drag the Bezier handles on the outer edge points to control the warp further. I dragged the intersection point in the upper-left further to the left to correct the distortion on the left column of the image. I tweaked other intersection points to straighten the

bottom and keep all edges perpendicular to the image plane (see Figure ⑥).

After pressing Enter to correct the distortion, I copied the result and pasted it into the main composition, naming this new layer Altar. I selected the Move tool and dragged the layer into position, allowing the figures on the left side to fall outside of the composition (see Figure ⑦). I wanted to continue my explorations into how color selections within paintings could results in well-composed abstract patterns, similar to the effect I achieved when I isolated the dot patterns in the *Abbazia* image (see Chapter 7, "Abbazia"). I selected the Wand tool from the toolbox, set the Tolerance to 44, and clicked the red garment of the figure in the lower-right of the Altar layer. I then chose Select, Similar to select all the red in the image, based on the 44 Tolerance range. With the reds selected, I clicked the mask tool in the Layers palette to hide everything except the red spots and brushstrokes. I set the blending mode for this layer to Hard Light to complete this first red layer (see Figure ⑧).

One of the things I regretted about the first placement of the Altar layer was the loss of the figures on the left side. Specifically, I liked the red robe of the saint in the lower-left corner. When I decided to superimpose another layer of red texture, I looked for ways to bring back the red-robed guy who bled off the left edge and did not appear in the composition. To do this, I duplicated the Altar layer by dragging it to the New Layer icon in the Layers palette, and I assigned the layer name of Altar Copy 1. I selected the Move tool and held down the Shift key while dragging to the right, restricting the vertical movement of the layer as I dragged. I positioned the red-robed saint in the lower-right corner of the composite and repeated the procedure to isolate the red color areas (I selected the red, created the mask, and set the blending mode to Hard Light).

Finishing the Image

The vertical red fragments on the left edge suggested that some additional framing could further enhance the subject. As I explored potential framing elements, I settled on the right edge

⑨ *The final image.*

molding from the Altar layer, which would run right down behind the red robe that was anchoring the lower-right corner of the composite. I tried the easiest approach of modifying the mask in the Altar layer to let the molding show through. The problem was that the Hard Light blending mode created too harsh an effect that felt awkward and disconnected.

I finally duplicated the Altar layer a third time and dragged it to the bottom of the layer stack, beneath the Madonna layer. This way I could leave the layer's blending mode at normal and introduce the edging into the composition. The final step was to add a mask to the Madonna layer along the right edge, allowing the molding to show through. I selected the Marquee tool and dragged down from the upper-right corner to create a thin vertical stripe. With the selection still active, I Option-clicked (Alt-clicked in Windows) the Add Layer Mask icon to hide the selected area. The finishing touch was to add the corner detail in the very bottom right (see Figure **⑨**).

VARIATIONS: EXPLORING THE HORIZONTAL

The primary variation for this image was to explore a horizontal format that introduced more of the *Assumption of the Virgin* photo. I was intrigued by the way the saints in the side panels seemed to interact with the Madonna's plight. They seemed to be reacting to it in an almost visceral way, shocked, repulsed, and in some cases, completely indifferent. I also liked the trio of cherubim that fly into the blue of Mary's hood and the way the saint in the lower-right corner seems to be talking with an empty red robe.

In addition, the saints seemed stained with the implied blood that was all over the image, and the gilded highlights and details on the molding in the upper-right echoed the shapes and textures on the handles of the swords.

In the end, I decided against this approach for the final image. I was primarily reacting to this shocking image of swords being plunged into a woman's chest, and the resulting pain and torment. These clever juxtapositions and commentaries seemed like distractions to the powerful imagery. I ultimately decided to get out of the way, crop it down, and let it stand on its own as much as I could.

Santissima Addolorata Image Design Log

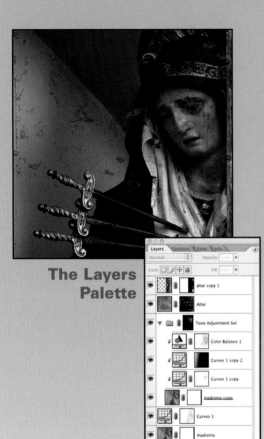

The Layers Palette

1. Open the *Madonna* file.

2. Select the Crop tool from the toolbox.

3. Press the Shift key and drag to draw a square crop from top of the Madonna's head to just below the swords. Double-click in the selection to apply the crop.

4. Select Curves from the Adjustment Layer pull-down menu at the bottom of the Layers palette.

5. In the Curves dialog box that appears, create three points, set to Input: 72, Output: 0; Input: 121, Output: 24; and Input: 207, Output: 130.

6. Set the Foreground color to black, select the Brush tool with a 200-pixel brush, and set the Opacity to 35%.

7. Paint the mask into the face area to lighten it.

8. Select New Layer Group from the Layers palette menu.

9. In the dialog box that appears, name the new group Tone Adjustment Set.

10. Select Duplicate layer in the Layers palette menu, and drag the Madonna layer to the Tone Adjustment Set group.

11. Select Curves from the Adjustment Layer pull-down menu in the Layers palette.

12. In the Curves dialog box that appears, create one point set to Input: 187, Output: 134.

13. Select Color Balance from the Adjustment Layer pull-down menu in the Layers palette.

14. In the Color Balance dialog box that appears, apply the following settings: Shadows -6, +5, +10; Midtones -4, +6, 0; and Highlights +23, +8, -6.

15. Highlight the Tone Adjustment Set in the Layers palette and Option-click (Alt-click in Windows) the Create Layer Mask icon.

16. Select a large feathered brush with white as the foreground color and an Opacity setting of 18%. Paint around the face to erase the mask.

17. Open the *Assumption of the Virgin* photo.

18. Select View, Show, Grid to turn on the grid overlay.

19. Double-click the Background layer of the *Assumption* photo. Click OK in the resulting dialog box to convert that layer from the Background layer to a standard layer.

20. Press ⌘-A (Ctrl-A in Windows) to select the entire image.

21. Select Edit, Transform, Warp to launch the Warp dialog box.

22. Drag the intersection point in the upper-left corner further to the left, correcting the distortion on the left column. Press Enter to apply the correction.

23. On the left edge, select the two middle points and Shift-drag them to the left to correct the perspective and line the left column up with the grid.

24. Select the lower-left point and drag it left and downward to align the bottom molding and the vertical column.

25. Select the modified *Assumption* image and copy/paste it into the composite image file as a new layer, independent of the Layer group.

26. Highlight the new layer name in the Layers palette and name it Altar.

27. Select the Move tool from the toolbox and Shift-drag the pasted layer into position.

28. Select the Wand tool from the toolbox, set the Tolerance to 44, and click the red garment of the figure in the lower-right corner.

29. Choose Select, Similar to select all the red in the image, based on the 44 Tolerance setting.

30. Option-click (Alt-click in Windows) the Add Layer Mask icon at the bottom of the Layers palette to hide everything except the red spots and brushstrokes.

31. Select Hard Light from the Blending Mode menu at the top of the Layers palette.

32. Drag the Altar layer to the New Layer icon at the bottom of the Layers palette to duplicate the layer.

33. Select the Move tool in the toolbox and Shift-drag the Altar Copy 1 layer to the right, until the red robe is in the lower-right corner.

34. Drag the Altar copy 1 layer to the New Layer icon at the bottom of the Layers palette, creating a new layer called Altar Copy 2.

35. Drag the Altar Copy 2 layer to the bottom of the layer stack in the Layers palette.

36. Highlight mask for Altar Copy 2 and click the Trash Can in the bottom right to delete the mask.

37. Select the Marquee tool from the toolbox and drag a 40-pixel-wide vertical stripe from the upper-right corner to the lower-right corner of the image.

38. Highlight the Madonna layer in the Layers palette.

39. Option-click (Alt-click in Windows) the Add Layer Mask icon at the bottom of the Layers palette to conceal the selected area, revealing the lower Altar layer.

40. Hide the visibility of the Madonna layer, revealing the Altar Copy 2 layer.

41. Select the Polygonal Lasso tool from the toolbox and click the corner points of the small molding area in the lower-right corner to select it.

42. Reactivate the visibility of the Madonna layer, click the Add Layer Mask icon at the bottom of the Layers palette to select it, and fill the selected area with black to add to the mask.

CHAPTER 11

PORTA ROSSA

DISCOVERING
EVOCATIVE DOORWAYS

The doors in Tuscany are extremely evocative and have long been the subject of photographers' attentions. I think part of the reason for this is the fact that the doors seem to collect and aggregate the marks, scrapes, and scuffs of history. They stand as immediate evidence that this is indeed a historic place where significant things have happened. And to be reminded of this historic legacy each time you enter a shop or dwelling is a very "Tuscan" way of integrating heritage into everyday life.

It's also interesting to consider the role that doors play in Tuscan culture. Yes, it's true that they sit on hinges and separate the inside from the outside, but Tuscany is full of even more of these separations. The cities themselves are a canvas of gray and ochre stone, separated from the lush landscape by gates that are nothing more than huge wooden doors. In addition, some of my most pleasant surprises in Tuscany have been to walk through an innocuous porta into an unexpectedly beautiful or significant environment.

And yet, despite all these contrasts and barriers, the region has an undeniably holistic consistency. The green landscapes, gray cities, and passionate people are interconnected in a way that belies the apparent discrepancies. Like two sides of the same coin, these individual characteristics combine to create a totality that is uniquely Tuscany.

Yellow Door

This door presented itself to me each morning as I left my Siena hotel. The first few times I noticed it, there was something that prevented me from setting up the shot; either the light wasn't quite right, or I was rushing to another site that I had somehow determined was more important. Finally, as I was returning to the hotel one afternoon, my patience (or perhaps procrastination) was rewarded. The sun was streaming into the narrow alley, bouncing off the opposite wall, creating a warm, diffuse glow. I set up my tripod and cable release and captured a bracketed set of images, ultimately settling on this one that was captured at 1/10 second at f/8.0.

The speck of blue string on the key, along with the subtle blue underpainting on the door really sets this image apart. In addition, I liked the horizontal and vertical divisions, along with the unique shapes that dictate the composition. As I was setting up, I was very careful to get the vertical and horizontal lines parallel with the edges of the frame. To make this happen, I had to keep the rear plane of the camera parallel to the door surface, ensuring that the lines wouldn't reveal any shifting perspective.

❶ Yellow Door
Nikon D2H
1/10 sec, f/8.0
Focal length 75mm

❷ *The cropped door.*

Building the Image

The first step in developing this composition was to get the right crop from the *Yellow Door* photo. The reality is that I could probably have created at least a half dozen good compositions from this one image because of the variety of image components and interesting details. I ultimately decided to go with a square format to stay consistent with the other images in this suite (as well as the overall format of this book).

So I selected the Crop tool from the toolbox and held down the Shift key to drag out crop areas that were restricted to a perfect square. As I explored the composition, I felt that I needed to maintain the triangular relationship between the thick vertical dividing line, the blue key, and the circular hole in the bottom center. The final crop emphasized this relationship while eliminating some of the information at the top of the photo (see Figure ❷).

Adding a Gradient Map

I selected Gradient Map from the Adjustment Layer pull-down menu in the Layers palette and double-clicked

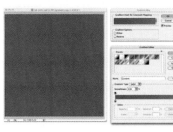

❸ *Adding the gradient.*

the gradient strip in the Gradient Map dialog box to launch the Gradient Editor. I was looking to veil the marks and scratches a bit, while integrating more dynamic, saturated color. In the Gradient Editor, I double-clicked the white color stop on the lower right of the gradient strip to launch the Color Picker, and selected a bright red (with RGB values of R158, G35, B35). I then double-clicked the black color stop on the lower left and selected a muted brown (with an RGB value of R96, G72, B48). This gradient created a strong color dominance while adding a graphic feel that was less photographic.

The result reduced the composition to a flat, low-contrast canvas (see Figure ❸). To add back some depth and a bit of visual tension, I added a mask to the Gradient Map layer and masked the areas over the dark crack between the two doors (see Figure ❹).

Bumping the Contrast

With the door crack at full contrast, the rest of the door scratches and scuffs felt a bit too muted. To bring back some of this lost detail, I added a Curves adjustment layer, applying an "S curve" to bring up contrast and saturation in the

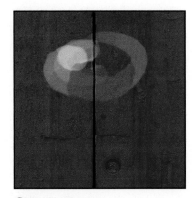

④ *Adding a Curves adjustment layer.*　⑤ *Setting the Opacity Jitter.*　⑥ *The final image.*

midtones area. I added two points to the curve, with values of Input: 77, Output: 55, and Input: 175, Output: 225. The resulting S-shaped curve lowers the shadow values and raises the highlights, creating a steeper curve in the midtones, which always translates to more contrast and detail (see Figure ⑤).

Crafting a Brush

At this point, I felt that I wanted to do some sort of drawing over the image to unify the composition. The muted door texture and the high-contrast black crack were working well together, but there didn't seem to be enough visual interest to complete the work.

As I thought about drawing over the image, I decided that I did not want to create some sort of textured brush that would emulate natural drawing materials, such as paper texture or charcoal markings. These kinds of simulated drawing marks always seem to fall short of their real-world counterparts in terms of their expressive qualities as well as their physicality. These results usually feel plastic or forced, lacking the gritty spontaneity of the real world.

I resisted the urge to create a textured brush and instead began to consider

what sort of marking would harmonize with the world of digital images. Because this world is full of photographs, gradients, and smooth tonal transitions, I decided to create a brush that had these same qualities.

I selected the Brush tool and chose Window, Brushes to launch the Brushes palette. In the Brush Tip Shape section of the dialog box, I set the Brush Tip diameter to 231 and left the other settings at their defaults. Having specified a large brush shape, I enabled the Shape Dynamics check box, set the Size Jitter slider to 40%, and set the Control drop-down menu to Pen Pressure because I was using a drawing tablet. The Pen Pressure setting would allow me to alter the size of the brush stroke based on the stylus pressure. (If you do not have a drawing tablet, set the Control menu to Off).

To define the smooth shape around the edge of the brush stroke, I enabled the Dual Brush check box and selected the Soft Round 200 brush from the brush thumbnails to serve as the secondary brush mask. (When the Show Tool Tips option is selected in the Preferences, General dialog box, hovering over a brush

thumbnail shows the brush name in a ToolTip). The Dual Brush option masks the primary brush shape through the secondary shape; in this case masking a 231-pixel brush through a 200-pixel mask, reducing and smoothing the stroke. Finally, I enabled the Other Dynamics check box and set the Opacity Jitter slider to 10%, with its associated Control menu set to Pen Pressure (see Figure ⑥). Finally, I saved the brush by choosing New Brush Preset from the Brushes palette menu and named my new brush Digital Brush in the dialog box that appeared.

Painting the Brush Strokes

To create a new layer to paint on, I clicked the New Layer button at the bottom of the Layers palette, double-clicked the layer's name and renamed the layer Drawing. I selected the Digital Brush I had just created from the Brush Preset Picker, and set the Opacity slider to 21% in the Options bar.

By drawing with gestural marks that increased in pressure, I was able to create an overlapping series of marks that took on a photographic feel, with varied opacity. It took several attempts to get the proper feel of the marks, erasing and undoing the results until I achieved the right balance (see Figure ⑦).

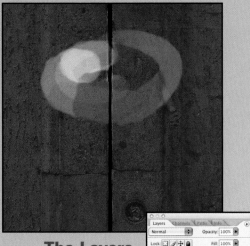

The Layers Palette

1. Open the *Yellow Door* photo.

2. Select the Crop tool from the toolbox.

3. Press the Shift key and drag to draw a square crop from the bottom to just below the top of the image, centering the composition on the vertical dark space between the doors. Double-click in the selection to apply the crop.

4. Select Gradient Map from the Adjustment Layer pull-down menu in the Layers palette.

5. Double-click the gradient strip in the Gradient Map dialog box to launch the Gradient Editor.

6. Double-click the white color stop beneath the gradient strip in the lower right to launch the Color Picker.

7. Select a bright-red color, entering the RGB values R158, G35, B35.

8. Double-click the black color stop beneath the gradient strip in the lower left to launch the Color Picker.

9. Select a brown color, entering the RGB values R96, G72, B48.

10. Highlight the mask icon in the Gradient Map layer.

11. Select the Brush tool from the toolbox with a 20-pixel soft brush, and set the foreground color to black.

12. Click once at the top of the dark strip between the doors. Hold down the Shift key and click again at the bottom of the dark strip, creating a vertical linear mask.

13. Touch up any irregularities in the mask shape as necessary.

14. Select Curves from the Adjustment Layer pull-down menu in the Layers palette. Double-click the layer name and rename it Curves Layer.

15. Add two points to the curve, with values of Input: 77, Output: 55, and Input: 175, Output: 225.

16. Choose Window, Brushes to launch the Brushes palette.

17. Click in the Brush Tip Shape section on the left side of the dialog box and set the Brush Tip diameter to 231. Leave the other settings at their defaults.

18. Enable the Shape Dynamics check box to activate this section. Set the Size Jitter slider to 40% and set its associated Control menu to Pen Pressure (ignore this setting if you're not using a drawing tablet).

19. Enable the Dual Brush check box to activate this section. Select the Soft Round 200 brush from the brush thumbnails.

20. Enable the Other Dynamics check box to activate this section. Set the Opacity Jitter slider to 10% and set its associated Control menu to Pen Pressure (ignore this setting if you're not using a drawing tablet).

21. Select New Brush Preset from the Brushes palette menu and name the brush you've just created Digital Brush in the dialog box that appears. Click OK to save the brush.

22. Click the Create New Layer button in the Layers palette to create a new layer. In the dialog box that appears, name the new layer Drawing.

23. Select the Brush tool from the toolbox and choose the Digital Brush preset from the Brush Preset Picker.

24. In the Options bar, set the Opacity slider to 21%.

25. Draw with gestural marks that increase in pressure. Undo or erase as necessary until you achieve the desired result.

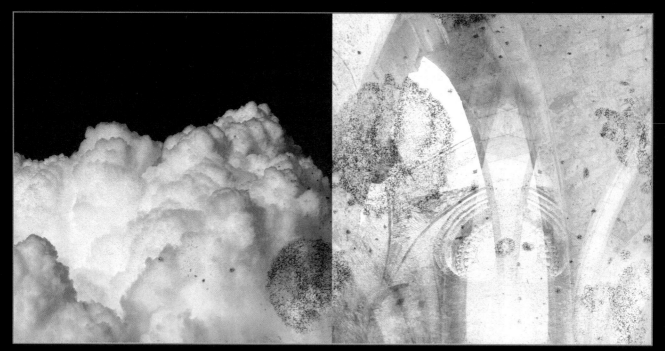

Molecola Sogni

MOLECOLA SOGNI

TOWARD
A WEIGHTLESS HISTORY

A Tuscan sky in summer is deep blue, with weightless, billowing clouds that create an effortless and dramatic backdrop. The sky contrasts with historic landscapes, cities, and monuments that sit solid and stoic, having endured generations of upheaval and change. It's as if the skies are constantly changing and evolving in a counterpoint to the landmarks, which seem unchanging and immovable.

As I started to define the direction for Molecola Sogni, I began to explore a reversal. What if the skies were fixed and immovable, and the buildings and cities were ethereal and transient? I began to push the archway photo of San Galgano from unflinching stone to shimmering weightlessness. The billowing clouds took on a heavy, gritty form beneath an ink-black sky, as if the clouds had been carved from stone and left to sit in one of the polluted city squares of Rome or Florence.

The comparison begs the basic question of what is unchanging and what is temporal. We're conditioned to see the earth's natural elements as enduring and the constructs of men as crumbling and entropic. And yet as I stood in San Galgano and so many other historic sites in Tuscany, I couldn't help but sense the residue of the countless individuals who walked within these walls. How did they live? What were they afraid of? What brought them peace? From there, it's a small jump to consider the enduring similarities: Were their desires the same as mine? These desires, longings, and hopes endure in a way that clouds and other molecular elements could never dream of—that is, if molecules could dream.

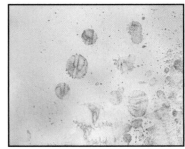

❶ Cathedral
Nikon D2H
1/180 sec, f/11
-1.33 EV
Focal length 36mm

❷ Campo Sky
Nikon D2H
1/320 sec, f/8.5
Focal length 120mm

❸ Drips Scan
Nikon D2H
1/10 sec, f/8.0
Focal length 75mm

Cathedral

The cathedral ruins at San Galgano in southwestern Tuscany are one of the few examples of gothic architecture in Italy. The amazing feature of this site is the open ceiling created by the long-departed wooden roof. The sky and clouds juxtaposed against the stone arches provided the initial exploration for this image. I set up my tripod and framed the shot, bracketing with the exposure compensation settings, finally selecting this frame which was shot at -1.33.

Campo Sky

Standing in the middle of Siena's main square, known as the Campo, was amazing. The entire region was preparing for the horse race known as the Palio. People were everywhere, the square was buzzing with activity...and yet I couldn't help but be amused as a big lazy cloud drifted by a tower that has stood firm and silent for more than 500 years. The abundance of light made it easy to hand-hold the shot, and I was careful to hold the verticality of the building, aligning it with the edges of the frame.

Drips Scan

I know lots of people who stubbornly try to create all of their effects within the computer, with no help from the atom-based world. I'm not one of those people. When I decided that I wanted to integrate drips and splatters into the Tuscany images, I got out some black ink, splattered some art paper, and ran them through the scanner. This image was transferred to paper through an intaglio press, which resulted in the light, ghosted image.

④ *Reduce to grayscale.*

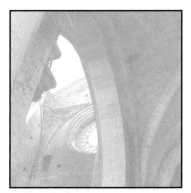

⑤ *Crop and reduce opacity.*

⑥ *Duplicate cathedral layers.*

Building the Image

The *Molecola Sogni* image starts out with a photo taken at San Galgano in southwestern Tuscany. In looking at the photo, I decided that the color was flat and a bit distracting. There were no dynamic or impactful colors; rather, it held an overall brown-gray patina. I selected the thumbnail in Bridge and then chose Open, Open in Camera Raw to launch the Camera Raw dialog box. (If using Photoshop CS or earlier versions, launch the file from the File Browser, which automatically opens in the Camera Raw dialog box).

In the Settings section, under the Adjust tab, I lightened the overall exposure for this image, moving the Exposure slider control to +2.30. This really opened up the shadow areas under the arches, flattened the sky to almost white, and brought up the details in the brick wall beneath the rose window. I set the Shadows slider to +6 to deepen the shadows to a pure black, and I set the Brightness to +94 and Contrast to +36. Finally, I set the Saturation slider to -100 to desaturate the color completely, reducing the image to black and white.

Switching to the Detail tab of the Camera Raw dialog box, I increased the Sharpness slider to 59, set Luminance Smoothing to 12, and finally clicked the Open button to open the photo in Photoshop (see Figure ④).

Cropping and Fading

When the modified photo opened, I selected the Crop tool and drew a square crop from the upper-left corner, holding down the Shift key to constrain the crop proportion to a square. I drew the crop to just above the ledge that buttressed the arches, showing a small piece of black archway in the lower-right corner. I double-clicked the crop to accept it.

I double-clicked the word *Background* on the Background layer to highlight it, and renamed the layer Cathedral 30%. Then I set the Opacity slider in the Layers palette to 30% to lighten the image. To introduce more translucency to the image, I clicked the Create New Layer icon at the bottom of the Layers palette and dragged the new layer to the bottom of the layers stack. I filled this new layer with white by selecting the Paintbucket, setting the foreground swatch in the toolbox to white, and

clicking in the image window (see Figure ⑥).

At this point, I had already decided to create a diptych, so I added additional canvas: I chose Image, Canvas Size and set the Width value to 2,967 pixels, clicked the right-top anchor square, and then clicked OK.

Multiple Cathedrals

To add complexity to the image, I dragged the Cathedral layer to the Create New Layer icon in the Layers palette, creating a duplicate layer. After setting the new layer's Opacity slider to 24%, I renamed the layer Cathedral 24%. To complete this layer, I added a layer mask and masked the lower-right corner, keeping it light and ethereal.

I duplicated the Cathedral 30% layer a second time and set the layer's blending mode to Soft Light. Then I selected Edit, Transform, Flip Horizontal to flip the layer, and used the Move tool to drag the layer to align with the cathedral images beneath it, placing it just above the Cathedral 24% layer. I added another layer mask and masked out the right side of the cathedral image (see Figure ⑥).

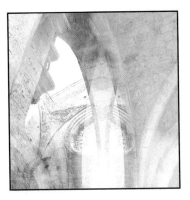
❼ *Add a Curves adjustment layer.*

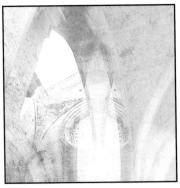
❽ *Mask the ledge.*

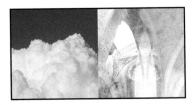
❾ *Crop to the clouds.*

Adding a Curve

The next step in preparing the cathedral section of the final diptych was to lighten the overall image using a Curves adjustment layer. After selecting Curves from the Adjustment Layer menu in the Layers palette, I added three data points: Input: 33, Output: 35; Input: 110, Output: 136; and Input: 202, Output: 241.

I initially applied this correction because I thought the tonal information in the stonework was flat, lacking in contrast and detail. This slight S-curve deepened the shadows a bit and lightened the midtones and highlight areas. An unexpected result of this adjustment was the added emphasis on the overlapping arch layers, which created an open, ethereal atmosphere (see Figure ❼).

Masking the Ledge

Now that the image was brighter, I started looking for other ways to emphasize the atmospheric patina

that was beginning to assert itself. In this particular example, I noticed the ledge that was jutting out into the white space in the upper-left of the composition. I felt it was intrusive and disruptive to the composition, and I wanted to find a way to interject a bit more white. The area I wanted to add to was white and flat. In addition, the area I wanted to remove was geometric and linear. These characteristics made the following edit pretty easy to achieve.

I selected the Polygonal Lasso tool and clicked at the point where the ledge shape juts into the white sky. I then clicked next to the column and continued clicking to outline the ledge shape. When the shape was selected, I clicked the Create New Layer button at the bottom of the Layers palette to add a new layer, just above the Curves 1 layer. I named the layer Ledge Mask in the dialog box that appeared and clicked OK. I set the foreground color to white and selected the Paintbucket tool. After checking the Options bar

to see that Foreground was selected in the Source pull-down menu and that the All Layers check box was disabled, I clicked in the active selection to fill it with white, masking the ledge in the layers beneath it (see Figure ❽).

Adding Clouds

To play off the bright, misty cathedral composition, I went looking for some clouds to tie into the cathedral image. The *Campo Clouds* photo that I ended up with featured bright, billowy clouds that rose into a deep blue sky. I cropped the photo to remove the bell tower and focused only on the clouds and sky, which I pasted into the left side of the composition (see Figure ❾).

Adding a Gradient Map

The clouds photo was solid, but it was far from harmonious with the right panel. The color was distracting, and the blue tint in the clouds looked a bit unnatural. Because the black-and-white color palette was

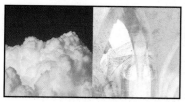  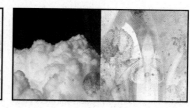

⑩ *Add a gradient map.*　　　⑪ *Add the drips.*　　　⑫ *The final image.*

working so well on the right side, it was a natural move to reduce the clouds on the left to black and white. With black and white set as my foreground and background colors, I selected the Gradient Map option from the Adjustment Layer menu in the Layers palette and clicked OK in the Gradient Map dialog box. I double-clicked the Gradient Map name in the Layers palette to select it and renamed the layer B&W Gradient Map.

Because the Gradient Map layer tended to darken the right side of the composition, I restricted the correction to only the clouds photo. To do this, I went to the Layers palette and positioned the cursor on the line between the Clouds layer and the B&W Gradient Map layer. Pressing the Option key (Alt key in Windows) with the mouse pointer in this position changes it to the Clipping Mask icon. Click to create a clipping mask, constraining the gradient map effect to only the Clouds layer (see Figure ⑩).

Adding Drips

The tonal range was now harmonious, but the overall composition felt a bit too clean and crisp. The two panels were still not harmonizing as much as I wanted, and I felt the need to mess them up a bit. To do this, I pasted a scan of some ink drips into the composition and dragged it into position so that two circular drips began to resonate with the rose window on the right (see Figure ⑪).

Inverting Drips

Now came the task of getting rid of the white substrate of the paper so that the black drips appeared to be splattered directly on the image. I tried the Darken blending mode but I lost the drips over parts of the Clouds layer. The Overlay mode lightened the underlying image too much. I finally got things to work by selecting Image, Adjustments, Invert to reverse the Drips layer and setting

the layer's blending mode to Difference.

This arrangement brought out the fibers and all the black pigmentation of the drips scan while preserving the tonality of the underlying layers. The entire composition felt more cohesive as well.

Having said that, a few of the drips were a bit distracting and needed to be masked out. Specifically, the gritty texture over the clouds in the lower-left area was a bit too heavy. With the Drips layer active, I clicked the Add Layer Mask button to create the mask. I selected the Brush tool with black as the foreground color and the Opacity slider in the Options bar set to 24%. I painted the mask in the clouds area to fade out the gritty texture and complete the image (see Figure ⑫).

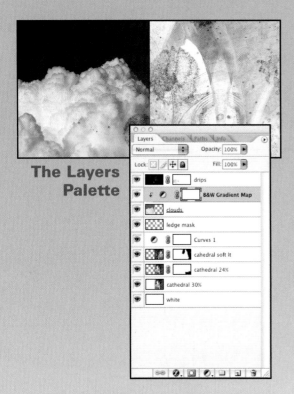

The Layers Palette

1. Open Adobe Bridge.

2. Navigate to San Galgano photo and highlight it.

3. Select Open, Open in Camera Raw to launch the Camera Raw dialog box.

4. On the Adjust tab in the Settings section, move the Exposure slider control to +2.30.

5. Set the Shadows slider to +6 to deepen the shadows to a pure black.

6. Set the Brightness slider to 94, the Contrast slider to +36, and the Saturation slider to -100 to desaturate the image completely.

7. Click the Detail tab in the Camera Raw dialog box.

8. Increase the Sharpness slider to 59, set Luminance Smoothing to 12, and click the Open button to open the adjusted photo in Photoshop.

9. Select the Crop tool and draw a square crop from the upper-left corner, holding down the Shift key to constrain the crop proportion to a square.

10. Double-click the crop to apply it.

11. Double-click the word *Background* in the Background layer to highlight it; rename the layer Cathedral 30%.

12. Set the Opacity slider in the Layers palette to 30%.

13. Click the Create New Layer icon at the bottom of the Layers palette and drag the new layer to the bottom of the layers stack.

14. Fill the new layer with white by selecting the Paintbucket tool, setting the foreground color to white, and clicking in the image window.

15. Double-click the new layer's title to highlight it and rename the layer White.

16. Choose Image, Canvas Size to launch the Canvas Size dialog box.

17. Set the Width value to 2,967 pixels (200%), click the right-top anchor square, and click OK.

18. Drag the Cathedral 30% layer to the Create New Layer icon in the Layers palette to create a duplicate layer.

19. Set the duplicate layer's Opacity slider to 24%. Then click the *Cathedral 30% Copy* text to highlight it and rename the layer Cathedral 24%.

20. Click the Add Layer Mask icon to add a mask to the Cathedral 24% layer.

21. Select the Brush tool with a 200-pixel brush, make black the foreground color, and set Opacity to 19%. Brush in the layer mask in the lower-right corner to lighten and blend the layers.

22. Drag the Cathedral 30% layer to the Create New Layer icon in the layers palette, creating another duplicate layer.

23. Set the layer's blending mode to Soft Light. Then double-click the layer's title and rename the layer Cathedral Soft Lt.

24. Choose Edit, Transform, Flip Horizontal to flip the Cathedral Soft Lt layer; use the Move tool to drag the layer to align with the cathedral images beneath it.

25. Click the Add Layer Mask icon to add a mask to the Cathedral Soft Lt layer.

26. Select the Brush tool with a 200-pixel brush, make black the foreground color, and set Opacity to 19%. Brush in the layer mask on the right side of the layer to lighten and blend the layers.

27. Select Curves from the Adjustment Layer pull-down menu in the Layers palette.

28. In the Curves dialog box that appears, add three data points to the curve: Input: 33, Output: 35; Input: 110, Output: 136; and Input: 202, Output: 241.

29. Select the Polygonal Lasso tool and click at the point where the ledge shape juts into the white sky. Continue clicking to outline the ledge shape as a selection.

30. Click the Add New Layer button at the bottom of the Layers palette to add a new layer. Name the layer Ledge Mask in the dialog box that appears and click OK.

31. Set the foreground color to white and select the Paintbucket tool.

32. Click in the active selection to fill it with white, masking the ledge in the layers beneath it.

33. Open the *Campo Clouds* file.

34. Select the Crop tool and Shift-drag to draw a square crop selection that selects only the clouds in the photo. Double-click to crop the image.

35. Copy the cropped photo and paste it into the composite. Highlight the new layer and rename it Clouds.

36. Select the Move tool and drag the Clouds layer into position on the left side of the composition.

37. Set the foreground and background colors to black and white.

38. Select the Gradient Map option from the Adjustment Layer menu at the bottom of the Layers palette; click OK in the Gradient Map dialog box.

39. Double-click the text *Gradient Map* in the Layers palette to select it and rename the layer B&W Gradient Map.

40. Position the mouse pointer on the line between the Clouds layer and the B&W Gradient Map layer. Option-click (Alt-click in Windows) to create a clipping mask.

41. Open the *Drips* file.

42. Copy the *Drips* file and paste into the composite. Highlight the new layer and rename it Drips.

43. Choose Image, Adjustments, Invert to reverse the Drips layer.

44. Set the Drips layer blending mode to Difference.

45. With the Drips layer active, click the Add Layer Mask icon at the bottom of the Layers palette to create a mask.

46. Select the Brush tool with black as the foreground color and the Opacity slider in the Options bar set to 24%.

47. Paint the mask in the clouds area in the lower-left corner to fade out the gritty texture from the Drips layer and complete the image.

Una Passione Perfetta
©2004 Daniel Giordan

CHAPTER 13

UNA PASSIONE PERFETTA

CREATING
DYNAMIC PRECISION

This image began with the extensive, multifaceted detail of the Florentine Church of Santa Maria Del Fiore, better known as the Duomo. It's an amazing structure, inlaid with all manner of green and coral marble, granite, and other cut stone, and dotted with perhaps more statuary than the eye can consciously consider. It's an overwhelming sight whose beauty and intricate details are almost unimaginable.

This detailed grid is contrasted with a scene from the ruins at San Galgano, whose details have been blunted and stripped away by time (along with the roof I might add), leaving a shell of the former building. And yet this shell still reflects the core spirit and passionate aesthetic of Tuscan art and architecture. With the ornate, man-made details worn smooth, San Galgano seems organic and natural. It's not about what some really talented guy did, it's more about how this structure reflects universal truths about geometry, art, and the human spirit.

And so the left side of the image bows inward, pressing emotionally and emphatically in on the viewers as they try to make their way through the passage. The experience is passionate, dynamic, perhaps even romantic. On the right, the image shows the technique and precision of Renaissance craftsmen, as the pattern comes through, providing structure and a framework. The name of this piece means "A Perfect Passion," and so it is that the best of these artists—the ones like Raphael and Michaelangelo—were able to walk that razor's edge between expression and precision, articulating a detailed vision of passionate specificity.

SOURCE
PHOTOS

① **Duomo Scaffold**
Nikon D2H
EV +.33
1/250 sec, f/4
Focal length 36mm

② **San Galgano 5**
Nikon D2H
1/80 sec, f/7.1
Focal length 18mm

❶

❷

Duomo Scaffold

It's no secret that air pollution and general tourist traffic are eroding many of Europe's most prominent landmarks. This has resulted in numerous restoration efforts in Tuscany that spare no expense to erase hundreds of years of dirt and grime. Although it's easy to applaud these efforts, it not necessarily easy to swallow when you have just a few days in Florence and your majestic view of the Duomo is shrouded in a lattice of steel pipes.

When I saw that the restoration wasn't going to allow me to take any traditional images of Florence's famous cathedral, I shifted gears and looked for an alternative composition. I was thankful that the skies were gray and overcast on that day, which minimized the shadows that were cast and saturated the colors. I set up my tripod and composed a photo that integrated the scaffolding with the façade of the building itself. After shooting a few dozen images like this, I caught this view as I was walking away and glanced over my shoulder for one last look. I didn't bother to set up the tripod, I just hand-held it and shot a bracketed set of images. This one used a +.33 EV compensation setting, which brought out the color definition just a bit more than the others.

San Galgano 5

By now you're getting the sense that San Galgano was one of my favorite landmarks in Tuscany (you've noticed that it's made several appearances in the images). This is one of the last photos I shot, taken just minutes before I was leaving. I had taken perhaps a few hundred photos that were cropped and composed more abstractly or dramatically, and I was making one more pass through the structure, capturing photos that were more documentary in nature. Similar to the *Duomo Scaffold* photo above, this was another quick-capture, hand-held shot that I selected because of its strong, intuitive composition.

❸ *Correct the perspective.*

Building the Image

This image began with explorations of the *Duomo Scaffold* photo. I was drawn to the strong geometric patterning and the horizontal and vertical lines. I wanted to straighten the perspective so that the lines ran parallel to the edges of the frame and so that the image appeared square to the viewer.

In Chapter 7, "Abbianza," I had a similar situation with the *Assumption of the Virgin* altarpiece photo. In that example, I used the Warp command to alter the perspective, but in this instance I used a simpler method. I pressed ⌘-A (Ctrl-A in Windows) to select the entire image, and then choose View, Show, Grid to display a grid overlay that would assist me with the alignment.

I then chose Edit, Transform, Distort. This command places a selection handle at each corner of the image, which I can then drag in any direction in or out of the image, independently of the other handles. I always drag the image window out as wide as possible when I do this,

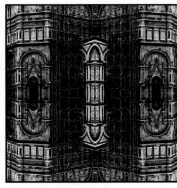

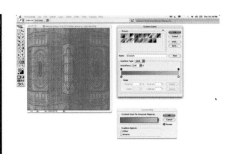

❹ *Crop and reduce opacity.* **❺** *Flip the pattern twice.* **❻** *Add Gradient Map layer.*

and zoom out of the photo if necessary (⌘--, Ctrl-- in Windows) so that there is enough gray border in which I can manipulate the image handles. I slightly pulled each top corner handle away from the image area to straighten the image vertically. I wasn't too concerned with the horizontal orientation because of all of the shifting planes and beveled surfaces, so I just left those as-is and double-clicked in the image area to apply the correction (see Figure **❸**).

Cropping and Setting Canvas

With the perspective corrected, I started looking for an interesting section of the photo to select as a crop. I knew I wanted to maintain the square format, so I selected the Crop tool from the toolbox and held down the Shift key to constrain the selection shape to a square. I dragged the selection around the scaffolding and included the main portal on the left, all the way to the right edge.

I then clicked the Background color swatch and selected black from the Color Picker to set the background color. I chose Image, Canvas Size

and set the width to 3384 pixels and the height to 3264 pixels (I used these values because of the geometry of the original image and how it doubles). I positioned the anchor square in the upper-left corner of the grid, set the canvas extension color to Background, and clicked OK to enlarge the canvas and fill it with black. I finished the layer by double-clicking its name in the Layers palette and naming the layer Cropped Image (see Figure **❹**).

Flipping the Pattern

I selected the Marquee tool and dragged a selection around the cropped photo pattern. To make sure that the selection was "pixel perfect," I double-clicked the Zoom tool to set the magnification to 100% and checked to see that the entire image was selected, excluding the black background. I then copied and pasted the image to duplicate the pattern on a separate layer. I chose Image, Transform, Flip Vertical to invert the pattern and then selected the Move tool and dragged the flipped layer beneath the original

pattern, creating a mirror image. I named this new layer Vert Flip.

I then drew another selection that surrounded both the original and the flipped pattern images, and selected Edit, Copy Merged. I pasted the copied selection to a new layer and chose Image, Transform, Flip Horizontal. I dragged the flipped image to the right to complete the grid pattern, assigning the name Horiz Flip to the newest layer (see Figure **❺**).

Applying a Gradient Mask

Now *this* is an interesting pattern! It's detailed and symmetrical, yet with some nuance. I found the color a bit distracting though, the blue and teal were an unexpected harmony that might have worked in other instances. I decided to add a Gradient Map layer to convert all of the color diversity to a smooth gradient transition.

I added a Gradient Map layer and clicked the gradient strip in the Gradient Map dialog box to launch the Gradient Editor. I clicked the left color stop to launch the Color Picker and chose a rust color with an RGB value of

7 *Add* San Galgano 5 *to the composite.*

8 *Add Linear Light blending mode.*

9 *Turn off the black layer.*

R130, G54, B3. I repeated the process with the right color stop, selecting a tan color with a value of R206, G190, B124 (see Figure **6**). After clicking OK to apply the gradient, I double-clicked the layer name in the Layers palette and named the layer Brown Gradient.

Adding San Galgano 5

At first glance, the *San Galgano 5* photo didn't feel like it was going to work with the composite. It has a vertical composition that didn't seem to relate at all to the square frame and detailed texture of the working composition. But as I thought about it and explored a few options, I liked the way the square format allowed me to place the right column of the *San Galgano 5* photo squarely in the lower-right corner of the pattern image, anchoring the entire right side. This arrangement would focus more emphasis on the arches and the doorway. I used the Rectangular Marquee tool from the toolbox and held down the Shift key to draw a square selection around the arches

and doorway. I copied the selection and pasted it into the composition.

The cropped *San Galgano 5* photo pasted into the composite at only about 25% of the composition's size, so I decided to scale it up. Although I could have scaled the pattern down to fit the *San Galgano 5* photo, I felt that the resolution held up enough, especially because there wasn't that much critical detail in the *San Galgano 5* photo. I selected Photoshop, Preferences, General (in Windows, choose Edit, Preferences, General) to launch the Preferences dialog box, and chose Bicubic Smoother from the Interpolation Method pull-down menu. This setting smoothes the details and reduces pixelization when scaling up an image. I clicked OK and then chose Edit, Free Transform. I dragged the *San Galgano 5* photo to the upper-left corner of the composite and dragged the lower-right handle out to the lower-right corner of the composition. Double-clicking in the image layer applied the transformation (see Figure **7**).

Integrating the Pattern

To integrate the underlying pattern with the *San Galgano 5* photo, I began trying out some blending modes. After considering various settings and experimenting with the Opacity slider, I set the blending mode to Linear Light and left the Opacity at 100%. With all layers turned on, the result was a high-contrast infusion of pattern and warmth (see Figure **8**).

The image now had a very illustrational feel, but it was loosing the uniqueness of this place. This could almost have been an industrial building or a tunnel. The color and texture were overshadowing the specificity created by the architecture.

After analyzing the layer structure, I realized that all the black in the Cropped Image layer (the original square of the Duomo facade) was creating much of the color distortion. I turned off the Cropped Image layer as well as the Vert Flip layer to tone things down. The result was a gently infused pattern on the right

⑩ *Warp the left side.*

⑪ *The final image.*

side that stopped around the center of the composition (see Figure **⑨**).

Adding Distortion

At this point, I'd love to tell you that I had this epiphany of genius that told me to distort the left side of the image to create the imbalance and juxtaposition shown in the final image. Unfortunately (or perhaps fortunately), this was not the case. In reality, I was in the process of exploring other options, and getting uninspired results, when someone posted a thread on the Photoshop CS2 beta message boards asking what people thought about the new Warp command.

Adobe maintains message boards for beta testers to ask questions and to facilitate a dialog between the software engineers and the testers, and I was obviously one of the beta team testers. I had the composite open as I was reading the question, so I highlighted the San Galgano 5 layer and selected Edit, Transform, Warp to launch the Warp grid over the

image, and I began to explore. After getting the hang of things, I backed out of the dialog box just long enough to select the left half of the image and then relaunched the Warp tool.

When you launch the Warp dialog box, a grid is superimposed over the image or selected area (in this case, the left side of the image). The grid is divided vertically and horizontally into three sections by two dividing lines. A warp distortion can be applied by dragging any intersection points of the grid in any direction. In addition, the outside corner points of the grid can be skewed by dragging the handles, just as you would with a Bezier Curve handle in a vector program.

I dragged the upper-right grid intersection down and slightly right, tweaking the lower and upper-right handles slightly to bow the distortion in the right side of the image. I nudged the grid a bit more, as shown in Figure **⑩**, to twist and bow the right wall as it recedes into

the image at the upper-left of the central arch. I double-clicked in the grid area to apply the distortion.

One of the things I found about the Warp tool was that I could drag the grid mesh quickly to create sweeping gestural distortions that felt fluid and natural. If I got too precise or tight with my edits, the warp seemed to loose much of its spontaneity; then I would quickly apply and undo the result and just start over.

Lightening the Pattern

The final edits in this image were simple. I decided that the pattern on the right side of the image was a bit too strong. To tone it down a bit, I selected the Horiz Flip layer and reduced its Opacity setting to 48%. I also selected the Dodge tool with the range set to Highlights and the exposure set to 11%. With a 300-pixel brush, I lightened the areas around the distorted left arch to add a diffuse glow to the distortion (see Figure **⑪**).

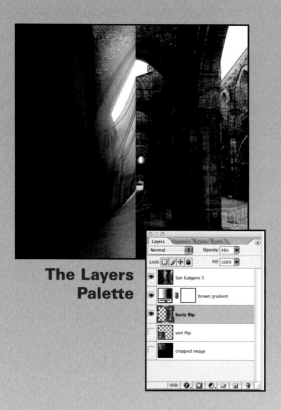

**The Layers
Palette**

1. Open the *Duomo Scaffold* photo.

2. Press ⌘-A (Ctrl-A in Windows) to select the entire image.

3. Choose View, Show, Grid to display the grid overlay.

4. Select Edit, Transform, Distort.

5. Drag the image window out as wide as possible and zoom out of the photo if necessary (press ⌘-- or Ctrl-- in Windows) so that there is enough gray border around the image to manipulate the image handles.

6. Pull each top-corner handle away from the image area to straighten the image vertically.

7. Select the Crop tool from the toolbox and press the Shift key as you're dragging to constrain the crop area to a square.

8. Drag the crop selection around the scaffolding to include the main portal on the left, all the way to the right edge of the photo.

9. Click the Background color swatch and select black from the Color Picker to set the background color.

10. Choose Image, Canvas Size and set the width to 3384 pixels and the height to 3264 pixels.

11. Position the anchor square in the upper-left corner of the grid and click OK to enlarge the canvas and fill it with black.

12. Double-click the layer name and rename the layer Cropped Image.

13. Select the Marquee tool and drag a selection around the cropped photo pattern.

14. Copy and paste the selected photo to duplicate the pattern on a separate layer.

15. Choose Edit, Transform, Flip Vertical to invert the pattern.

16. Select the Move tool and drag the pasted layer vertically below the original pattern, creating a mirror image.

17. Double-click the layer name and rename the layer Vert Flip.

18. Select the Marquee tool and drag a selection around the Vert Flip and Cropped Image layers.

19. Select Edit, Copy Merged, and paste the selection to duplicate the pattern on a separate layer.

20. Choose Edit, Transform, Flip Horizontal to flip the pattern.

21. Select the Move tool and drag the pasted layer horizontally to the right of the original pattern, creating a mirror image.

22. Double-click the layer name and rename the layer Horiz Flip.

23. Select Gradient Map from the Adjustment Layer pull-down menu in the Layers palette.

24. Click the gradient strip in the Gradient Map dialog box to launch the Gradient Editor.

25. Double-click the left color stop to launch the Color Picker and choose a rust color with an RGB value of R130, G54, B3. Repeat the process with the right color stop, selecting a tan color with a value of R206, G190, B124.

26. Click OK to apply the gradient.

27. Double-click the layer name and rename the layer Brown Gradient.

28. Open the file *San Galgano 5*.

29. Select the Rectangular Marquee tool from the toolbox and draw a square selection around the arches and doorway.

30. Copy the selection and paste it into the pattern composition.

31. Choose Photoshop, Preferences, General to launch the Preferences dialog box (in Windows, choose Edit,

Preferences, General) and select Bicubic Smoother from the Interpolation Method pull-down menu. Click OK to close the dialog box.

32. Choose Image, Free Transform and drag the cropped San Galgano 5 photo to the upper-left corner of the composite. Then drag its lower-right handle out to the lower-right corner of the composition.

33. Double-click in the image area to apply the transformation.

34. Double-click the layer name and rename the layer San Galgano 5.

35. Select Linear light from the blending modes menu in the Layers palette.

36. In the Layers palette, turn off visibility for the Cropped Image and Vert Flip layers.

37. Choose the Rectangular Marquee from the toolbox and drag a selection vertically around the left side of the composite.

38. Choose Edit, Transform, Warp to load the warp grid over the selected area.

39. Drag the upper-right grid intersection down and slightly left, pulling the lower- and upper-right handles out slightly to bow the distortion in the lower part of the image.

40. Drag the grid intersection points to twist and bow the right wall as it recedes into the image at the upper-left corner of the central arch.

41. Double-click in the grid area to apply the distortion.

42. Select the Horiz Flip layer and reduce the layer's Opacity to 48%.

43. Select the Dodge tool and set the range to Highlights and the Exposure to 11%. Choose a 300-pixel brush and lighten the areas around the distorted left arch in the San Galgano 5 layer.

Parte Interna

PARTE INTERNA

BUILDING
VISUAL TENSION

The simplistic duality of the Punto design (refer to Chapter 9, "Punto") has been blown apart in Parte Interna. The place to sit and get your bearings has been veiled and obscured, and we're forced to visually make our way through the layers and objects in an effort to find our own equilibrium.

Not only has the visual space gotten more complex, the design also features similar textured and tonal areas that resonate with each other. The white of the sun cast through the windows echoes the white of the grassy area on the lower right. The gray of the drips echoes the gray of the texture on the left side. And the black asserts itself strongly, from the tree trunk silhouettes to the ambiguous center, to the dark shadows on the right, behind the bench. These tones are woven together and play off each other quite well. There are textural references as well: The texture of the wall behind the bench echoes the texture of the drips as well as the cloudy tree texture in the upper right.

As your eye makes its way through the composition, it's constantly pulled from one area to the next. It goes left to right, but it also goes front to back, creating a visual tension that never quite resolves itself. The title Parte Interna means "inner part," and it refers to the way the image pulls viewers into itself and engages them in the act of looking, seeing, and exploring.

Orcia Landscape

This is the same photo used in the *Punto* image from Chapter 9, a landscape taken in the Orcia valley. The morning light and saturated colors set this photo apart, as does the composition and division of space.

Galgano Bench

This is another photo used in the *Punto* composition; a bench in a chapel on the grounds of San Galgano. I think the simplicity and boldness of shapes helped make this a useful photo in my compositing and montage efforts.

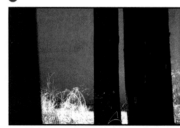

Sant Olivetto Woods

The brilliant light of the Tuscany region really made this photo work. The sun was strong and directional, breaking through a bank of foliage, backlighting the main trees. This cast a strong reflected light on the subject tree, bringing out details while maintaining an interesting contrast ratio.

Pink Trees

This photo was all about the pink wall. It was shot in the same area as the *Sant Olivetto* photo, basking in the same directional light. I set the exposure to emphasize and saturate the wall, intentionally overexposing and blowing out the grass. The strong color, bold stripes of the trees, and bright grass give this photo an abstract quality.

Drips2

I used a scanned image in the *Molecola Sogni* image similar to this one. I created random ink drips on paper and transferred them using an intaglio printing press to another sheet. The resulting image was scanned on a flatbed scanner to create this digital file.

❻ *Create texture.*

❼ *Add the bench.*

Building the Image

It's interesting that this image began as a variation of the *Punto* image discussed in Chapter 9, yet feels so different. Because there is some degree of redundancy between the two chapters regarding how the image was built, I'll be a bit more succinct in certain areas of this chapter. Full details are spelled out in the Image Log in the *Punto* chapter.

Cropping and Optimizing

I opened the *Orcia Landscape* photo and sharpened it using the High Pass filter. To do this, I dragged the Background layer to the New Layer icon in the Layers palette to create a copy. I then chose Filter, Other, High Pass, set the Radius slider to 3.6 pixels, and clicked OK to apply the effect. I set the blending mode for the Background Copy layer to Overlay to complete the sharpening effect. Then I chose Merge Down from the Layers palette menu to simplify the layer stack. To complete the effect, I cropped the image's vertical orientation to a

square and changed the layer name to Landscape.

To change the image into a flat texture, I started by duplicating the Landscape layer: I dragged the Landscape layer to the New Layer icon in the Layers palette, creating a new layer called Landscape Copy. I renamed the new layer Flipped Landscape, and with that layer still active, I chose Edit, Transform, Flip Vertical to flip the layer upside down, and selected Darken from the Blending Modes pop-up menu. The Darken blending mode looks at the overlapping pixels and displays only the darker of the two. In this case, the blending mode hides the sky by displaying the darker tree texture instead (see Figure ❻).

Adding the Bench

I found the *Galgano Bench* photo and cropped it to the square format to fit the composition. After doubling the canvas size in the main image to create the horizontal format, I copied the cropped bench photo and pasted it into the

composition, dragging it to the right side. I then set the Bench layer's blending mode to Hard Light, which created deep shadows and high contrast (see Figure ❼).

Optimizing Pink Trees

The next step was to optimize the *Pink Trees* photo and prepare it for integration into the main image. I started by applying an Unsharp Mask filter to bring back a bit more detail.

Although the strong saturated color was working well for the photo on its own, I was concerned that it would be a bit too intense and saccharine when added to the composition. Specifically, I felt that the bright greens and yellows in the grassy area were distracting and artificial, and I wanted them to have more of a flat, *photogram effect*. To tone things down, I chose Image, Adjustments, Hue/ Saturation. In the dialog box, I moved the Saturation slider to -52 and clicked OK.

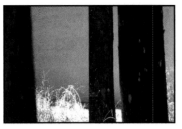
❽ *The Pink Trees selection area.*

❾ *Add Pink Trees.*

❿ *Linear Light blending mode.*

I then selected the Rectangular Marquee tool and held down the Shift key as I dragged a selection, constraining the selection area to a square. I chose an area that focused on the pink color and that allowed the tree trunks on the right to bleed of the right edge. I was anticipating that these dark trunks would provide a tonal transition between the left and right sides of the composite (see Figure ❽).

The Pink That Transforms

I copied the photo, pasted the Pink Trees selection into the composite, and dragged the layer beneath the Galgano Bench layer in the Layers palette. I then used the Move tool to drag the Pink Trees into position on the left side of the composition. I kept the *Pink Trees* photo open throughout this process in case I had to go back and recrop slightly.

The interesting thing about this step in the process is that it really transformed the image from a contemplative, compartmental diptych to a cohesive image with more of a singular focus. As I mentioned in the description of this photo, *Pink Trees* has a strong graphic presence with

these vertical black tree trunks dividing the space, and the strong pink color flattening the space.

The trees began to blend with the bench image on the right, just as I hoped they would. But the texture from the Landscape layers was gone, and the contrast in the rest of the Pink Trees image was a bit flat (see Figure ❾).

Bringing Out the Texture

I knew I needed to find a blending mode that would let the texture in the Landscape and Landscape Flipped layers show through without completely obliterating the Pink Trees layer. I also wanted to darken the tree trunks on the right so that they would blend more seamlessly with the dark shadows in the Galgano Bench layer.

After exploring a range of options, I selected Linear Light from the Layers palette Blending Mode menu. This gave me deep blacks that kept up with the blacks created by the Hard Light mode in the Galgano Bench layer. It also let the trees texture from the Landscape layers push through the pink wall area (see Figure ❿).

Hard Choices

At this point, a part of me would have been happy to call it a day. I really liked the saturated warm red on the left side, and I was happy with the way the tree trunks blended with the Galgano Bench image. And yet the image wasn't pushing far enough. It felt as though, if I had stopped, I would have been playing it safe, too easily satisfied with a nice color set and competent composition.

I decided to pull out the color on the left side and run with a monochromatic texture in an effort to push the piece further. I created a new layer by clicking the Create a New Layer icon in the Layers palette; I double-clicked the layer title to select it and named it Solid Black. After selecting the Paintbucket and filling the layer with black, I set the blending mode for this new layer to Color. The Color blending mode applies the color of the top layer to the lower composite, without changing the tonal properties. This action desaturates the lower layers, reducing everything beneath the Solid Black layer to black and white.

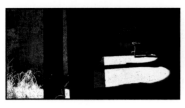

⓫ *Add Tree Bark texture.*

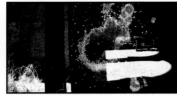

⓬ *Add Drips scan.*

⓭ *The final image.*

Adding Sant Olivetto Woods

Most of the broad strokes were in place at this point, so I decided to explore the addition of nuance and detail. This came in the sun-dappled form of the *Sant Olivetto Woods* photograph.

I thought that the texture on the tree trunk as well as the light patterns in the background created an interesting organic pattern that would harmonize with the all-over foliage pattern on the left side of the composite, while adding differentiation and specificity.

I copied the photo and pasted it into the main composite, giving it the layer name Tree Bark 2. After using the Move tool to drag the tree bark layer to the upper-left corner of the composition, I dragged its layer position below the Solid Black layer in the layer stack, just above the Pink Trees layer. Finally I set the layer's blending mode to Soft Light and its Opacity value to 62% (see Figure ⓫). I liked the way the texture of the tree trunk on the left echoed the stone texture on the back wall behind the bench on the right.

Adding Drips2

The final image addition came from my scan archive as I pulled out a scan of ink drips similar to the one I used in the *Molecola Sogni* image in Chapter 12, "Molecola Sogni.

I opened the file, pasted it in at the top of the layer stack, and renamed it Drips 2. To integrate the image with the lower layers, I set the layer's blending mode to Linear Light. This resulted in a light transparent background in which the midtones of the lower composite image showed through the blacks in the Drips scan. I wanted to knock out the white area and make the drips more visible against the background.

At first I thought that a simple image inversion would do the trick, but I wanted more control over the tonal range. So I decided to invert with the Curves command. After selecting Curves from the Adjustment Layer pull-down menu in the Layers palette, I dragged the curve handle in the upper right to the lower left (from Input: 255 to Output: 0). I then dragged the handle in the lower left to the upper right, which action inverted the

tones in the image. As a final tweak, I dragged a point downward (Input: 66, Output: 1o1) to darken the layer and eliminate some of the distracting detail (see Figure ⓬).

Masking Drips 2

At this point, the drips were bright white, which resonated with the bright white grassy area in the lower-left corner of the composite. What I didn't like was that they all but obscured the bench on the right.

I wanted to tone down the Drips layer to something like a 50% opacity, but still leave myself room to make local revisions in specific areas of the drip pattern. This meant that I couldn't just lower the Opacity slider. Instead, I clicked the Add Layer Mask icon in the Layers palette, set the foreground color to an RGB value of R128, G128, B128 (a 50% gray), selected the Paintbucket tool, and clicked in the image to mask the entire image by 50%.

I then selected the Brush tool and set the foreground color to white. I lowered the Opacity for the brush to 1o% in the Options bar and lightened the mask around the left side of the central drip shape to add back a bit more contrast and detail (see Figure ⓭).

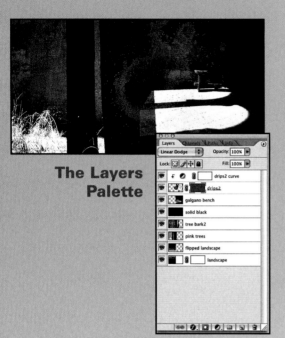

The Layers Palette

1. Open the *Orcia Landscape* photo.

2. Double-click the background layer and rename it Landscape.

3. Drag the Landscape layer to the New Layer icon in the Layers palette to duplicate the Landscape layer.

4. Choose Filter, Other, High Pass to launch the High Pass dialog box.

5. Set the Radius slider to 3.6 pixels and click OK to apply the effect.

6. Set the blending mode for the Landscape Copy layer to Darken.

7. Select Merge Down from the Layers palette menu to merge the two Landscape layers.

8. Select the Crop tool and Shift-drag to draw a square cropping area in the lower-center of the image. Double-click within the crop selection to apply the crop.

9. Drag the Landscape layer to the New Layer icon in the Layers palette to duplicate the Landscape layer.

10. Double-click the Landscape Copy layer title and give the new layer the name Flipped Landscape.

11. Choose Image, Transform, Flip Vertical to flip the layer.

12. Select the Move tool, press the Shift key to constrain horizontal movement, and drag the Flipped Landscape layer 130 pixels higher in the composition.

13. Select the Darken blending mode from the Layers palette for the Flipped Landscape layer to complete the foliage texture layers.

14. Choose Image, Canvas Size. In the dialog box that appears, set the Width value to 3210, and set the anchor box to the upper-left corner. Click OK to enlarge the canvas.

15. Open the *Galgano Bench* photo.

16. Select the Crop tool and Shift-drag to draw a square cropping area around the center of the image. Double-click within the crop selection to apply the crop.

17. Choose Select, All to copy the cropped *Galgano Bench* photo.

18. Choose Edit, Copy, activate the image composite, and choose Edit, Paste.

19. Select the Move tool from the toolbox and drag the new layer to the blank canvas area on the right.

20. Double-click the layer name in the Layers palette and rename it Galgano Bench.

21. Select Hard Light from the Blending Mode pull-down menu in the Layers palette.

22. Open the *Pink Trees* photo.

23. Choose Filter, Sharpen, Unsharp Mask. Set the Amount slider to 60%, the Radius slider to 0.7 pixels, and leave the Threshold slider at 0. Click OK to sharpen.

24. Choose Image, Adjustments, Hue/Saturation. In the dialog box, move the middle Saturation slider to -52.

25. Select the Rectangular Marquee tool and Shift-drag a square selection, focusing on the pink wall, allowing the trees to bleed off the right edge.

26. Choose Edit, Copy, activate the composite image, and choose Edit, Paste.

27. In the Layers palette, drag the pasted image beneath the Galgano Bench layer, double-click the new layer to highlight it, and name it Pink Trees.

28. Select Linear Light from the Layers palette Blending Mode menu.

29. Click the Create a New Layer icon in the Layers palette, double-click the layer title to select it, and name the new layer Solid Black.

31. Set foreground color to black, select the Paintbucket from the toolbox, and click to fill the new layer with black.

31. Set the blending mode for this new layer to Color.

32. Open the *Sant Olivetto Woods* photo.

33. Choose Select, All.

34. Choose Edit, Copy, activate the image composite, and choose Edit, Paste.

35. Select the Move tool and drag the pasted layer to the upper-left corner of the composition.

36. In the Layers palette, drag the Tree Bark 2 layer below the Solid Black layer in the layer stack, just above Pink Trees. Double-click the layer name and name the layer Tree Bark 2.

37. Set the layer's blending mode to Soft Light and set its Opacity value to 62%.

38. Open the Drips 2 scanned image file.

39. Choose Select, All. Then choose Edit, Copy, activate the image composite, and choose Edit, Paste. Name the new layer Drips2.

40. Select the Move tool and drag the pasted layer to the center of the composition.

41. Select Linear Light from the Blending Mode pull-down menu in the Layers palette.

42. Choose Image, Adjust, Curves.

43. Set the curve points to Input: 255, Output: 0; Input: 66, Output: 101; and Input: 0, Output: 255.

44. Click the Add Layer Mask icon in the Layers palette to add a mask.

45. Set the foreground color to an RGB value of R128, G128, B128 (50% gray), select the Paintbucket tool, and click in the image to mask the entire image by 50%.

46. Select the Brush tool, set the foreground color to white, and lower the Opacity slider to 10% in the Options bar. Lighten the mask around the left side of the central drip shape.

GLOSSARY

active autofocus

A kind of focusing system in which the camera sends out an infrared signal that is reflected by the subject, allowing the camera to calculate the distance to the subject and set the focus. See also *passive autofocus*.

aperture

The opening of a lens as measured in f-stop values.

ASA/ISO rating

A single measurement value for film speed, represented by two organizations—the American Standards Association and the International Standards Organization.

bit depth

The number of data bits contained in an image file that determines the number of colors that can be used to describe an image. The most common image files use 8 bits to render 256 shades of gray. Many digital cameras can capture 16-bit files, which can render 65,536 shades of gray.

bracket

To make exposures above and below the anticipated exposure setting, potentially overriding the camera's autoexposure setting. This technique is useful for capturing an accurate exposure in difficult lighting conditions.

burst exposure

A camera setting or shooting mode that captures a fast sequence of exposures by continuously holding down the exposure button.

center-weighted metering

An in-camera metering system that emphasizes the tonal information found in the center portion of the frame.

chromatic aberration

A misalignment of color channels that is sometimes visible at the edges of digital images. Notice the colored fringing that appears as a red, cyan, blue, or yellow discoloration around high-contrast edges.

combing

Empty spaces or gaps within the tonal range of an image that appear as a result of over-processing. The histogram of such images have the shape of a comb.

crop

To select a portion of a full-frame image as the final composition.

depth of field

The distance within a scene that records the subject on film as being in sharp focus. Depth of field is determined by the focal length of the lens, the f-stop setting, and the distance from the camera to the subject. It can be shallow or deep, and can be totally controlled by the photographer.

duplex metering

An exposure method that uses an incident meter to measure front- and backlighting values relative to the subject. The results are averaged to determine the final exposure value. This is a good method to use when an image is strongly backlit.

exposure

The amount of light that enters the camera lens and strikes the film or image sensor. The components of exposure are the lens opening (aperture) and duration of light exposure (shutter speed). Exposure is a combination of light intensity and duration.

exposure compensation

Also called EV settings. An on-camera exposure compensation system that allows you to override the camera's metered exposure settings. EV settings are centered at 0, with -2, -1, +1, and +2 settings to indicate an increase or decrease from the default 0 setting. The EV settings increase or decrease exposure in 1-stop increments.

Exposure Lock feature

A method used by some digital cameras to allow an exposure reading to be registered and held while the photographer recomposes the image. The process usually involves pressing the shutter halfway to register a reading, pressing an exposure lock button to lock it in place, recomposing the scene, and taking the final image as usual.

file format

The data structure of a computer file that determines how the information is organized. File format determines the compatibility of a file with various software applications.

file type

See *file format*.

focusing rails

A tripod-based focusing system, consisting of a pair of rails and a camera mount. A turn wheel moves the camera along the rails in very small, controlled increments, shifting the focus point in the image. This tool is valuable for close-up photography and other situations in which there is an extremely narrow depth of field.

f-stop

A fractional value that measures the opening of a lens. The value is arrived at by dividing the focal length of the lens by the diameter. The wider the opening, the lower the f-number, which lets more light through the lens. Each f-stop value represents a halving or doubling of light.

grayscale

A digital image containing 256 shades of gray.

histogram

A graphical scale that represents the tonal values for each pixel within an image. The horizontal axis represents the entire tonal range from black to white. The vertical values indicate the number of pixels within the image that have that tonal value.

image buffer

Dedicated in-camera memory that temporarily stores digital image data, before recording it to a data card.

incident reading
A metering system that measures the light falling on the subject, rather than the light reflecting off it. Handheld meters with dome receptors are examples of incident meters, which are held next to the subject and pointed back towards the camera.

JPEG
Joint Photographic Experts Group (the committee responsible for the file format's standards and applications). A file format designed for use with graphics, photos, and other color bitmaps. The JPEG format uses compression algorithms and processes that average pixels of the same or similar value to create files that are smaller than equivalent uncompressed files.

lossless compression
Any compression method that reduces file size without sacrificing any image data.

LZW compression
Lempel-Ziv-Welch compression. This lossless compression method is named for Israeli researchers Abraham Lempel and Jacob Zif who published the original IEEE papers on compression in 1977 and 1978.

monochrome
An image that contains multiple shades of a single color.

monopod
A mobile camera support consisting of a single telescoping leg, on which a camera is mounted.

passive autofocus
A kind of focusing system in which the camera determines the subject's distance based on the light and contrast in the subject matter. See also *active autofocus*.

quartertones
The area of the tonal range that falls between the highlights and the midtones. Numerically, the pixel values for quartertones fall in the range between 160 and 224.

reflected metering
A metering system that reads light reflected from the subject. All in-camera meters use reflected light meters.

sharpness
The crisp, hard-edged details that occur in an image when it is in focus.

shutter speed
An exposure variable that describes the duration of time in which light is allowed to strike the film or sensor.

spot metering

The act of taking an exposure reading from a specific portion of the frame, either through the camera lens or with a hand-held light meter.

through-the-lens (TTL) metering

An in-camera metering system that reads and measures the light coming through the lens.

TIFF

Tagged Image File Format. A digital file format used for digital photo images. TIFF images store image data in tagged fields in the file structure.

tripod

A mobile camera support device consisting of three tele-scoping legs and a center column, on which a camera is mounted.

video tripod

A mobile camera support device consisting of three telescoping legs and a center column, on which a video camera is mounted. Because of the smaller size and weight of most video cameras, video tripods are usually lighter and more compact than camera tripods.

zone system

An exposure system popular-ized by Ansel Adams that previ-sualizes the scene as a set of nine zones; the photographer exposes and develops the image to place the tones in the image into one of the zones.

zone system

INDEX

Parte Interna
image building
example

T

TIFF files